Sentiments and Acts

COMMUNICATION AND SOCIAL ORDER

An Aldine de Gruyter Series of Texts and Monographs

Series Editor

David R. Maines, Wayne State University

Advisory Editors

Bruce Gronbeck • Peter K. Manning • William K. Rawlins

David L. Altheide and Robert Snow, **Media Worlds in the Postjournalism Era**

Joseph Bensman and Robert Lilienfeld, **Craft and Consciousness: Occupational Technique and the Development of World Images** (*Second Edition*)

Valerie Malhotra Bentz, **Becoming Mature: Childhood Ghosts and Spirits in Adult Life**

Herbert Blumer, **Industrialization as an Agent of Social Change: A Critical Analysis** (*Edited with an Introduction by David R. Maines and Thomas J. Morrione*)

Dennis Brissett and Charles Edgley (*editors*), **Life as Theater: A Dramaturgical Sourcebook** (*Second Edition*)

Richard Harvey Brown (*editor*), **Writing the Social Text: Poetics and Politics in Social Science Discourse**

Norman K. Denzin, **Hollywood Shot by Shot: Alcoholism in American Cinema**

Irwin Deutscher, Fred P. Pestello, and H. Frances G. Pestello, **Sentiments and Acts**

Bruce E. Gronbeck, **Rhetoric and Socioculture**

J. T. Hansen, A. Susan Owen, and Michael Patrick Madden, **Parallels: The Soldiers' Knowledge and the Oral History of Contemporary Warfare**

Emmanuel Lazega, **The Micropolitics of Knowledge: Communication and Interaction in Work Groups**

Nicklas Luhmann, **Risk: A Sociological Theory**

David R. Maines (*editor*), **Social Organization and Social Process: Essays in Honor of Anselm Strauss**

Peter K. Manning, **Organizational Communication**

Stjepan G. Meštrović, **Durkheim and Postmodernist Culture**

R. S. Perinbanayagam, **Discursive Acts**

William K. Rawlins, **Friendship Matters: Communication, Dialectics, and the Life Course**

Vladimir Shlapentokh and Dmitry Shlapentokh, **Ideological Trends in Soviet Movies**

Jim Thomas, **Communicating Prison Culture: The Deconstruction of Social Existence**

Jacqueline P. Wiseman, **The Other Half: Wives of Alcoholics and Their Social-Psychological Situation**

Sentiments and Acts

Irwin Deutscher
Fred P. Pestello and H. Frances G. Pestello

ALDINE DE GRUYTER

New York

About the Authors

Irwin Deutscher is Professor Emeritus, University of Akron. He is past President of the Society for the Study of Social Problems and the North Central Sociological Association and has been elected to the council of the American Sociological Association. Deutscher is currently President Elect of the Society for Applied Sociology.

Fred P. Pestello is an Associate Professor of Sociology at the University of Dayton. He received a Ph.D. degree in 1985 from the joint doctoral program in sociology between The University of Akron and Kent State University. His current research interest is in advancing the direct investigation of the relationship between sentiments and acts.

H. Frances G. Pestello is an Associate Professor of Sociology at the University of Dayton. She received a Ph.D. degree in 1983 from the joint doctoral program in sociology between the University of Akron and Kent State University. Her current research interests are at-risk adolescents and the ways in which spouses are able to combine careers and families.

ALDINE DE GRUYTER
A division of Walter de Gruyter, Inc.
200 Saw Mill River Road
Hawthorne, New York 10532

This publication is printed on acid-free paper ∞

Library of Congress Cataloging-in-Publication Data
Deutscher, Irwin, 1923–
Sentiments and acts / Irwin Deutscher, Fred P. Pestello, H.
  Frances G. Pestello.
        p. cm. — (Communication and social order)
    Includes bibliographical references and index.
    ISBN 0-202-30444-2 (alk. paper). — ISBN 0-202-30445-0 (pbk. :
alk. paper)
    1. Social psychology—Research. 2. Attitude (Psychology)
3. Personality and situation. I. Pestello, Fred P., 1952– .
II. Pestello, H. Frances G., 1951– . III. Title. IV. Series.
HM291.D467 1993
302'.072—dc20   92-27887
                                                                      CIP

Manufactured in the United States of America
10 9 8 7 6 5 4 3 2 1

302.072

D486s

262185

Contents

Preface　　*ix*

I. WHAT'S THE PROBLEM?

1　Sentiments and Acts: The Sequel

The Four Flaws   3
Hopeful Signs for the Seventies   4
The Biography of a Problem   5
Retrieval and Synthesis: Old and New   7
The Double Screen   8
Training and Education and Knowledge   12

2　A Problem Found and Lost: The Temper of the
Times and the Mystique of Science

Epistemology and Research Methods   19
Notes   29

3　Bits of Evidence

And That's Only the Beginning   31
Sometimes Consistency   34
What Else Could You Expect?   35

4　A Cumulative Science?

The Test of Time   43
Looking Backward   46
A Half-Century of "Progress"   56
A Fourth Study   58
Conclusion: What Validates What?   64

v

II. METHODS: THE CREDIBILITY OF EVIDENCE

5   How Do We Know We Know?

The Validity Problem   69
The Other Side   78
The Last Word   80
Notes   85

6   Anyone May Lie a Bit, Cheat a Bit, and Try to Be
    Helpful

Getting in Our Own Way   87
The Problem with Talking to People:
    Surveys and Interviews   91

7   Speaking in Tongues

Language and Social Research   99
Speaking Out of Context: Questionnaires and
    Formal Interviews   99
Speaking in Context: Participant Observation   110

8   What Can You Believe Nowadays?

Subjects Are People Too   117
Systematic Distortion: The Ubiquitous Type I
    Error   123
Can the Weakness of One Be the Strength of the
    Other?   125

9   The Logic of Our Procedures

What Is an Inconsistency?   129
Methodology as Theory: Are Observed
    Inconsistencies More Apparent Than Real?   136

III. A HATFUL OF EXPLANATIONS

10 The Social Situation: Does Bad Company Cause
Naughty Behavior?

Public and Private Opinion 141
Compartmentalization 144
Toward a Situational Sociology 146
Implications: Take Care of the Company You
Keep! 149
Current Fad or Telling Signpost? The Sociology
of Emotions 157
All the World *Is* a Stage 160

11 Stimulus-Response Is for Animals (Symbols Are
for People)

It's What's in Between That Counts 163
The Legacy of Blumer 165
A Small Step Forward: The Discovery of
"Intervening Variables" 167

12 Rising Expectations and Later Disappointments:
Research in the 1980s

The Hopeful Sign of Research in the Late Sixties
and the Early Seventies 173
The Disappointment of Research in the Eighties 180

13 Concepts and How Their Confusion Can Mess
You Up

Making Distinctions and Connections 187
On Adding Apples and Oranges 189
Attitude: Something That Cannot Be Defined 193
Behavior: Something That Should Not Be
Observed 198
Beyond Concepts: A Hatful of Explanations 201
Notes 205

14   A Phenomenological Approach: Toward a
     Situational Sociology

         Social Reality as a Social Creature   207
         The Subject as Methodologist   212
         It Makes a Difference   218

15   Toward the Twenty-First Century

         How Much Improvement?   223
         Fiddling with People's Lives   226

References   235

Index   258

Preface

Although this book, like its predecessor, is an unlikely inspiration for a movie, it is indeed a sequel. The manuscript for the first one was shipped to the editor in the summer of 1970, and in the fall of 1973 *What We Say/What We Do: Sentiments and Acts* was published. Both volumes are about the relationship between talk and action.

We have again avoided in our title, the traditional distinction, "attitudes and behaviors," because of the connotational paraphernalia attached to these terms. Any dichotomy does an injustice to the problem; it is, in fact, necessary to draw much finer distinctions in order to make sense of the great variety of frequently inconsistent evidence considered here. There can be any number of sentimental orientations toward a given object and the evidence in Chapter 13 suggests that values, norms, and beliefs are not necessarily related to one another. In like manner, there can be any number of action orientations toward the same object. Aware of the risk, we have chosen to avoid stylistic monotony by varying our terminology. We employ "attitudes," "sentiments," and "words" as if they were synonymous. We know they are not. We also shift among "acts," "deeds," and "behaviors" even though these terms mask very different kinds of orientations as well.

How is this volume different from its predecessor? Clearly it is a revision of *What We Say/What We Do* with many pages lifted verbatim from that book. On the other hand, much of the earlier book has been omitted from this one. The supporting articles are no longer reprinted in each chapter, imposing on the readers the responsibility of studying the first volume or original sources in order to do their own screening of the evidence. This book also explores areas and concerns that did not exist, or were just emerging, two decades ago. Perhaps the most radical change in the biography of this study is that "we" are now plural. This volume unlike its predecessor is a collaboration. At the other extreme are such stylistic changes as the elimination of the extensive footnoting and the sexist language of the early seventies.

This book is truly a sequel in the sense that it focuses on a set of issues posed in its predecessor and asks the question: What has happened since then? It was the two younger authors who raised this question and the three of us ferreted out what we considered to be some of the issues raised in *What We Say/What We Do*. As with many such collaborations, the division of labor among authors is often blurred. The basis from the older book by Deutscher is obvious. Deutscher also wrote the initial draft of the first chapter of this book and the closing section, "Fiddling With Peoples' Lives." The analysis of recent literature on sentiments and acts, as well as its place in the history of this issue, is the work of the Pestellos. So too is most of the other updating and all of the daily work involved in producing a manuscript. With the help of BITNET we were in nearly constant electronic communication and much of what resulted is a blend of all three of us.

The major problems identified in the predecessor to this volume, *What We Say/What We Do*, are summarized in the first chapter. In that volume, the story simply unfolded; in the fashion of some mystery writers, Deutscher did not know how it would end until he finished writing it. When it was published in the early 1970s he saw hopeful signs of change beginning to appear in the literature and considered these new directions in a section entitled "Looking Forward: Research in the Late Sixties and Early Seventies."

This book, on the other hand, deliberately attempts to explore a new literature and the manner in which it reflects upon certain flaws identified in the first. Rather than keep the reader in suspense, we will be candid in confessing now a disappointing degree of inaccuracy in our projections of a rosier future for social research. Conditions did not change as much as we thought and hoped they would.

Although it is imprecise, for convenience we will refer to the literature analyzed in the 1973 book as "pre-1970." Papers published between 1970 and 1972 were most likely to be mentioned in the section called "Looking Forward." The review and updating of that section appears in Chapters 11 and 12 of this volume. The retrieval methods employed for the more recent literature are straightforward. Although we refer to that literature as "post–1970," much of it does, in fact, encompass the years 1982 through 1985. It was early in 1986 when we began this reassessment and we thought that the work of the four preceding years would provide a reasonable picture of how things had changed since the ancient days of pre-1970.

Unlike Wicker (1969), Schuman and Johnson (1976), and Hill (1981), our interest is not in chronicling research in this field. Rather we will attempt to assess the area as it stands today. We do so, in part, by building upon two papers that critique the post–1970 literature (F. G.

Pestello and F. P. Pestello 1991; F. P. Pestello and F. G. Pestello 1991). The literature we considered in those papers came from our search of twenty-two journals.

We started with a list of journals likely to have articles on the attitude-behavior relationship. The list was expanded as we examined other journals referenced in relevant articles. We uncovered sixty-two articles, a comment, and a rejoinder. Fifty of the articles report on one or more original studies (for a listing of the sixty-four pieces see F. P. Pestello and H. F. G. Pestello 1991). These articles are cited below as they become relevant to our comparison between then (pre-1970) and now.

Many people facilitated our work. Foremost among them is David Maines. David initiated this project with great enthusiasm. Without his encouragement this book would not have been written. We are also grateful for the enduring support of our colleagues at the Department of Sociology at the University of Akron and the Department of Sociology and Anthropology at the University of Dayton, particularly that of Pat Donnelly, head of the department at Dayton. Sincere thanks are due Charlie Chantell, former acting dean of the College of Arts and Sciences at the University of Dayton, who provided funds for a student assistant, and Nancy Schiml for her outstanding secretarial work in helping us prepare the manuscript. Students Melissa Atkins, Kathy Blessing, Kelly Driscoll, and Bridget McKeever also assisted us at various stages in the preparation of the manuscript. We would also like to thank Laura Hengehold for constructing the index. Brenda Donnelly, of the Center for the Study of Family Development at the University of Dayton, was instrumental in providing technical assistance with computer software. We are especially grateful for the tolerance and support of our loving families. Finally, we thank Arlene Perazzini for her skill and patience in ushering this manuscript through the production process.

This book is gratefully dedicated to the memory of C. Wright Mills, who inspired us to improve our intellectual craft, who reminded us of the difference between training and education, and who emphasized the importance for each social scientist to be his or her own methodologist. Mills's methodological proscriptions, including the crucial intersection between biography and history and the need to appropriately discount all kinds of evidence, guided the construction of this book.

I.D.
F.P.P.
H.F.G.P.

I

What's the Problem?

1

Sentiments and Acts:
The Sequel

This sequel, like the original text that inspired it, is about the relation-ship between what people say and what they otherwise do. Our concern does not lie with superficial hypocrisy or deceit, although it surely exists. Liars often make themselves apparent and may be exposed with relative ease. We barely consider simulation, pretense, or any deliberate feigning either in response to questions or in observable actions. It is our aim to improve our understanding of how people with integrity may *honestly* express a sentiment and yet act contrary to that expression. It will become apparent that the problem of what we say and what we do is endemic. The objects of saying and doing may be anything or anyone.

How might one explain the near random relationship between senti-ments and acts found in the pre-1970 literature? It was not that most evidence suggested a random relationship. If it had, the problem would have been solved. Only *some* of the evidence suggested a random rela-tionship between what people say and what they do. On the other hand, *some* of the evidence suggested that there is a very close relation-ship between the two and, finally, *some* of the evidence suggested that people are likely to do the opposite of what they say—an inverse rela-tionship! All of this evidence had been discounted as it filtered through our double screen of methodology and conceptual clarity. We will return to the double screen and the discounting process.

The Four Flaws

Four major flaws were proposed as possibly accounting for the con-fused findings in the pre-1970 studies. These flaws are related to data gathering, concepts, assumptions, and theory. The evidence and argu-ments regarding these flaws are discussed in detail in later chapters (see also Pestello, Pestello, and Deutscher 1992). In brief, the four flaws in-volve:

3

1.   An insufficient attention to validity: One indicator of an improvement of research on the relationship between attitudes and behaviors would be an increase in the attention paid to the validity of the data (see Chapter 5).

2.   A need for conceptual clarification: A second indicator of an improvement of research on the relationship between attitudes and behaviors would be an increase in the precision of the conceptual distinction under study (see Chapter 13).

3.   The assumption of a psychological need for consistency: A third set of indicators of an improvement of research on the relationship between attitudes and behaviors would include a recognition that ordinary people may perceive no discrepancy in a logical inconsistency or, if they do, may not define it as problematic (see Chapter 10).

4.   The neglect of intervening social processes: The fourth set of indicators of an improvement of research on the relationship between attitudes and behaviors would be increased emphasis on the intervening process rather than on dependent and independent variables. Indicators may include not only increased use of unobtrusive research, but also increased efforts to deal with the subjects' or respondents' definitions of the situation in which the attitudes or behaviors are elicited (see Chapter 11).

Hopeful Signs for the Seventies

In the earlier volume it was observed that, since the midsixties, some students of the relationship between attitudes and behaviors had demonstrated an increasing awareness of the need to study what is in between. Although that emerging wave of research remained couched in terms of variable analysis, it suggested movement in a desirable direction. There was less concentration on the dichotomy and more on such intervening processes as "social constraint," "reference groups," "public and private conditions," "opportunity," and "competence." This body of literature is reviewed in Chapter 11.

Although these remained studies of variables, they represented progress in conceptualization. In fact, the research program begun by Albrecht (1973) in the early seventies, exploring the relationship between what people say and what others expect of them, signaled an emerging awareness of the need to account for the manner in which people define the social situation. The signal provided by Albrecht may have been a weak one.

In a 1969 summary of the state of the attitude-behavior literature, Wicker seemed discouraged. He observed on the one hand that there was increasing agreement among researchers that situational factors are important, but on the other hand he could locate practically no research that took them into account. Part of the problem may lie in the fact that recognition of the need to understand intervening processes implies a different style of research from what was fashionable during the pre-1970 period. If it is necessary to grasp action from the perspective of those who act, then the investigator must have what Blumer (1956) describes as an "intimate familiarity" with the world as those actors experience it. It is then no accident that participant-observation techniques are closely related to the research demands of this issue.

A few years after the publication of *What We Say/What We Do*, another comprehensive review of the field was attempted. The Schuman and Johnson (1976) summary was based largely on research done while *What We Say/What We Do* was in production and in the years immediately following. They were encouraged by what they found, arguing that "research over the past few years has begun to identify factors that account for or help specify A-B relationships" (p. 199). Five years later, Hill (1981) published his assessment of the area and was even more encouraged than Schuman and Johnson. He concludes that the debate over an attitude-behavior relationship "can be put to rest. . . . Under a variety of conditions attitudes have at least modest utility in predicting behavior, and behavior has at least modest utility in predicting attitude change" (p. 373).

We shall discover later that the criteria for credible evidence we employ are somewhat different from these optimistic authors. Nevertheless, their optimism and our own will be tested in this book, as we attempt to assess the extent to which there has, in fact, been an improvement in the voluminous research published since 1970. This was a domain of great importance, which appeared to be stagnant, if not regressive, up to that decade. In summary, our major criteria for evaluation are the issues of technique, concepts, assumptions, and theory, found in the four flaws mentioned above.

The Biography of a Problem

There is a customary style for reporting any research. That style generally moves with cool logic from the statement of the problem, through a review of literature, to a listing of hypotheses and their sources, a description of methods, a report of the data, and finally to a set of conclusions and, sometimes, recommendations (either for further research or for policy). With minor variations, this is the way scientists report their findings, and, with minor variations, this is the way they are reported here. In *What We Say/What We Do*, data were reported in the form of reprinted articles, which were key sources for the conclusions we drew. In this volume, such data are properly referenced and described in a fragmentary way as we consider relevant issues. The conscientious reader may still examine these bits of evidence by resorting to the library or to the earlier volume.

This conventional style of reporting scientific findings should not, however, be confused with the actual biography of any piece of research. Although each is guided by its own logic and, although each logic may be reasonable enough, the description of the process as it appears in writing may be quite different from the process as it actually happened. This provides our first example of the general problem addressed in this book: *How people do research is not always the same as how they say they do it.*

Writers of methodology textbooks generally ignore this distinction between how discoveries are initially made and how they are later written, suggesting rather that the manner in which research is reported is the manner in which it ought properly to be conducted. This orthodoxy persists even in the face of blatantly irregular procedures that occasionally result in findings of such great importance that they must be incorporated into the standard literature of a field. Michael Polanyi reports that "when Einstein discovered rationality in nature, unaided by any observation that had not been available for at least fifty years before, our positivistic textbooks covered up the scandal by an appropriately embellished account of his discovery" (1958, p. 11; for a summary of some leading philosophers of science on this topic see Dalton 1964, pp. 51–53; see also Scheff 1990, pp. 144–45).

In *What We Say/What We Do*, we referred in the preface to an itch to examine the relationship between what people say and what they otherwise do. That itch resulted from reading Richard LaPiere's "Attitudes vs. Actions" (1934). As the evidence is developed in Chapter 2, the reasons for our concern will become clear. For the moment let us note only that in the early 1930s a study reported that all but one of the 251 restaurants and motels approached by a minority couple did, in fact, accommodate them; all but one of these establishments, which responded to a mailed questionnaire, said they would not serve such minorities. In the previous book, as in the present one, we made our best effort to begin to find an honest answer to an honest question: What is the relationship between what people say and what they do? Furthermore, if there should be an occasional incongruity between the two, under what conditions is it likely to occur and how can it be explained?

LaPiere's study provided the impetus to begin considering the problem. It deals with the relationship between racial prejudice and racial discrimination. But that is only one case of the more general issue of the relationship between attitudes and acts. The first step was to locate whatever literature might exist in any field of human behavior. Our little file of six references had grown to 450 items by the time the earlier volume was published.

At that time we observed that about half the literature resulted from the discovery of older materials, but that the other half was the result of an outburst of research reports, theoretical treatises, and methodological articles that had occurred in the late sixties and early seventies. After a long period of quiescence, the issue of attitudes vs. behavior had come to life. Since then the literature has continued to grow and we have stopped counting. Our major task in this book is to consider the more recent literature and determine what has happened since publication of *What We Say/What We Do.*

As we studied the materials, the bibliography sometimes shrank as well as grew. Although we did not call it that at the time, we had already begun to "screen" for relevance and credibility. Some items, in spite of their seductive titles, turned out to have nothing to do with our problem. Others turned out to be unbelievable, regardless of their conclusions. This was the crude beginning of a process we would later come to think of as our *double screen*. If we were reporting our procedures in standard research style, we would probably begin with a discussion of the double screen, as if we had methodically planned our work in that manner. That might make a more reasonable narrative, but it would not be true. We will return to the double screen later.

Retrieval and Synthesis: Old and New

The retrieval technique in the first volume simply emerged. It was unplanned, although it could be reported in traditional style as if it were a systematic procedure designed prior to the research. That technique for handling the wealth of materials closely parallels the procedure described by Glaser and Strauss (1967). They are concerned primarily with field data although they do mention library research in their Chapter 7. We also found C. Wright Mills's appendix on intellectual craft (1959, pp. 195–226) to be useful in this respect. It is interesting to compare these older techniques for synthesizing materials to the currently more fashionable processes of meta-analysis and postmodern analysis.

Meta-analysis is a device for providing a quantitative synthesis of several studies dealing with the same question (Glass, McGaw, and Smith 1981; Mullen 1989; Wachter and Straf 1990). It permits the analyst to assess the findings of a set of studies "objectively." With this procedure, the investigator is not required to think about the methods employed, the strengths or weaknesses of the studies, their theoretical orientations or perspectives, or anything else that might introduce bias into scientific judgment. All that is required is that each study report uniform data such as the standard error of the mean. It is assumed that the only studies worth considering are those which employ measurement techniques that can be manipulated to yield mean scores. This severely restricts the kinds of observations that can be considered in assessing the state of knowledge. All of LaPiere's research would have to be omitted from such an analysis as would other useful high-validity studies such as Warriner's (1958) analysis of the attitudes and behaviors of Kansans toward drinking or Lohman and Reitzes's (1954) study of the variation in white workers' attitudes toward black co-workers as the situation is moved from the work setting to the residential neighborhood. Meta-analysis is not an appropriate device for synthesizing knowledge primarily because it excludes nearly all valid information.

The postmodernists are at the other extreme. They are deeply concerned with the agenda and perspective of an author. Characteristics of authors—sex, race, social class, sexual orientation, and so forth—are used to discount their writings. Through the practice of "deconstruction," texts, like other cultural products, are critically analyzed (e.g., Denzin 1990a). Authors are stripped of their pretense of authority and published works are stripped of their pretense of objectivity. Science, natural and social, is seen as rhetoric: "Truth and knowledge are ideological constructions, based on the power formations that exist in any society at any moment in time" (Denzin 1990b, p. 148; see also Richardson 1988, pp. 200–2).

Although our double screen may have anticipated postmodernist ideology, it was not a self-conscious effort in that direction. The postmodern movement was not yet flourishing when *What We Say/What We Do* was written. Rather, that book followed the lead of C. Wright Mills in attempting to properly discount sources.

The Double Screen

The problem of making sense out of a wide variety of sometimes contradictory findings is an attribute of any research endeavor. We have described the first step: scanning the literature in order to create a bibliography that provides a reasonable sample of thinking and observations concerned with sentiments and acts. At the time, it seemed that the rest would be routine. One needed only to read the materials and determine the conditions under which the observations were made and then tabulate the results. Surely when we counted and sorted the various conclusions, there would appear quantitative evidence of the extent to which sentiments and acts are related under different conditions. We did, in fact, make an abortive effort at this sort of primitive meta-analysis. But the almost random hodgepodge of findings—sometimes entailing contradictions among studies exploring the same phenomena—in conjunction with the growing suspicion that the only clear relationship that was emerging was between the method employed and conclusions reached, caused us to take a step back.

It was not difficult to discard materials that were blatantly incredible. But after a while it became clear that this procedure needed to be made more explicit and more systematic: We discovered the need for what S. M. Miller calls a "crap detector" [he attributes the term to Hemingway, who actually spoke of a "built-in, shock-proof, shit detector" (1963)]. With few exceptions it is difficult to make a clear distinction between evidence that is crap and evidence that is not. Although there is a charm in Miller's earthy language, C. Wright Mills comes rather closer to the kind of screening that is necessary. Mills (1940a) refers to a process he calls *discounting*. He reminds us that an intelligent interpretation of historical data requires some knowledge of who wrote it, under what conditions, and why. When we understand this context, we can then properly discount the data. That means that rather than *discarding* much of what is reported as "crap," we instead *discount* it and interpret it; we do use it but not necessarily with as much confidence or even in the same manner as the original author would have it.

History and biography are routinely discounted according to what is known about the author. If, for example, we are given an account of a battle, we want to know, among other things: Was the author a soldier and, if so, a private or a general? Was the writer on the winning or the losing side? Note that we attempt to locate sources of perspective (what might be called biases) and then we take them into account by discounting the report to the degree and in the direction that seems appropriate. We do not discard reports merely because of biases or flaws. If we did there would be no history, as some postmodernists insist. But history does exist and it is recognizable as a presentation by people who have some sort of stake in the matters of which they write, who are located somewhere in their own society and tend to see the world from that perspective, and whose work is more or less open to methodological criticism. This same observation can be made of all discourse, including social science reports:

> Here sociologists can garner suggestions from critical historiography which attempts to locate (culturally and biographically) observers (e.g., Roman popes) of social events in order properly to discount their recorded observations. This method is aware of the differences of societal occurrences as seen and written of by variously situated reporters. (Mills 1940a, p. 330, note 37)

Whether our data are derived from surveys, interviews, observations, laboratory experiments, or whatever, they require discounting—but rarely discarding! It is in this sense that nearly everything is admissible as evidence, but some evidence is more credible than others. We have no rules for the assessment of credibility, except do it. Inevitably, different scholars will apply different criteria.

This process of discounting is the first component of our double screen. It is primarily a methodological screen and it can be seen in nearly every chapter of this book. There are students of the relationship between attitude and behavior who believe that once methodological problems are resolved, nearly all apparent discrepancies between what we say and what we do disappear. One may draw this implication from Donald Campbell's (1964) analysis of "Pseudoinconsistency in the Attitude Literature," which we discuss in Chapter 9. Howard Ehrlich (1969) is explicit in this matter, although he adds the second element of the double screen to his explanation: "[T]he evidence for inconsistency may be rejected on both methodological and conceptual grounds, and . . . there is no necessary incompatibility between a theory of attitudes and theories of interpersonal or intergroup behavior" (p. 29). Ehrlich's notion of intervening variables is central to the analysis found in Chapter 11.

We concur in the observation that much of the variance is explained by methodological difficulties and still more is explained when conceptual problems are clarified. In addition, we will attempt to document the position that much of the variance can only be explained by the fact that, under many conditions, people simply fail to act as they say they do. *Some* of the observed discrepancy between sentiments and acts is in fact more apparent than real; *some* of it is also very real.

Ehrlich has introduced the second component of the double screen. It may be that if reports are judged carefully on methodological grounds, discrepant findings will get sifted out and each one of the remaining studies will agree with the others. But this is unlikely. In the analysis of documents for this volume, the remaining evidence seemed to make more sense after methodological screening, but it was still far from coherent. Early in the game, we were inclined to treat with contempt critics who argued about what "attitudes" really are, or what "behavior" really is. We were willing to settle for comparisons between what people say and what they do. And when some critics reminded us that speech is behavior too, we shrugged impatiently at their petulance and snarled, "O.K., what people say and what they *otherwise* do!" And that is how we proceeded.

The first time one of us seriously considered this issue in print, he wrote (using italics for emphasis):

> We still do not know much about the relationship between what people
> say and what they do—attitudes and behavior, sentiments and acts, ver-
> balizations and interactions, words and deeds. *We know so little that I can't
> even find an adequate vocabulary to make the distinction!* (Deutscher 1966,
> p. 242)

It was not until later, under the influence of evidence such as Westie's
test of "The American Dilemma" (1965) and Rodman's study of illegitimacy in the Caribbean (1966), that it became clear how concepts
and their confusion can mess one up—more of this in Chapter 13. Having arrived at a conceptual as well as a methodological screening process, we began to ask to what extent different studies are in fact addressing different issues under the same labels. Surely, if they are talking
about different things, then their findings may be different but not inconsistent. By the time the information has filtered through the double
screen—when it has been sorted for both credibility and for conceptual
consistency—it can be assumed that the residual findings represent the
kinds of differences between sentiments and acts that actually occur
among people under the various conditions that make up their everyday
lives.

Early in this research it was assumed that actions speak louder than
words, but gradually it became apparent that words may speak louder
and more eloquently than actions. Merton clearly articulates this possibility and questions the assumption that overt behavior is "more real"
than verbal behavior: "The assumption is both unwarranted and scien-
tifically meaningless. . . . The a priori assumption that verbal responses
are simply epiphenomena is to be accorded no greater weight than the
assumption that words do not deceive nor actions lie" (1940, p. 21).

The process of discounting involves an infinite regression, since the
observations of the discounter must also be discounted. Attempts to
discount materials treated in this volume have been made, but our own
biases, from whatever sources, must also be taken into account by the
reader. *Argumentum ad hominem* is rightly viewed with disapproval in
considering the merits of any issue, but in considering the works of a
scholar, the person's location in society becomes a basis for interpretation and evaluation. This is a central theme in Alvin Gouldner's *The
Coming Crisis in Western Sociology* (1970). It is Gouldner's call for a "reflex-
ive sociology," which is being echoed here. The close kinship between
the present volume and Derek Phillips's *Knowledge from What* is reflected
in a statement on his opening page:

> In a book that raises many questions about the so-called objectivity of
> sociological research, it seems almost obligatory for me to provide some

biographical information so that the reader can better understand my vantage point in doing this book. For it is my belief that, despite protestations to the contrary, the writer is always present in his narrative. (1971, p. xi)

We believe this view to be correct. There is no such thing as a pure, objective, detached sociology. Sociology is done by sociologists whose own humanity inevitably interferes with what they do. With proper discipline, sociologists may become inhumane, but they cannot become inhuman.

Training and Education and Knowledge

The distinction between training and education is Mills's, not ours. Here is the problem with training:

Since one can be *trained* only in what is already known, training sometimes incapacitates one from learning new ways; it makes one rebel against what is bound to be at first loose and even sloppy. But you must cling to such vague images and notions, if they are yours, and you must work them out. For it is in such forms that original ideas, if any, almost always first appear. (Mills 1959, p. 212)

In this volume as in its predecessor, there is no intention to train anyone in anything. There is no body of information we would like to convey. We do hope to make some slight dent in the trained incapacity we all acquire in our attempts to become educated. We are not convinced that social scientists know a great deal about the social world or how it works or what can be done about it. In the earlier book, the belief was expressed that such knowledge is close at hand and that the primary requisite for it is to help a new generation of students to remove the blinders that so narrow the vision of the rest of us. We suggested then that, rather than building on what we know, they learn from our mistakes. Chapter 4 focuses on this issue. Even with the passage of years, we retain our faith.

Some of the failure to realize our hopes may be attributed to a dismal academic job market, which left even the best of young scholars scratching to find jobs, to hold those jobs, and to obtain tenure. Under such economic conditions tenure became a matter of job security rather than of academic freedom as it was originally intended. It would not have been in the career interests of any young scholar to risk original work or original thinking. Better to stick to the ritual requirements for advancement and to think only those great thoughts that their mentors had thought. The easiest route to publication (and thus to security) was to verify the works of those eminent scholars who came before. As the last decade of the twentieth century is under way, the academic marketplace is improving. We think that the amount of intellectual risk-taking will improve with it.

We are appalled by the notion entertained by some radical sociologists that sociology is the tool of the establishment—some tool! We may be accused of being servants of the power structure, but we are hardly a useful tool for anyone. Phillips is surprised by the

apparent belief that sociologists actually know something that could be used *for* those in power and *against* [those not in power]. . . . [That] radical sociologist[s] should share with the sociological elite the belief that sociologists possess some unique knowledge that can be put to the use of one or another segment of the society was unexpected by me. (1971, pp. xv–xvi, emphasis in original)

Our ignorance can be illustrated in the effort of two sociologists to create "an inventory of scientific findings" about human behavior. Berelson and Steiner's (1964) whole book is a disappointment to the student, largely because of their integrity. When such honest scholars attempt to list propositions, this is what sometimes happens: One proposition is the statement that "the lower classes presumably violate the law more frequently than the upper classes." This is immediately followed by the qualification, "in any case, they are more likely to get caught and punished." After musing over the possibility of recording bias, they conclude that "it is not at all clear what the fact is" (p. 488). The fact is that they do not know; we do not know; no one knows! This isolated illustration may help clarify our reservations about training.

The idea of a dictionary does not die easily. Peter Hamilton has "selected and translated" Boudon and Bourricaud's *A Critical Dictionary of Sociology* (1989). As if a dictionary of the unknown was not sufficiently distressing, one that selects and translates it is even more. This more recent effort is, however, superior to earlier ones since it provides an historical background and critique of the terms.

Other than noting the improvement in sociological dictionaries, we have reviewed several major and minor ways in which this book differs from its predecessor. Furthermore, we have traced the biography of our interest in questions about what people say and what they do. These materials have been provided as an aid to readers so that they may better discount what we have to say. Although they are not reviewed here, our own personal and professional biographies must be a part of our analysis. Credibility is a relatively simple matter in a volume such as this since all of the raw data—the literature cited—are readily available for reanalysis. Although we use the relationship between sentiments and acts as a point of departure, our problem entails most of the crucial theoretical and methodological issues that continue to plague contemporary social science.

It should be clear that if one is to understand the meaning of the evidence with which one deals, if one is to make the judgments required in order to assess credibility and conceptual clarity (our double screen), if one is to put all of this together in a logical and empirically sound manner, if one is to do all of these things, then there is no choice but to attempt to live up to C. Wright Mills's mandate to "be a good craftsman." And let us forgive him the archaic generic masculine form of a quarter-century ago:

> Let every man be his own methodologist; let every man be his own theorist; let theory and method again become part of the practice of a craft. Stand for the primacy of the individual scholar; stand opposed to the ascendancy of research teams of technicians. Be one mind that is on its own confronting the problems of man and society. (1959, p. 224)

Let us get to it!

2

A Problem Found and Lost:
The Temper of the Times
and the Mystique
of Science

There are three avenues through which social scientists can seek to understand human behavior: (1) We can observe it in process; (2) we can view the written or otherwise artifactual records of people; and (3) we can ask questions and listen to answers. There are different techniques for implementing these approaches and they may be employed in various combinations. Among sociologists, it is the last—the verbal approach—that is most commonly used (Wells and Picou 1981, pp. 148–52). We survey; we poll; we interview. Although we are often constrained to use verbal elicitation techniques, it is actually behavior in which we are more often interested. Assuming the old-fashioned, but still dominant, textbook definition of attitudes as "tendencies to act," we frequently proceed to draw conclusions about the behavior of people on the basis of what they tell us.

In his classic volume on interviewing, Hyman makes this assumption explicit: "If one could wait around indefinitely," he writes, "the natural environment would ultimately liberate behavior relevant to a given inference. However, practical limitations preclude such lengthy procedures" (Hyman 1954, pp. 17–18). Martin Fishbein has built a prolific line of attitude-behavior research on this same assumption:

> Since direct behavioral observation is often impossible and always time-consuming and costly, our options are rather limited. I personally feel that the insistence of many investigators on direct behavioral observation . . . has not only been inappropriate, but it has actually impeded rather than advanced scientific knowledge. (1980, p. 78)

Such reasoning is carried to its extreme in an example provided by Whyte (1984, pp. 86–87). Whyte reports that George Strauss (1952) attended every meeting of a union for a year. He learned all the regular members' names and closely observed how they sat on both sides of a central aisle. Strauss noted that those who sat on one side favored the incumbent leaders, while those on the other side opposed them. "Furthermore, as Strauss observed a shift in the number of members seated on the two sides of the aisle, he was able to predict correctly that the incumbent officers would lose in the next election" (Whyte 1984, p. 87). His paper was published in *Sociometry:*

> The editor accepted the article with obvious reservations because he insisted that Strauss change the title of his article, making it "Direct Observation as a Source of Quasi-Sociometric Information." In effect, he was saying that what Strauss really should have done was circulate a questionnaire among the members attending the meeting to ask them what other members they would like to sit next to, and so on. Unfortunately, he had not used the sociometric method, so the editor was willing to settle for the next best thing: observation of actual behavior. (p. 87)

Extensive reliance on survey techniques reflects a basic assumption of contemporary social science. Oral and written reports of actions, past or intended, are taken as accurate measures of behavior. But ever since encountering Richard LaPiere's "Attitudes vs. Actions" (1934), we have been haunted by the suspicion that this may be untenable.

Employing methods that are equal if not superior to more recent research on the problem, LaPiere finds that what people say about a despised minority is not only unrelated to what they do when confronted with that minority; *it is inversely related.* People do the opposite of what they say—at least in this case. The evidence is powerful and the differences large—evidence that has discomforted many social scientists since that time. Scholars who insist on believing that people are consistent beings persist in their efforts to prove that LaPiere's study does not really show people to be inconsistent (e.g., Lord, Lepper, and Mackie 1984). It is clear that even if the analyst chooses to heavily discount this isolated bit of 1934 evidence, it cannot be discarded completely.

Richard LaPiere's quest has a history (see Deutscher 1973, p. 13).[1] This history culminated in his 1934 article "Attitudes and Actions"—the "first well-known attempt to study the relationship between attitudes and behavior" (Sjoberg 1982, p. 283). The study upon which the article is based consisted of a carefully designed and controlled experiment that consumed two years in the field and over ten thousand miles of driving.

During that time LaPiere recorded the treatment a Chinese couple received in hotels, auto camps, tourist homes, and restaurants. *Of the*

251 establishments approached, only one auto camp refused to accommodate them. Here then was an estimate of Caucasian-Oriental intergroup *behavior.* Allowing a time lapse of six months, a questionnaire was sent to each establishment. They were asked, "Would you accept members of the Chinese race as guests in your establishment?" *Only one yes response was received.* Here then was an estimate of Caucasian *attitudes* toward Orientals. Most important is the juxtapositioning of these two estimates: We have, in 1934, strong empirical evidence not only that there may be no relationship between what people say and what they do, but that under some conditions there may be a highly inverse relationship between the two. LaPiere concludes that "if we would know the extent to which (an individual's belief) restrains his behavior, it is to his behavior that we must look, not to his questionnaire response" (1934, p. 235).

In LaPiere's work we find a line of continuity leading toward new theoretical insights into human behavior, new methods for attaining knowledge, and new kinds of evidence, which could be used with confidence by policymakers bent on reducing some of the problems of the contemporary world. Yet, for the most part, social scientists have failed to pursue the path followed by LaPiere. LaPiere contends that no one has ever challenged his argument that what people say and what they do are not always in concordance. "On the other hand," he writes, "it seems to have had no effect at all on the sociological faith in the value of data gathered via opinion, attitude and other kinds of questionnaires. The 'Attitude vs. Action' paper was," he continues, "cited for years by almost everyone who wrote on attitudes or opinions as a sort of caution not to take their data too seriously; whereupon each author promptly ignored the caution and proceeded to assume that his data was indicative of what people would actually do in real-life circumstances."

LaPiere is not completely correct. Campbell's piece (1964) on "Pseudoinconsistency in the Attitude Literature" is a challenge, although not an effective one. [Raden's (1977) empirical explanation of Campbell's logic seems to support our skepticism.] Much of the work done since the middle seventies, which attributes observed discrepancies between sentiments and acts to methodological flaws, also poses a challenge to LaPiere's conclusion.

LaPiere was certainly not alone; there were other voices crying in the wilderness. In the late thirties, some of the best young minds in American sociology were concerned with the problem. Robert K. Merton, in a paper published in 1940, was critical of his own recently acquired survey data on attitudes toward blacks. The article provides an extended discussion of Merton's concerns about the theoretical and methodological adequacy of opinionnaires. He spends most of the paper detailing the ways in which attitude measures cannot accurately measure attitudes.

Merton reflects on the possibility that "Northerners treat Negroes less 'favorably' than they talk about them and Southerners talk about Negroes less 'favorably' than they treat them" (1940, pp. 21–22). Decades later, with the "discovery" of de facto segregation, the invention of such euphemisms as "neighborhood schools" and "law and order," antibusing riots in "liberal" northern cities like Boston, and the periodic murders of blacks who happen through white neighborhoods in the northeastern states, it became obvious to nearly everyone that at least one of these possibilities was reality; there was, in fact, a considerable discrepancy between the manner in which northern whites related to blacks and the empty rhetoric they employed in chastising their southern cousins. In 1938, Merton asked, "May we assume the amount and direction of spread between opinion and action to be relatively constant for members of different groups? To my knowledge," he continues, "no systematic research on this problem has been carried out" (1940, p. 21).

At the same time as Merton, C. Wright Mills argued, "Perhaps the central methodological problem of the social sciences springs from recognition that often there is a disparity between lingual and social-motor types of behavior" (1940a, p. 328). Mills suggested that we need to know "*how much* and *in what direction* disparities between talk and action will probably go" (p. 328, emphasis in original). It is interesting that both of these young visionaries should identify the same problem as critical (in contrast to most of their distinguished contemporaries), should do so at about the same time, and should suggest social-structural explanations. Merton speculates about the possibility of consistent group differences in the spread between opinion and action. Both Merton and Mills suspect that the location of people in particular strata of the society needs to be considered if one is to understand discrepancies between sentiments and acts. This is partly true, but Herbert Blumer employs a different perspective and, we think, with considerably more explanatory potential.

Blumer was the most consistent spokesperson for the point of view suggested by LaPiere's data. Since 1931 he has argued the logic of this position, in terms of theory, method, and substantive fields such as industrial relations and public opinion polling. In his presidential address to the American Sociological Society in 1956, Blumer suggests that, not only do we know nothing about behavior or the relation between attitudes and behavior, but that we don't know much about attitudes either:

The thousands of "variable" studies of attitudes, for instance, have not contributed to our knowledge of the abstract nature of an attitude; in a similar way the studies of "social cohesion," "social integration," "authority," or "group morale" have done nothing, so far as I can detect, to clarify or augment generic knowledge of these categories. (p. 684)

Why have both the empirical evidence and the theoretical rationale been ignored? Six decades ago LaPiere's explanation was couched in terms of economy and reliability: "The questionnaire," he observed,

> is cheap, easy, and mechanical. The study of human behavior is time consuming, intellectually fatiguing, and depends for its success upon the ability of the investigator. The former method gives quantitative results, the latter mainly qualitative. Quantitative measurements are quantitatively accurate; qualitative evaluations are always subject to the errors of human judgment.

"Yet," he concludes, "it would seem far more worthwhile to make a shrewd guess regarding that which is essential than to accurately measure that which is likely to prove quite irrelevant" (1934, p. 237).

Others, like Mills, have assumed a more cynical explanation. Turning to the sources of research finance, he suggests:

> Many foundation administrators like to give money for projects that are thought to be safe from political or public attack, that are large-scale, hence easier "to administer" than more numerous handicraft projects, and that are scientific with a capital S, which often only means made "safe" by trivialization.

"Accordingly," Mills concludes, "the big money tends to encourage the large-scale bureaucratic style of research into small-scale problems as carried on by The Scientists" (1954, p. 22). These explanations have persisted and most of them remain as valid today as they were in the past, but we suspect that they reflect a deeper and perhaps more basic problem. It is possible that the apparent anomaly of acknowledging the correctness of one position while pursuing another can best be explained in terms of the sociology of knowledge.

Epistemology and Research Methods

The sociology of knowledge has to do with the way in which the temper of the times and the ideological milieu in which we are immersed affect the kinds of questions we ask, the kinds of answers that form a permissible range, and the kinds of methods we employ to seek those answers. It "is devoted to digging up the social roots of knowledge, to searching out the ways in which knowledge and thought are affected by the environing social structure" (Merton 1957, p. 440). We may indeed have some roots to dig in our attempt to understand the directions taken by American sociology during the last six decades. The perceptions of knowledge—notions of the proper or appropriate ways of knowing—that were fashionable during the late twenties and early thirties, when sociology had its choices to make, surely impinged upon those choices.

Men like LaPiere and Blumer and, later, Mills are arguing from a basically antipositivistic position at a time when a century or more of cumulative positivistic science was resulting in a massive payoff in our knowledge and control of physical forces. And sociology had its alternatives. L. L. Thurstone was giving birth to what was to become modern scale analysis. Emery Bogardus was translating some of these ideas into sociological scales of contemporary relevance. And men like George Lundberg and Stuart Chapin were creating the theoretical and methodological rationale for the new "science" [see Bannister (1987) for an extended discussion of the pre-1940 quest for sociology to become a science]. Incisive critiques of the new sociology and the logic of its quantitative methods were plentiful. Merton (1940), for example, raises serious questions about the logic of scaling. He questions the meaning of the summed scores of groups' responses, and the linear continuity of the scales. He points out that scale items are not interchangeable. He concludes that Thurstone scales "rank, but they do not 'measure,' opinions" (p. 18). Merton also observes a number of sociological inadequacies of the Thurstone Attitude Scale, including the possibility that *people can simultaneously hold conflicting opinions.*

Such basic issues have been assiduously avoided in favor of systematic improvement in scaling *technique.* Thus we have "advanced" from Bogardus to Guttman to LISREL, without ever addressing the basic critique. If we listen to LaPiere's (1964) recollections of the temper of the times it becomes apparent that logic may not have been the deciding factor. His account is, of course, retrospective, perhaps distorted in some ways, certainly flavored by what has happened since, but nevertheless an eyewitness report by a deeply involved participant:

> American sociologists of the first two decades of this century were—with some few exceptions, of which Cooley is the only one that immediately comes to mind—just moralistic reformers in scientists' clothing. . . . Well into the 1930's the status of sociology and hence of sociologists was abominable, both within and outside the academic community. The public image of the sociologist was that of a blue-nosed reformer, ever ready to pronounce moral judgments and against all pleasurable forms of social conduct. . . .
> It is my impression, one that I cannot document, that most of the men

who came out of the Chicago department . . . [through the 1920s] were fairly passive disciples of the "Chicago School"—mostly trained in the ideas of Park, if not by him—and that they went out to spread the good word with a strong sense of mission. . . . The men who were to shape sociology during the 1930's were, for the most part, products of one or two men departments (e.g., Columbia) of low status within their universities. They were therefore to a considerable degree self-trained and without a doctrinaire viewpoint, and they were exceedingly conscious of the low esteem in which sociology was held.

Such men, and I was one among them, were determined to prove—at least to themselves—that sociology is a science, that sociologists are not moralists, and that sociology deserves recognition and support comparable to that being given psychology and economics. It was, I think, to this end that toward the end of the 20's scientific sociology came to be identified with quantitative methods in sociology, and the latter in turn with reliance upon the questionnaire as the one valid tool of investigation. Keep in mind that our number was few, that we were widely scattered, and the majority of well-established sociologists were products of or at least adherents to the Chicago School. What had we to offer; what had we to distinguish ourselves from the prescientific sociologists; what certainty that we too were not just moralists in disguise? Why, statistics, of course! Once this discovery had been made—and I suspect Stuart Chapin was as important in this as anyone else—the rest followed more or less automatically; and by the mid-thirties American sociologists were split into two antagonistic camps—the moralists, now usually described as "armchair theorists," and the scientists, whose distinguishing mark was the table of weights and measures.

About 1935 the scientists attempted an organizational purification of sociology proposing that membership in the ASS be limited to true sociologists and the rather considerable body of social workers, social reformers, and crack-pots be driven from our ranks. Like Luther, they discovered that it is impossible to reform from within, so they established the now long-defunct Sociological Research Association, with membership limited by charter to 100.[2] By this time, the Chicago department had lost its homogeneity, and the conflict between quantitativists and qualitativists raged there as elsewhere. So some Chicago men were admitted to the inner circle—and so, for some reason, was I. But admission was by election, and before long the original criteria for membership was [sic] forgotten, and by 1940 the organization consisted of 50 or so self-defined great men who could agree upon nothing except that the supply of great men had been exhausted.

Now as to my own uncertain part in all this. I was one of the Young Turks, and I shared with Lundberg, Bain, Stouffer, etc., the distaste for sociology as it had been and the hurt of its lowly status. But unlike the majority of the rebels, I did not share their belief that the cure for bad sociology was quantification. (letter to Irwin Deutscher, October 23, 1964)

LaPiere sees the history of American sociology between the two world wars as an effort not to build knowledge, but to achieve respectability and acceptability (see also Rhoades 1981, pp. 24–26). In terms of this goal, he believes we were successful (LaPiere 1969): "For it has in considerable measure been sociological reliance on quantitative methods that has won for sociology the repute and financial support that it now enjoys. That in gaining fame sociology may have become a pseudoscience is another, and quite different, matter" (letter to Irwin Deutscher, October 23, 1964).

It is possible to document a great sensitivity to public opinion on the part of sociologists who were seeking a bit more academic respect than, say, driver education has today. It becomes clear that this defensiveness of repute persisted into the 1940s when we examine an event that took place in 1947. The setting is the annual meeting of the American Sociological Society. Herbert Blumer (1948), reading his paper, "Public Opinion and Public Opinion Polling," is the villain in the drama.

In brief, Blumer issues a challenge to the empirical relevance of public opinion sampling procedures. His arguments tend to be logically and empirically unimpeachable. For example, he suggests that although each person may carry equal weight in an opinion poll, people do not carry equal weight in influencing policy, implementing decisions, or otherwise acting on their opinions. It follows that, to the extent that we are interested in what is likely to happen at some future time, we ought to do something other than randomly sample the population. An alternative is to sample those who have power and influence to effect the anticipated action or not to effect it. We should sample only those to whom the issues are salient, relevant, meaningful!

In the present context, the substance of Blumer's remarks is unimportant. What is curious is that, within the context of the professional meetings, the discussants also treated the substance of Blumer's remarks as unimportant. The two distinguished discussants, Julian Woodward and Theodore Newcomb, were indeed terribly distressed, but it was about something else.

Newcomb appears to have missed Blumer's point. He allows that there are certainly bad pollsters as well as good ones: "Some of them, I suppose, do not even know whether their respondents are archbishops or itinerant laborers" (Newcomb 1948, p. 550). The point is less what they are, than it is how influential they are and how salient the particular issue is to them. Cesar Chavez and Lech Walesa are laborers, but their opinions are of a different order from that of some other laborers (even though it may be the same opinion). Because, we suspect, of his scientific blinders, Newcomb finds Blumer's argument about sampling elusive: "I wish [Blumer] had shown some inherent connection between sampling and failure to obtain adequate information" (p. 550). The question is not one of adequacy of information; it is one of relevance to action.

When Newcomb pounces he reveals what is really irritating him: "I happen to believe that Professor Blumer's stand is one which delays scientific progress" (1948, p. 551). Fishbein's 1980 thoughts (quoted earlier) suggest that Newcomb's sentiments persist. As we read Blumer, it becomes clear that this was in fact his intention. He had made a choice between attempting to understand human behavior or advancing that perspective which sociologists call "science."

Woodward appears to have a better grasp on what Blumer is trying to sell, but he won't buy. He does suggest that surveys could measure the intensity with which opinions are held, the affiliation of respondents, and the influence of respondents. Like Newcomb, however, it is the science and respectability dimension that bothers him. He is embarrassed by Blumer's comments and is worried about what others will think of sociology and sociologists:

> Unhappily this is exactly what people outside the academic world, and not a few in the other disciplines inside it, have come to expect of the sociologist. . . . It is perhaps permissible to call attention to the need that we sociologists pay attention to our own problem of mass communication and our own impact on public opinion. Fortunately very few of the practicing pollsters are here today . . . but . . . if they were present, these public opinion survey people, who so far owe very little to the sociologists . . . would hardly go away from the meeting convinced that they owe much more in the future. I am afraid Blumer's paper would increase, rather than narrow, the distance between practitioner and professor. . . . This is too bad. (Woodward 1948, p. 554)

Blumer may be a prophet without honor. Some seventeen years after this encounter, Angus Campbell recollects Blumer's comments with a touch of nostalgia and no little remorse: "It is curious," Campbell writes, "that Blumer's hopes for the functional analysis of public opinion have been so little realized. The ability to conduct effective research on the problems he would have selected seems to elude us. The direction research has actually taken has been heavily influenced by the methods available" (1965, p. 633).

In those unhappy days we were an uneasy discipline, reaching simultaneously for knowledge and respectability. It may have been the very nature of our work that evoked an inherent contradiction between these two goals. In attempting to assume the stance of physical science, we have necessarily assumed its epistemology—its assumptions about the nature of knowledge and the appropriate means of knowing, including the rules of scientific evidence.

The requirement of clean empirical demonstration of the effects of isolated variables, in a manner that can be replicated, led to the creation, by definition, of such factors or variables. We knew that human behavior was rarely if ever directly influenced or explained by an isolated variable; we knew that it was impossible to assume that any set of such variables was additive (with or without weighting); we knew that the complex mathematics of the interaction among any set of variables, much less their interaction with external variables, was incomprehensible to us. In effect, although we knew the variables did not exist, we defined them into being (see Phillips 1971).

As Blumer's (1956) incisive critique of variable analysis implies, uncontrolled catalytic agents may be expected to be the rule rather than the exception in social processes. If that is so, then research designed to capture those processes by controlling the relationship among preidentified variables may lead us up a blind alley. That alley is all the more vicious because it is endless as well as blind. There are always other variables to consider and so we never discover that it is a dead end (Liska 1984; Sherman and Fazio 1983). We will explore this further in Chapter 12 when we consider the "moderating variable" approach.

It is also true that the excellent tools we have been developing may not be appropriate for the job we need to do. The argument that if our tools are inappropriate we ought to select problems that fit them, is so specious that it is hardly worth comment. The point is that otherwise good tools may be doing the wrong job or unimportant jobs. The best of shovels is not very useful for chopping down trees and it is difficult to dig a hole with even the finest axe. Sometimes such operations are attempted in social research.

We were not satisfied with creating variables. They had to be stripped of what little meaning they had in order that they might be operational, i.e., that they have their measurement built into their definition. One consequence then, was to break down human behavior in a way that was not only artificial but that did not jibe with the manner in which that behavior was observed. Having laid these foundations—and because the accretion of knowledge is a cumulative affair—we began to construct layer upon layer.

Merton suggests that the cumulative nature of science requires a high degree of consensus among scientists and leads, therefore, to an inevitable enchantment with problems of reliability (Merton 1957; see also Weigert 1970). All knowledge, whether scientific or not, is cumulative and all people who think or write stand on the shoulders of those who have thought or have written before. Merton would, we hope, view this "inevitable consensus" and the resulting fascination with reliability as dysfunctional: that is, as an unintended consequence and one that is contrary to some of the accepted goals of science—the discovery of new perspectives, new methods, and new knowledge. Surely these cannot be attained when everyone is committed to agreeing with everyone else.

It does, nevertheless, appear that the adoption of the scientific model in the social sciences has resulted in an uncommon concern for methodological problems centering on issues of reliability, to the concomitant neglect of problems of validity. We have, in our pursuit of reliability, been absorbed in measuring the amount of error that results from inconsistency among interviewers or inconsistency among items on our instruments. We concentrate on whether we are consistently right or wrong. As a consequence we may have been learning a great deal about how to pursue an incorrect course with maximum precision.

It is not our intent to disparage the importance of reliability per se; it is the obsession with it to which we refer. As we observe in Chapter 5, zero reliability must result in zero validity. Without stable measurement we cannot get at what we intend. But the relationship is not linear, since infinite perfection of reliability (zero error) may also be associated with zero validity. That is, our measurement may be very stable, but still fail to get at what we intend.

Whether or not one wishes to emulate the scientist and whatever methods may be applied in the quest for knowledge, we must make estimates of, allowances for, and attempts to reduce the extent to which our methods distort our findings. We hope this puts us on record as considering reliability a matter of serious concern. However, after this chapter the remainder of this book will be much more attentive to her neglected stepsister—validity.

It is because of the reliability issue that C. Wright Mills identifies the "disparities between talk and action" as "the central *methodological* problem of the social sciences" (Mills 1940a, p. 329, emphasis added). Mills's plea for systematic investigations into the differences between words and deeds is based on the need for the "methodologist to build into his methods standard margins of error" (p. 329). Just as Mills is concerned about reliability in the historical method, Hyman has documented the need for estimates of reliability in social-anthropological and clinical-psychiatric observations. He reminds us that the village of Tepotzlan as described by Oscar Lewis is quite different from the same village as it was described earlier by Robert Redfield. More recently, Freeman (1983) created a scandal with his challenge to Margaret Mead's (1928) observations of Samoans.

One of the few positive consequences of our decades of "scientific" orientation is the incorporation into the sociological mentality of a self-consciousness about methods—regardless of what methods are employed. As a result, sociologists who bring ethnological field techniques to bear on their problems are constrained to contemplate methodological issues and to publish methodological observations. This was notable in the series of articles that Howard S. Becker and Blanche Geer began publishing in the late 1950s (see Deutscher 1973, p. 42). Barney Glaser and Anselm Strauss (1967) were the first to systematically codify and justify the procedures and the logic employed in such sociological fieldwork. Shortly thereafter, a host of publications concerned with qualitative techniques began to appear.

In 1973 *Urban Life and Culture* (later retitled *Urban Life* and more recently *Journal of Contemporary Ethnography*) was started and five years later *Qualitative Sociology* began. Each has served as a medium for consideration of qualitative procedures. Scores of books on qualitative methods have also been published over the last two decades and Sage Publications recently (1986) began a series in qualitative methodology.

Several other outlets favoring the publication of qualitative studies have arisen since the early 1970s. These include the journal *Symbolic Interaction*, and the research annual *Studies in Symbolic Interaction*. Along with other journals that have consistently been open to qualitative work, like *Sociological Quarterly*, these avenues for publication serve as essential alternatives to the discipline's flagship journals.

Despite protestations of its defensive editors (Bonacich 1990, p. 327; see also Marwell 1991; Stryker 1982) the leading journal of the American Sociological Association, the *American Sociological Review*, is edited with an overwhelming bias toward quantitative content (Becker 1990, p. 323). The association's journal devoted to the study of social interaction, *Social Psychology Quarterly*, appears to be similarly biased. Scheff charges that this focus rewards reliability. He laments that "in most studies, reliability is purchased at the price of lessened attention to theory, validity, relevance, etc." (1991, p. 5).

Regardless of the importance of reliability, there remains a danger that in our obsession with it, the goals—the purposes for which we seek knowledge—and the phenomena about which we seek knowledge may become obscured. Scheff provides an example from a review done with his colleagues on quantitative studies of self-esteem:

> We showed that after more than 10,000 studies using more than 200 different scales, little or no advancement in knowledge or benefit to the public good had resulted. By focusing on reliability at the expense of theory and validity, studies of this type have become the sorcerer's apprentice, an industry that is mechanically producing a flood of studies of no obvious value. All of the human sciences are dominated by an enchantment with procedural rationality. (1991, p. 5)

One of the less desirable consequences of our neglect of the relationship between words and deeds has been the development of a technology that is inappropriate to the understanding of human behavior, and conversely, the almost complete absence of a technology that can facilitate our learning about the conditions under which people in various categories do or do not "put their monies where their mouths are." Under what conditions will people behave as they talk? Under what conditions is there no relationship? And under what conditions do they say one thing and behave in a manner exactly the opposite? In spite of the fact that all of these combinations have been empirically observed and reported, few efforts have been made to order such observations.

Perhaps of even greater importance, we do not know under what conditions a change in attitude anticipates a change in behavior or under what conditions a change in behavior anticipates a change in attitude. Again, both phenomena have been empirically observed and recorded. Overt action can be understood and interpreted only within the context of its meaning to the actors, just as verbal reports can be understood and interpreted only within the context of their meaning to respondents. And in large part the context of each is the other. "Where but in social situations," asks Erving Goffman, "does speaking go on?" (1964, p. 134). But the fact remains that one of the methodological consequences of our recent history is that we are barely beginning to develop a technology for observing, ordering, analyzing, and interpreting overt behavior— especially as such behavior relates to attitudes, norms, aspirations, opinions, values, and other sentiments.

One abortive approach to the study of overt behavior, time and motion studies (e.g., Tausky and Piedmont 1968), is inadequate because it leaves one with no understanding of what the flow of action means to the actors (Maines 1987; Denzin 1987). On the other hand, such understanding is not, in itself, adequate. For example, Roebuck and Spray (1967) provide a description of sexual maneuvering in a cocktail lounge that reeks of validity (see also the early volumes of *Urban Life and Culture*, which contain many articles reporting essentially raw data). The credibility of their observational account with its rich sense of subtle interactional ploys is unimpeachable. But what does one do with it? Implications and applications and relationships with other social phenomena are left to the reader to tease out. We submit that data, even very good data, cannot stand on its own.

The development of a new technology could take any number of directions. Ideally, we should seek to refine the model provided by LaPiere, whereby we obtain information from the same population on sentiments and acts under natural social conditions. Surely the kind of cleverness that creates situational apparatuses for the psychological laboratory could also create refined situational designs for research under conditions that have meaning for the actors. The theoretical and methodological rationalization of participant-observer field techniques begun by Becker and Geer and further systematized by Glaser and Strauss is a promising alternative. There may be as yet untapped possibilities in contrived laboratory experiments—if we can learn how to contrive them in such a way that their results are not denuded of any general meaning by the artificial specificity of the situations. If someday reliable and valid projective instruments are developed, we may have made a significant technological step forward.

Novel methodological innovations do lie buried in the literature. Kohn and Williams (1956), for example, have suggested a method of deliberately introducing new factors into natural situations for observational purposes. This is a device for applying rigorous experimental controls to everyday life without creating unintended and undesirable reaction effects (for other examples, see Steffensmeier and Terry 1975). Occasionally, a social psychologist devises a laboratory experiment with such diabolical cunning that the situation must surely appear real to the subjects. The study by Stanley Milgram (1964) is one such experiment. Zimbardo's (1972) prison experiment provides an example in which the situation became real even for the experimenter and his colleagues (Haney 1976). Some psychologists have evolved a design that enables them to exploit the subject's definition of a dummy experimental situation, in order to conceal the actual nature of the experiment, which appears as a natural event unrelated to the experiment (Himmelstein and Moore 1963).

There was a time earlier in this century when sociologists came to a crossroads. We could choose, on the one hand, to undertake neat, orderly studies of measurable phenomena. This alternative carried with it all of the gratifications of conforming to the prestigious methods of pursuing knowledge then in vogue, of having access to considerable sums of monies through the granting procedures of large foundations and governmental agencies, of a comfortable sense of satisfaction derived from dealing rigorously and precisely with small isolated problems that were cleanly defined, of moving for fifty years down one track in an increasingly rigorous, refined, and reliable manner, while simultaneously disposing of the problems of validity by the semantic trickery of operational definitions.

On the other hand, we could have tackled the messy world as we knew it to exist, a world where the same people will make different utterances under different conditions and will behave differently in different situations and will say one thing while doing another. We could have tackled a world where control of relevant variables was impossible not only because we didn't know what they were, but because we didn't know how they interacted with each other. We could have accepted the conclusion of almost every variant of contemporary philosophy of science that the notion of cause and effect (and therefore of stimulus and response or of independent and dependent variables) was untenable. We eschewed this formidable challenge. This was the hard way. We chose the easy way.

Yet the easy way provides one set of results and the hard way provides another. The easy way for Merton in 1938 would have been simply to present his survey findings in as sophisticated a manner as possible and to return for more data on additional samples if there were questions unanswered. He chose instead to think about the potential impact of different group associations on the strength and direction of his findings and thus to seriously question their meaning. The easy way for Blumer in 1947 would have been to demonstrate his disciplinary loyalty by showing pollsters how his ingenuity could help them obtain better samples, rather than questioning the basic assumptions of polling methods. The easy way for LaPiere in 1934 would have been to conduct as rigorous as possible a survey of attitudes of hotel and restaurant managers toward Orientals. But this leads to a set of conclusions that are the opposite of what he finds when he does it the hard way, i.e., traveling thousands of miles in order to confront those managers with Orientals.

A short typescript paper by David Hanson (1965; see also Hanson 1969) reviews some of the literature on the relationship between attitudes and overt behavior. He concludes that laboratory experimental studies tend to show a positive correlation between attitudes and behavior, while observational field studies tend to show no such correlation. Although there are important exceptions to this rule, it serves as a reminder that our choice of methods may not be unrelated to our conclusions. Let us turn from polemics to evidence. What observations can be found that reveal the empirical relationship between sentiments and acts? This is the central question of Chapter 3.

Notes

1.   Quotations attributed to LaPiere in this chapter and not otherwise identified, are from a lengthy communication of his reminiscences to Irwin Deutscher, October 23, 1964.

2.   The Sociological Research Association was not as defunct as LaPiere believed (or hoped). Galliher and Hagan (1989) report that the group still exists and shares a meal together at the national meetings each year. The interested reader should see Bannister (1987) for a history of the organization.

3

Bits of Evidence

And That's Only the Beginning

In the mid-sixties Linton Freeman calmly announced to a gathering of busy researchers that there should be an immediate national moratorium on all data gathering. At the time he was interested in data banks and information retrieval systems, so the source of such a ridiculous notion was understandable, but of course none of the assembled sociologists could believe he was serious. Freeman was sensitive to the large amounts of unanalyzed and partially analyzed data on just about everything, gathering dust in files everywhere. As we began to locate and read materials on the relationship between sentiments and acts we were persuaded to take Freeman's suggestion seriously.

We would still insist that when we are very clear about what we need to know it is imperative to design research that will ferret out that specific bit of knowledge and to gather the necessary data. It may also at times be desirable to gather data for the purpose of verifying something that appears to be correct but that requires somewhat more evidence in order for us to be comfortable with it. There may be very good reasons for data gathering. But as we have come more and more to suspect, a great deal of data gathering is ritual duplication—unnecessary, unproductive, and, mostly, not at all useful to anyone.

We do not think it a contradiction to suggest that, on the one hand, little attention has been paid to the problems raised by LaPiere in his pioneering study and that, on the other hand, a great deal of data are available on those same issues. These statements can be consistent because, without any necessary awareness or concern for the problem of sentiments and acts, hundreds of observers have recorded information on how people behave, how they talk, and sometimes even on how they do both. The data are in the library, but they are raw data in the sense that the investigators must perform the analytic task of relating them to each other and to the problem that concerns them.

31

The trick, in this kind of research, is to locate empirical data that inform one on the relationship between what people say and what they otherwise do, regardless of the labels attached to dimensions and regardless of the author's original intent. But why go to all this trouble, largely on the grounds of a primitive field study on a Chinese couple done during the Great Depression and the persistent polemics of Herbert Blumer? First of all, we personally consider the LaPiere study a masterpiece and we have gradually come to realize that Blumer makes very good sense. Others may disagree with both of these judgments. But it is difficult to disagree with the observation that LaPiere identified a problem of central importance to the understanding of human behavior and one that far transcends (1) American attitudes, (2) Chinese minorities, (3) relationships between restaurateurs and motel keepers with minority customers, (4) the decade of the thirties, or (5) problems of minority groups in general. Let us consider this last point.

The richest empirical observations on the relationship between what people say and what they do are found in the study of race and ethnic relations. Confrontation by scholars with a public language of race and ethnic relations that is frequently at odds with public behavior toward minorities has led to a clear conceptual distinction between prejudice on the one hand and discrimination on the other. Merton (1949) developed a typology of the relationship between prejudicial sentiments and discriminatory actions, which clearly suggested that the two do not always go together. Once made, the conceptual distinction directs investigators, in their observations, analyses, and conclusions, toward the fact that verbalizations and subjective states of mind are not necessarily related to objective actions toward others.

Without such an empirical and conceptual confrontation the social scientist is prone to ignore the possibility that people do not always do as they say and, in fact, may do the exact opposite. The old adage, Do as I say, not as I do, suggests that ordinary people may be aware of this contradiction. Warriner (1958) cautions us to be alert to differences between public and private sentiments and, by inference, public and private actions. He finds that Kansans in a small, "dry," rural community publicly support prohibition and condemn drinkers. Many of these people, however, drink in their homes. Warriner does not attribute this discrepancy to hypocrisy, but rather suggests that "whenever the members of the community acted within the context of the community, their behavior conformed to and expressed the explicit canons of the official morality" (p. 166). The honest expression of opinion in a relatively public situation thus becomes something quite different from the equally honest expression of opinion in a relatively private situation. Gusfield (1967,

1981) suggests that a public morality serves a symbolic function for the community, even when it is not enforced.

In spite of the conceptual advantage offered to students of race and ethnic relations, there is evidence that suggests that the problem of sentiments and acts is endemic. It has been reported that small-time steel wholesalers mouthed patriotism while undercutting the national economy in wartime (Kriesberg 1956), that the head of an automobile company promised not to make one cent of "blood money" off of a war but the corporation turned an enormous profit from the defense contracts it secured (Lacey 1986, Chapter 9), that the behavior of mothers toward their children is unrelated to their attitude toward them (Zunich 1962), that attitudes toward and participation in riots are discordant (Ransford 1968), that natural food devotees believe that white sugar is poison but sometimes eat it (Pestello 1985), and that pedestrians observed crossing an intersection against a Don't Walk light frequently stated that they never engaged in such behavior and, even more frequently, expressed the sentiment that it is a naughty thing to do (Dannick 1969).

In the midfifties, a pair of industrial psychologists, interested in assessing the state of knowledge regarding the relationship between employee attitudes and employee performance, covered all of the literature in that area through 1954 (Brayfield and Crockett 1955). Treating various classes of studies separately, they found in every category minimal or no relationship between the attitudes of the employees and their performance. In other words, what workers say about their work and how they evaluate it has nothing to do with how they act on the job. The post-1970s literature we collected contained several studies where the researchers found either that attitudes are highly unstable and contribute little to predicting behavior beyond knowing past behavior (e.g., Acock and Fuller 1984; Davidson, Yantis, Norwood, and Montano 1985; Fredericks and Dossett 1983), or that the entire model tested, which included attitude variables, explains little variance in behavior (e.g., Baumann and Chenowith 1984; Hill, Gardner, and Rassaby 1985; Kantola, Syme, and Campbell 1982).

Everyone has learned some painful lessons lately about attitude-behavior discrepancy. In the 1970s we learned that the leaders of a White House team elected on a strong "law and order" platform behaved quite contrary to their rhetoric. In the 1980s we discovered that some conservative Republican congressmen (Bauman and Lukens), who aligned themselves with Reagan and his call for a return to "traditional values," were involved in sordid homo- and heterosexual affairs with juveniles. We also found out that two prominent television evangelists (Bakker and

Swaggart), who passionately preached about morality, were engaging in untoward sexual behaviors.

Perhaps now the reader can better understand why we see no contradiction in suggesting, on the one hand, a neglect of the problem of sentiments and acts and, on the other hand, a plethora of available data. The parameters of the issue seem to us to have been adequately identified. In this case, at least, we would agree with Freeman. There is no need to gather any more data describing the relationship between what people say and do.

Freeman and Ataöv (1960) illustrate the problem of inconsistencies in a student sample. They create a situation in which they can determine whether students cheat when correcting their own exams. Several weeks later, these students are presented with a questionnaire asking a number of indirect questions about cheating, along with a direct question about whether they have ever cheated on an exam. All correlations between behavior, the direct question, and their three types of indirect questions were *not* significant.

Sometimes Consistency

It would be a serious selective distortion of the existing evidence to suggest that all of it indicates an incongruence between what people say and what they do. Consumers sometimes do change their buying habits in ways that they say they will (Martin 1963), people frequently do vote as they tell pollsters they will (but not when race confounds the issue as in the Virginia gubernatorial election of 1989), urban relocation populations may accurately predict to interviewers the type of housing they will attempt to obtain (Cagle and Deutscher 1970), local party politicians do in fact employ the campaign tactics that they believe to be most effective (Frost 1961), youngsters will provide survey researchers with self-reports of their delinquency that are consistent with official measures of delinquency (Elliott and Ageton 1980), and an expectant mother's attitudes and intentions regarding breast-feeding vs. bottle-feeding are related to the type of feeding the infant receives (Manstead, Profitt, and Smart 1983; Manstead, Plevin, and Smart 1984). The empirical evidence can best be summarized as reflecting wide variation in the relationships between sentiments and acts.

As a result of their review of all of the studies on employee attitudes and performance, Brayfield and Crockett observe,

> the scarcity of relationships, either positive or negative, demonstrated to date even among the best designed of the available studies leads us to question whether or not methodological changes alone would lead to a

> substantial increase in the magnitude of the obtained relationships. (1955, p. 415)

Having arrived at the point where they are able to question the assumption that a relationship must obtain between what people say and what they do, these authors can now question whether or not the failure to observe such a relationship is necessarily a consequence of the inefficiency of the measuring instruments.

This observation parallels that made by Warriner in his study of Kansas drinkers. "In most studies," he declares, "an inconsistency is explained away by searching for some bias in the observational technique . . . . He continues, "Our thesis is that at least one class of these inconsistencies is real (i.e., is not a function of faulty observational techniques) and has been inadequately accounted for in the past" (1958, p. 165). It seems to us that any research is open to methodological criticisms and that for investigators to attribute their findings to that source when they do not get what they expect is something of a ruse.

It is possible to attribute any findings to methodological deficiencies—whether they suggest no relationship, an inverse relationship, or a positive relationship. What Brayfield and Crockett (1955) and Warriner (1958) are suggesting is that methodological faults do not account for all of the observations. This is an important breakthrough since it permits them, and us, to look at alternative explanations, including conceptual considerations.

What Else Could You Expect?

A core assumption in the attitude-behavior literature is that attitudes direct behavior. Few researchers question it. Yet, consider for a moment some of the more popular conceptual frameworks entertained by social scientists. They all suggest that no matter what one's theoretical orientation may be, there is no reason to expect congruence between sentiments and acts and every reason to expect discrepancies between them.

The expectation for incongruence is true even of the varieties of balance theory, popular in social science. Neofunctionalism in sociology and anthropology, and dissonance in psychology, may posit a drive or strain toward consistency but such an image of people and society must carry with it the assumption that, at any point in time, a condition of imbalance or dissonance or inconsistency obtains. A drive toward balance could not be a viable force unless we were constantly in a state of imbalance!

If one chooses, on the other hand, to work with such psychoanalytic concepts as the unconscious or the subconscious or the various defense mechanisms, then it must be assumed that people cannot themselves know how they might behave under specified conditions. Furthermore, such mechanisms as repression or rationalization suggest that respondents may not be able to tell an interviewer how they have behaved in the past. Turning to such dissimilar sociological ancestors as Charles H. Cooley and Emile Durkheim, we find that they built their concepts of people in society around the assumption that human nature requires social constraints. Under such conditions there is an inherent conflict between a person's private self and social self; hence the area of role theory is developed to help us understand some of the devices by which a person is constrained to act appropriately in diverse social situations. Goffman (1959) develops this split between private and public self into a dramaturgic model incorporating the ideas of "backstage" vs. "frontstage" behavior.

On the gross societal level (macrosociological analysis), such concepts as social disorganization, anomie, and cultural lag suggest that people can be caught up in discrepant little worlds, which make conflicting demands upon them. These concepts are rooted in inconsistencies between attitudes and behaviors! When we consider the behavior of groups smaller than societies, we frequently think in terms such as situational contingencies, the definition of the situation, public and private behavior, or reference group theory—all of which relate what one does or what one says to the immediate context, both as it exists objectively and as it exists in the mind of the actor. Do we not expect attitudes and behaviors to vary as the definition of the situation is altered or as different reference groups are brought to bear?

The symbolic interactionists have traditionally exhibited the greatest sensitivity to this problem in sociology. Among others, both Blumer and LaPiere have insisted that we act, either verbally or overtly, in response to the symbolic meaning the confronting object has for us in the given situation. A question posed by an interviewer concerning feelings about Armenian women forces one to respond to the words and to the interviewer; standing face-to-face with a real flesh-and-blood Armenian woman, one is constrained to act toward a very different set of symbols. Is there any reason to assume that behavior should be the same in these two radically different symbolic situations?

In his distinction between the psychology of prejudice and the sociology of intergroup relations, Arnold Rose (1956) has developed a vigorous symbolic interactionist argument regarding the theoretical and empirical independence of attitudes and behaviors. Underpinning this conceptual framework is Herbert Blumer's interpretation of the social philosophy of George Herbert Mead. From such a perspective, verbal behavior and overt behavior may be seen as different segments of a single act in process. Apparent inconsistencies can be conceptualized as resulting from errors in interpretation on the part of the actor, or from reinterpretation of the meaning of the act during the interval between the moment of verbal expression and the moment of overt behavior. This formulation also sensitizes the investigator to the possibility that the apparent inconsistency is a result of the actor's perception of the verbalization and the overt behavior as segments of two different acts; i.e., regardless of the investigator's intent, the word and the deed may be perceived by the actor as relating to different objects. Or, employing a distinction created by Rokeach (1970), people may have attitudes toward objects and they may have attitudes toward situations and the two need not be related.

One conceptual framework that we tend to neglect lies in the study of talk, language, or conversation. Although symbolic interactionists have been most sensitive to the importance of language for social interaction, they have tended to implicitly accept the importance of language without explicitly examining its role in interaction (Maines 1981; Boden 1990). There is a variety of ways to approach the study of language, ranging from formal linguistics, which focuses on the structure of sound and meaning, to syntactics, where the emphasis is upon grammatical structures (Grimshaw 1981). The central problem of meaning—the semantic dimension of language—suffered neglect for many years primarily because investigators were prone to avoid as "unscientific," subjective phenomena that appeared to be difficult to measure. In addition to its other features, the study of talk should deal with an analysis of the meanings of verbal communication in context: Researchers should reveal how speech works in social interaction (Grimshaw 1981, p. 201). The problem of attitudes and actions is probably best informed by this semantic dimension, for it is here that issues of understanding and misunderstanding are addressed.

Although latent, there has been a concern throughout the history of American sociology with the importance of language. It can be found in both Cooley's and Mead's fascination with the use of personal pronouns in the development of the social self, as well as in fragments of discontinuous work by sociologists like Everett Hughes (Hughes and Hughes 1952), C. Wright Mills (1939, 1940a, 1940b, 1963), Leonard Schatzman and Anselm Strauss (1955), and James H. S. Bossard (1945). We have not been sufficiently concerned with whether people understood our responses as we intend (Atkinson 1988, p. 455; Goffman 1981). Furthermore, as Benney and Hughes have put it, "The interview, as itself a form of social rhetoric, is not merely a tool of sociology but a part of its very subject matter" (1956, p. 138). Collins makes a similar point about questionnaires, "[H]ighly technical question surveys which fail to examine the situation of question-answering in regard to the other reality-constructing activities of respondents' (and sociologists') lives are naive" (1975, pp. 108–9).

Ethnomethodologists contributed to a resurgent interest in everyday natural speech as sociological data (Garfinkel 1967; Cicourel 1967; Jacobs 1967; Scott and Lyman 1968). They challenged the taken-for-granted nature of the social world. Social and verbal interaction is based on trust. Social actors do not question whether others have a rationale for what they do and say. It is assumed that words and actions are linked (Collins 1975). A difficulty with ethnomethodology is its greater concern with the method of studying everyday talk than explaining it (Collins 1975; Atkinson 1988). "Ethnomethodology has tended to act as if there were no regularities at all in the way people affect each other, which might be called 'social structure'" (Collins 1975, p. 109). In at least some versions of ethnomethodology, the imagery has become asocial and subjective, rather than intersubjective (Maines 1981), and intention and meaning have been eliminated in favor of understanding methods of generating orderly sequences (Atkinson 1988).

Growing out of ethnomethodology is another promising approach to language or talk, conversation analysis. Boden (1990) suggests that talk is "language-in-action." Conversation analysis and symbolic interactionism converge at the point where thought becomes action through talk (Boden 1990). Conversational analysts have focused on the sequencing of talk in natural settings. In so doing, they have reduced the multidimensional nature of temporality in social life to a unidimensional form (Atkinson 1988; Maines 1987). The main departure between these two approaches is again methodological. What is the best way to observe talk: recordings or ethnographic accounts? Repeatedly hearing a sequence of talk alone may not be enough; to understand meaning, we need to know about the relationships and context (McCall and Wittner 1990).

A linguistic approach is in its infancy in providing a foundation for understanding the relationship between what people say and what they do. What differences in meaning can be conveyed by different people with the same words? Crew demonstrates that even the supposedly simple and straightforward Likert responses can be interpreted very differently by respondents than researchers intend and presume:

> Many of the questions on the interview schedule were Likert type items ranging from "very much" to "very little" or from "very good" to "very poor." The problem was that in the colloquial language of the region, the word "very" apparently has an idiomatic usage which is closer to what we mean by "fairly" or even "poorly." . . . In many cases the coded response

was quite likely the exact opposite of the respondent's opinion. (1983, p. 225)

In an address in 1965, we raised the question (only half seriously) of whether one could safely assume that the dichotomy between a negative response and an affirmative response was as easily translatable as it seemed to be: "Should we assume that a response of 'yah,' 'da,' 'si,' 'oui,' or 'yes' all really mean exactly the same thing in response to the same question? Or may there be different kinds of affirmative connotations in different languages?" (Deutscher 1966, p. 249). We have since discovered that this was a more serious question than we had thought. For example, Glenn (1954) found that an English no tends to be interpreted as yes by members of the Arabic culture, if the no is not emphasized. A simple no indicates that negotiation should occur. Conversely, a nonemphasized yes is likely to be interpreted as a polite refusal. Hunt, Crane, and Wahlke were informed by an Austrian respondent that "every 'yes' has its 'however,' and every 'no' its 'if.'" They also reported that "it was not possible to find a French equivalent for 'may or may not' as a check-list response" (1964, p. 66).

As it happens, this problem is not restricted to exotic languages and cultures. It occurred to us that part of the conventional wisdom of some young American men is that when a woman says no she may mean yes. Concerns with acquaintance rape point to the potential seriousness for this type of "misunderstanding." He assumes he is carrying out her real wishes, while she feels supremely violated [see Scully and Marolla (1985) on rapists' justifications and excuses].

Even more revealing is David Riesman's finding that, in effect, there is something of the Arab in English-speaking American professors. Riesman personally interviewed survey respondents to the Lazarsfeld and Thielens Teacher Apprehension Study. He asked the professors about their responses to precoded alternatives and concluded that, "it sometimes happens that people torn between 'yes' and 'no,' will answer in one direction and then add qualifications in the other, showing for example that their 'yes' doesn't quite mean 'yes,' and may even lean toward 'no'" (Riesman 1958, p. 277, footnote 11).

We would suggest that it may be impossible to accurately translate most words in any language to any other language. Words are fragments of linguistic configurations; they mean nothing in isolation from the configuration. We have a great deal to learn from linguistics if we can bring ourselves to view language from the perspective of the symbolic interactionist and the ethnomethodologist—as social and cultural symbolism. Clearly, we have developed a certain respect for the explanatory power of the symbolic interactionist perspective. We do not believe that we held (much less understood) this position when we first began to look at the attitude-behavior relationship in 1964. It came to appear to us as one of the more reasonable and empirically correct modes of explanation as we tried to make sense out of the morass of data in which we were drowning. It is, however, not our purpose at this point to urge anyone's conversion to a symbolic interactionist perspective. We will be satisfied if the reader will agree that no matter what perspective is taken, there is no basis for assuming consistency between what people say and what they do.

Let us suggest that, as an intellectual exercise, you take whatever other conceptual frameworks to which you may be partial and determine whether or not they permit you to assume that you can expect people to act in accordance with their words. If we had only LaPiere's verbal data to go on, surely we would suggest to minority peoples that they are unlikely to find food or lodging on a cross-country auto trip. His behavioral indicators lead to no such recommendation. It seems clear to us that there are implications in all this for the role of social science research in policy recommendations. Research aimed at evaluation or demonstration frequently makes precisely the assumption that we have challenged: that what people say is a predictor of what they will do.

There is a body of folk wisdom encased in such aphorisms as: The proof of the pudding is in the eating, Put up or shut up, and Talk is cheap. These suggest that in the commonsense world of the person on the street, everyday life may be governed in part by a rule that implies doubt as to the probability or the intention of others acting as they speak. If there is an "aha!" quality about all this, then we suspect that that is what sociology is all about. It is true that the commonsense world of the sociologist is not the same as the commonsense world of the person on the street. But it is not at all clear which of the two incorporates the most effective methodology for understanding and dealing with recurrent problems of human interaction and social processes.

This we take to be the central theme of ethnomethodology, as Harold Garfinkel has named it. The position deserves to be considered with respect. Under incessant needling by a group of prominent sociologists, Garfinkel makes it clear that he intends no irony in his choice of terms (Hill and Crittenden 1968). He contrasts ethnomethodology with such fields as ethnobotany or ethnoastronomy, which, he suggests, are ironic. By this he means that the ethnoastronomer (or whatever) studies the curious (perhaps naive and certainly "unscientific") manner by which primitive people explain the workings of the solar system and the celestial universe. This primitive folk knowledge is evaluated and judged by the standards of Western science. It is essentially an ethnocentric procedure whereby we see how close the simple folk have guessed the truth as we know it to be. Ethnomethodology, in contrast, assumes that the person on the street governs everyday relations with others by a set of rules. It is these rules which, taken for granted though they may be, constitute an effective methodology for human relations. We suspect that sociologists have been remiss in not being more attentive to the fact that every person must indeed be a social scientist if survival at any level in a human society is to be guaranteed.

We suspect, furthermore, that we need to make a more deliberate effort to discover what every person knows but takes for granted in negotiating everyday life with others. The more orthodox symbolic interactionists deliberately involve themselves in the little worlds they study precisely in order to discover that "aha!" quality of those worlds—to render their social processes and perspectives explicit. The ethnomethodologist, although operating on some of the same assumptions for the same purposes, takes a somewhat different methodological stance. Since members of little social worlds are seen as behaving according to rules that they take for granted, the researcher must maintain a certain distance in order to avoid being seduced into those taken-for-granted worlds. Only by maintaining a degree of detachment—as a stranger—can the investigator perceive what members routinely assume.

But why do we fuss so? Science is a cumulative affair and sociology is young. Given time to build a body of knowledge, we will discover our mistakes, rectify them, and systemically move ahead. Yet it sometimes seems that we aren't getting anywhere. This may be a myopic view, but in Chapter 4 we will examine more closely, using a case study approach, the "progress" we have been making in understanding the relationship between sentiments and acts.

4

A Cumulative Science?

The Test of Time

Research done in the fifties left the impression that we were not being informed much beyond what we had learned from LaPiere's 1934 article. Then, in 1965, Lawrence Linn published "Verbal Attitudes and Overt Behavior." That paper provided an opportunity to undertake a partial test of our cumulative knowledge about sentiments and acts. Up until Linn's 1965 article, the only credible piece of research that was clearly comparable to LaPiere's had been Melvin DeFleur and Frank Westie's 1958 article, "Verbal Attitudes and Overt Acts: An Experiment in the Salience of Attitudes." Linn provided a third point on the time line. A search of the post-1970 literature turned up a roughly comparable study by Charles Lord, Mark Lepper, and Diane Mackie published in 1984, "Attitude Prototypes as Determinants of Attitude-Behavior Consistency." It provides the fourth point in our time line and brings us to the present state of research.

Obviously these four studies are far from identical and, in some ways, not comparable. On the other hand, we could not have learned anything about continuity in knowledge if all we had were replications, since, in that case, each study would simply duplicate the logical and methodological errors (or truths) of the previous one. What makes these studies useful for our purposes is, first, that each represents an acceptable degree of craft for its time. The studies are not straw people, but are, rather, reasonable exemplars of social science research. Second, it is fortuitous that they are well spaced over a fifty-year period.

There are four other qualities that these studies share. Most important is the fact that each deals with the relationship between verbal expressions and overt acts, and in each, both the word and the deed are recorded for the same population. Furthermore, each employs the same substantive problem situation: dominant-group attitudes and acts toward a minority. In addition, each is an empirical study that attempts to

43

rigorously design and control the research situation. Finally, all of them employ the same style of reporting the problems, the methods, and the results, and all four are published.

Early in 1969, the first author of this book published a paper providing a detailed comparative analysis of the 1934, 1958, and 1965 articles. That paper provoked a lively exchange. The remainder of this chapter and much of the next one are based on the critique made in the 1969 article. But there have been modifications, largely as a result of the extensive and thoughtful feedback that followed its publication (Ajzen, Timko, and White 1982; Ewans 1969; L. Gordon 1969; Lastrucci 1970). The most comprehensive critique came from a group of Illinois psychologists and is discussed in Chapter 5.

What follows, then, is an analysis of four cases that provide an opportunity to improve upon our guess about the extent to which we have been progressing methodologically in the kind of social research that is the concern of this volume. The test is only partial, but it is nevertheless an improvement over the hunch. *Let us examine the progress of five decades of sociological pursuit of answers to the same question!*

Looking Backward

Linn

We will begin with an analysis of Linn (1965) and establish the criteria that emerged as the 1934, 1958, and 1965 articles were read comparatively. Linn "is concerned with the relationship between verbal attitudes as expressed through response items on an attitude questionnaire and subsequent behavior" (p. 353). He is interested ultimately in achieving prediction of behavior from written attitude scores. The attitude of his white female subjects is obtained by asking them if they would be willing to pose for hypothetical photographs with black men. A graded series of conditions under which the pictures would be used, ranging from strictly scientific use to propaganda, provides a "scale" from which an estimate of prejudice is made. Selected subjects are asked at a later point if they would be willing to cooperate with a psychological testing agency by permitting their photos actually to be taken with blacks. Under these supposedly real conditions, the subjects are asked to sign a series of photographic releases, that series being graded along the same lines as the conditions in the attitude scale. As Linn puts it, "attitude objects (items on the questionnaires) [are] identical to the behavior observed (the signing of photographic releases)" (p. 357).

This cleverly indirect technique for establishing the relationship between attitude and behavior suffers from at least five types of defects. The first of these is the emphasis on prediction.

Criterion 1: Prediction. Prediction is a primitive scientific notion that assumes a direct, uninterrupted, straight-line flow of behavior. The idea of such simple cause-and-effect relationships between two variables has by and large been discarded in the philosophy of science. Among social scientists, however, the idea sometimes survives as what Weigert (1970) has called "the magical rhetoric of methodology." According to Weigert, "A common designation of magic is the attribution of empirical efficaciousness to minutely observed rites without understanding the causal link between rite and effect" (p. 116). Prediction is, in fact, as closely related to magic as it is to science.

One may accurately predict without ever understanding why the prediction works. Malaria, for example, could be related to the presence of stagnant water in warm climates and effectively brought under control without any knowledge of the particular breed of mosquito that carried it, much less of what that mosquito carried. In a similar case, the discovery of the spread of AIDS led to the closing of public baths, without much understanding of what caused the disease and exactly how it was transmitted (Shilts 1987). This is effective and valuable social action in the public health arena; it has nothing to do with science.

Herbert Blumer has argued repeatedly that prediction of a later phase of a social act is not possible solely on the basis of knowledge of an earlier phase. As Blumer points out, the act is a process in constant development: It is being constructed. The earlier dimension tapped does not determine any later dimension that may be tapped. The determination is made during the course of the intervening period and may be heavily influenced by factors in the immediate situation in which the act or attitude is called forth. In Blumer's own words:

> Between the initiating agent and the overt expression the act is built up. In this construction of the act the individual is engaged in defining what confronts him in his situation and is engaged in the process of making indications to himself in doing so. It is out of this process that he shapes his overt behavior. In other words, how he acts overtly is formed primarily out of what he takes into account and how he molds what he takes into account. The deficiencies of essentially all schemes, including that which reasons from attitude to overt behavior, lie in the failure to accommodate this intervening process of constructing the act. I do not know whether there is much likelihood, given the temper of contemporary thought, for sociologists to see this simple and obvious point. (personal communication to Irwin Deutscher, March 29, 1966)

The fact remains that science is concerned with "input" and "output" only in marginal ways. Any study that takes prediction to be a major goal of research is confusing science and magic. Clearly one of the several available devices for confirming either a magical or scientific claim is the predictive test. If we say to you that the sun will be blotted out at high noon tomorrow because the gods are displeased, and if it is blotted out, our magic has been put to a predictive test and passed. If we inform you that there will be a total eclipse of the sun at precisely noon tomorrow because our calculations indicate that the moon will pass between the earth and the sun at that moment, and if there is a total eclipse, our science has been put to a predictive test and also passed. It is a legitimate and persuasive test, but it is not the primary concern of scientific research.

Criterion 2: The Sample. Linn's sample is small and select—too small and too select! It consists of 34 eighteen- and nineteen-year-old women enrolled in an introductory sociology course at a state university. The selectivity is compounded by the fact that only volunteers from among those who took the attitude test were exposed to the behavior test. The investigator concedes that his subjects have had few or no contacts with members of the minority group during their young lives, therefore leaving doubt as to the salience of the research situation to them.

We see nothing wrong with either a small sample or a homogeneous one, but it ought to be at least large enough to allow the intended statistical operations. And it ought to be homogeneous according to characteristics of people who make a difference when we generalize for others like them. In terms of Blumer's argument about public opinion (see Chapter 3), we may pose the question: How appropriate or relevant is it to ask or observe anything with this particular public? They have no influence, no understanding, no experience, no sensitivity, and no importance in relation to the particular situation studied.

Criterion 3: Experimental Design. We are particularly taken with the power of evidence derived from a study that incorporates experimental controls. Such a study need not, of course, be constructed under synthetic laboratory conditions, but to us the important kind of control (from among many types) is the one that provides a comparison between those who do and do not receive the experimental treatment. In Linn's case, the question unanswered by the lack of such controls is, To what extent were the women who took the behavioral test influenced by the fact that they had previously taken an attitudinal test regarding this same matter? This is a question of reactivity and it is, in our opinion, a very important one. Linn's questionnaire items dealing with photo releases must have seemed unusual even to questionnaire-conditioned undergraduates. It is possible that they not only remembered them, but that they thought about them and, in Blumer's terms, had begun constructing an act that terminated when they were confronted with the behavioral test.

This is what we mean when we say that the behavioral test may have been influenced by the attitudinal test. Although it may not always be possible to avoid such reactivity if one wishes to expose subjects to similar stimuli at different points in time, experimental controls would at least permit us to estimate how much reactivity is present. In this case, what would be the difference between the subjects and a matched group of women who had not taken the original attitudinal test? If we knew that Linn's design was not reactive, we could have much greater confidence in his conclusions. Since we do not know this, we must continue to entertain considerable doubt.

Linn could also have strengthened the explanatory power of his study by controlling for sex and race. In submitting samples of black males, black females, and white males to the attitudinal and the behavioral tests, it would become possible to obtain estimates of the amount of variance attributable to sex, race, and the interaction between them.

Criterion 4: Assumptions Related to Scaling and Scalability. Linn had to make several assumptions about the scalability of his seven items in the two presumed scales. In transforming the noun, *a scale*, into a verb, *to scale*, Louis Guttman (1959) achieved not only a technical, but also a methodological innovation. He created a new way of thinking about how you go about accumulating evidence. Campbell achieves much the same end in his widely cited work on the relationship between attitudes and behavior, "Social Attitudes and Other Acquired Dispositions" (1964). Linn, however, does not entertain questions about the way in which responses to one item on his "scale" relate to responses on other items. In effect he fails to employ the verb form introduced by Guttman and retains instead the older noun type notion employed by Bogardus in his social distance scales. There is no evidence whether or not or to what degree these seven items do, in fact, form a scale.

Related to the above issue is the question of how large a discrepancy between ratings on the attitude scale and on the behavior scale can be assumed to represent an inconsistency. Linn reports that 59 percent of the women had discrepancies of two or more intervals between attitude and behavior. A 2-point discrepancy on a 7-point scale is not necessarily indicative of gross inconsistency. Finally, there is empirical evidence that unit intervals at one end of an attitude scale are not necessarily the same size as their presumed equivalents at the other end of the scale.

Reanalyzing data from several previously published studies, Jordan concludes that

> in these experiments a "positive attitude" or "positive affect" does not have an effect upon "measured behavior" oppositely equivalent to the effect of a "negative attitude" or "negative effect." The universal symmetry underlying present-day thinking on the subject is questionable. (1965, p. 315)

Jordan denounces as unjustifiable the custom of finding an arithmetic average of attitude ratings that includes both positive and negative ratings. Linn's evidence, based on his scales, seems not very powerful.

Criterion 5: Statistical Treatment.   There are numerous assumptions required by the statistical procedures employed by Linn without any evidence that these assumptions are met: sampling assumptions, assumptions about the populations, assumptions of additivity, assumptions related to the size and symmetry of the scale intervals, and in the case of his coefficient of correlation, assumptions about linearity. This latter assumption is clearly not met! A cursory review of the theoretical underpinnings of the various statistical procedures employed by Linn suggests that this is only the beginning of his failure to meet assumptions.

We do not mean to be picky on this issue and there is already extant a large body of literature related to the misuse of statistics in social science research (e.g., Blalock 1989; Lieberson 1985), but we find that there are two types of statistical assumptions. One is the ideal type, which makes logical sense and which we strive to approximate. The requirement for a normal distribution that underlies some procedures is an example. Obviously, one is unlikely to encounter a normal distribution when dealing with empirical social data. The ideal-type assumption simply warns us that if the curve is of a very different type, we ought to consider other techniques. It has been demonstrated that a high degree of skewness can be tolerated in applying techniques that ideally require a normal curve.

There is, however, another type of assumption that needs to be taken much more literally, a mathematical assumption. For example, in applying analysis of variance, it must be assumed that cell frequencies are equal or proportional to one another. If they are not (or if we do not take steps to simulate that assumption) then our results are such that one and one does not add up to two (see Blalock 1979, pp. 366–67). It is intolerable to breach that kind of assumption. This is precisely what Linn does when he applies a correlation technique that assumes linearity in a relationship that he knows to be nonlinear.

Linn also encounters considerable loss of degrees of freedom resulting from his grouping of data and from other computational procedures. Of even greater importance, the use of the statistics he selects is questionable. One of these is a 3×3 chi-square analysis. Interpretation of a 2×2 matrix is difficult enough; the 3×3 is much more problematic. In Linn's analysis, frequencies of less than 5 would be expected in seven of the nine cells. Although there is nothing magical about the number five, it is customary to limit chi-square analysis to tables in which at least 5 observations are expected to occur in each cell. (The test assumes that the sample frequencies for each cell are normally distributed about the expected value. The distribution cannot be normal when expected values are small since obtained frequencies cannot be much below the expected value, but they can be way above it.) Furthermore, this seems to us a reasonable enough custom since large differences in the chi-square can result from relocation of a single observation when very small frequencies are expected. This problem is most serious in small matrices, with the likelihood of distortion decreasing as the number of degrees of freedom increases.

The other statistic employed by Linn is the simple Pearsonian coefficient of correlation. As mentioned above, this is questionable under conditions where the author has already posited nonlinearity and where two variables are correlated that by definition are limited in their fluctuations to a range between 1 and 7. What would be a random or chance coefficient under these conditions? Certainly not zero! On the basis of tests employing the chi-square and the Pearsonian coefficient, Linn concludes that "neither test showed the variables to be significantly related, thus confirming the hypothesis that individuals with either positive or negative verbal attitudes do not necessarily act in accord with those attitudes in an overt situation" (Linn 1965, p. 358). In what seems to be a direct contradiction to this conclusion, Linn states in a footnote that if his sample had been larger, the differences would probably have been significant. By the time we have finished discounting Linn's research, we conclude that no matter what his findings, they are not very credible.

In spite of its tone, this is not an attack on Linn per se. His procedures conform to commonly accepted practices in sociology at that time. Unfortunately, those practices persist into this time. Some of these criticisms have to do with problems of techniques that are endemic to sociological research—problems with which we have by and large learned to live. What is important is not so much that Linn or DeFleur and Westie (like nearly everyone else) can be taken to task on these grounds, but that it is possible to avoid such troublesome distortions of the empirical world, as we shall see! Sociological research does not *have* to be incredible.

One must treat the Linn study with the respect it deserves. If the reader should mistakenly be inclined to view either Linn or DeFleur and Westie contemptuously, let us here note that they laid the most important groundwork for future research at the time they were writing. Linn was one of the first to draw attention to the need to look at intervening processes rather than at the simple attitude-behavior relationship. DeFleur and his associates have also made major contributions to the understanding of this problem.

DeFleur and Westie

Having established the criteria of judgment in the analysis of Linn's 1965 article, consider the DeFleur and Westie (1958) undertaking, which preceded Linn by seven years. They, too, address themselves to the relationship between verbal attitudes and overt acts, and Linn's design closely parallels theirs. But the two studies are sufficiently different that they cannot be considered replications. It is therefore legitimate to attribute any convergence in conclusions to the validity of the studies rather than to the fact that they find the same things because they proceed in the same manner.

DeFleur and Westie are methodologically oriented. They observe that "in the face of the steady stream of studies of the verbal dimension of attitudinal behavior, the paucity of investigations of the overt-action correlates of such verbal behavior is indeed striking" (p. 667). Their major goal is the development of standardized situations or instruments "enabling the investigator to quantify, on a positive-negative continuum, an acceptance or avoidance act for a set of subjects, with other conditions held constant" (p. 667).

Their behavioral test is identical with that employed later by Linn: a request to have the white subject's picture taken with a black and to sign a graded series of releases for the use of the picture. The identity ends here. In the DeFleur-Westie study, the attitudinal dimension is derived from an occupational social distance scale that asks for acceptance or rejection of a large number of occupations when the incumbents are white and when they are black. The sum of the differences of ratings of blacks and whites provides a prejudice score. Extremely prejudiced and unprejudiced group quartiles were identified, and a multifactor matching procedure resulted in matched samples of twenty-three prejudiced and twenty-three unprejudiced undergraduate sociology students. Measures of attitude toward and behavior toward the minority group were available for forty-six subjects. Using the five criteria employed in the analysis of the Linn study, what kinds of progress can be detected during the seven-year period that separates these two articles?

Criterion 1: Prediction. Coupled with their determination to reduce apparent methodological difficulties in sociological research, DeFleur and Westie explicitly reject the notion of prediction as a central concern. They observe that "the relationship between these verbal and overt attitudinal dimensions, while significant, is not a simple one-to-one correspondence" (p. 672). There is a clear awareness here that it is unreasonable to assume simple prediction from one variable to another. There remains, nevertheless, the implicit assumption of a direct, if nonlinear, relationship between an independent and a dependent variable—the notion of cause and effect: "Further advances in the prediction of overt behavior from attitude measuring instruments may require both systematic measures of the social anchorages of individual psychological orientations and careful studies of their translation into overt action" (p. 673). Although their stance may not fully meet the requirements of criterion 1, the authors of this older research seem to us more sophisticated in this respect than their descendant.

Criterion 2: The Sample. Although the DeFleur-Westie sample was small, it was larger than Linn's later sample—forty-six subjects compared to thirty-six. In the earlier study the sexes are equally represented and the introduction of a matching procedure reduces the probability of self-selective differences between prejudiced and unprejudiced volunteers. Although DeFleur and Westie's midwestern university (Indiana) is further south than Linn's (Wisconsin) and has a less liberal tradition, the salience of the questions to the subjects remains problematic, especially in terms of the perceived consequences of their responses.

The notion of demand characteristics in research with students was not articulated by Orne until 1962. Even though there was good reason to suspect that the behavior of students in experiments was more a consequence of being in an experiment than of anything else, DeFleur and Westie may be excused for being insensitive to this possibility, but by 1965, Linn ought to have been aware of this problem. The possibility of student expectations and felt obligations as subjects in research conducted by their professors is one that demands attention (see Rosenthal and Rosnow 1975). Although still defective, it seems to us that the sampling procedures employed by DeFleur and Westie in 1958 were superior to those employed by Linn in 1965.

Criterion 3: Experimental Design. Like Linn, DeFleur and Westie are essentially lacking in experimental controls. Some controls are implicit in this earlier study since both sexes are represented and other matching factors appear equally in both the prejudiced and the unprejudiced groups (quartiles). Although in this respect the earlier study has a poten tially superior design, neither piece of research attempts to control for any effect it may have created when it administered the original verbal test. With the benefit of hindsight, we can see how both sets of investigators could have greatly improved the power of their evidence by subjecting an untreated control group to the behavioral test.

Criterion 4: Assumptions Related to Scaling and Scalability. The conclusions of both Linn and DeFleur and Westie are based upon reflections or differences between attitude and behavior on scales constructed for the purpose of estimating those two dimensions and the differences between them. DeFleur and Westie, unlike Linn, treat the issue of scalability self-consciously. In this earlier study, the derivation of the rank order of the scale is described and its validity argued on the basis of a high rate of agreement among a panel of expert judges. Although no scale analysis is possible because of sample limitations, high transitivity is reported: Only three irregularities in the cumulative feature of the instrument occur in the forty-six cases. Extremely prejudiced and unprejudiced scorers are used in the earlier study and the subjects are classified behaviorally according to whether or not they signed the releases at a level above or below the mean of the total sample. As a result of these procedures in classifying both attitude and behavior, DeFleur and Westie do not encounter a problem found in Linn's later work—the need to arbitrarily assume that a 2-point discrepancy on the scales reflects inconsistency. By scaling criteria, the earlier study appears to be superior to the later one.

Criterion 5: Statistical Treatment. DeFleur and Westie employ no correlation analysis. This means that they did not need to make as many assumptions as Linn would later require. This superior assumptional parsimony may, however, be nullified by their need to assume that differences in rating the black and white occupations are additive, and by the loss of additional degrees of freedom consequent to computing the mean level at which photographic releases were signed. The application of chi-square analysis by DeFleur and Westie in 1958 is clearly more sophisticated than its use by Linn in 1965. In spite of their larger sample, the earlier investigators hold their chi-square down to a 2×2 matrix that is easily interpreted and they manage to achieve sufficient expected frequencies in each cell. Although Ajzen and his colleagues (Ajzen, Darroch, Fishbein, and Hornick 1970) find a computational error in this chi-square, it seems to make no difference in the conclusions.

On the basis of the chi-square analysis, DeFleur and Westie reach the opposite conclusion from what Linn was to come up with seven years later:

In this situation, there was clearly a greater tendency for the prejudiced persons than the unprejudiced to avoid being photographed with a Negro. The relationship is significant, suggesting some correspondence in this case between attitudes measured by verbal scales and an acceptance-avoidance act toward the attitude object. (1958, p. 671)

This conclusion is followed immediately by a qualification:

In spite of the statistical significance, however, there were some preju-diced persons who signed the agreement without hesitation at the highest level, as well as some unprejudiced persons who were not willing to sign at any level. Thus the relationship between these verbal and overt attitudi-nal dimensions . . . is not a simple one-to-one correspondence. (p. 671)

In spite of the fact that the probability is 99 out of 100 that the distribu-tion in the chi-square table is attributable to something other than chance (presumably to the relationship between attitude and behavior), the fact remains that 30 percent of the cases are deviant: fourteen of the forty-six subjects were either prejudiced people who showed a willing-ness to sign releases or unprejudiced people who showed an unwilling-ness to sign releases. These two types of inconsistencies are very differ-ent and require special treatment. Certainly the DeFleur-Westie evidence, reported in 1958, is weak and inconclusive, but the disturbing observation is that it seems more credible than the 1965 study.

LaPiere

LaPiere's article precedes DeFleur and Westie by twenty-four years and is thirty-one years older than Linn's. Let us look all the way back. You will remember that LaPiere, like the others, seeks to document the relationship between verbal attitudes and overt acts toward members of a minority racial group. In this case the minority group is Chinese rather than black. LaPiere employs Chinese confederates who seek to obtain services from entrepreneurs who are actually operating businesses. Two hundred and fifty-one such behavioral observations were made and the acceptance-avoidance results recorded. From among these, 128 attitude observations were obtained by allowing a six-month time lapse and then sending each of the entrepreneurs a questionnaire in which they were asked if they would service Chinese people in their establishment. Let us expose LaPiere to the five criteria used to evaluate the 1965 and 1958 studies.

Criterion 1: Prediction. Linn, it will be recalled, is committed to a primitive notion of prediction. In DeFleur and Westie we found a deliberate effort to set aside that notion, although many of its concomitant assumptions remain. LaPiere openly challenges the theoretical tenability of posing a causal relationship between attitude and behavior toward the same object. Attitude and behavior, he suggests, are discrete phenomena that are theoretically independent of each other. He argues throughout the last two pages of his article that it is unreasonable to posit a prediction of behavior on the basis of attitudes. For example, "Only a verbal reaction to an entirely symbolic situation can be secured by the questionnaire. It may indicate what the responder would actually do when confronted with the situation symbolized in the question, but there is no assurance that it will" (p. 237).

Even without LaPiere's precedent, Linn should have suspected this, since his young women subjects told him as much. As one of Linn's respondents with an unprejudiced attitude explained to him (when asked why she did not show up for her photograph): "I wanted to but couldn't." It seems to us that LaPiere, back in 1934, had a clearer grasp of this issue than either of the experimenters who followed him over the next thirty years. In spite of his efforts, however, he, like the rest of us, finds it difficult not to think in the causal terms with which we have all been so deeply imbued.

Criterion 2: The Sample.   LaPiere's sample consists not of thirty-four or forty-six captive undergraduates, but of 128 mature adults engaged in the conduct of responsible business. The number is not only larger but the probability of self-selectivity is considerably less. Linn and DeFleur-Westie both coerced their total samples to participate in the verbal dimension of the study (at least neither investigator reports any refusals of students to cooperate with that phase of the study), but both permitted voluntary withdrawal from the overt behavior test. LaPiere's study, on the other hand, is designed to coerce the total sample to participate in the behavioral test (every entrepreneur is confronted with an acceptance-avoidance choice) but permits voluntary refusal to respond to the verbal test. With this difference in mind and also the fact that the DeFleur-Westie sample was reduced by their matching procedure as well as by noncooperation, the percentages of voluntary withdrawal between these two earlier studies can be compared. (Linn reports only that the women were told that "participation is completely voluntary." There is no indication of how many subjects did not volunteer. We know only that the students who had previously responded to the attitude questionnaire "were asked to volunteer.")

In the DeFleur-Westie study, the combined loss resulting from the matching procedure, the use of only extreme quartiles, and voluntary withdrawal was 81.6 percent (these three sources are indistinguishable in their report). In contrast, LaPiere lost a total of 49 percent. To the extent that rates of voluntary withdrawal of subjects provide an index of self-selectivity, LaPiere appears less self-selective in his sample than the investigators who followed him. The universe from which this oldest sample is drawn also represents an improvement in sampling procedure over its two descendants. We no longer have undergraduate students for whom the verbal dimension is of doubtful salience. The LaPiere sample is drawn from a population that must make choices both in terms of intent and in terms of action choices they perceive as having real consequences in the conduct of their daily activities. It is our impression that LaPiere's 1934 sample and his sampling procedures inspire greater confidence than those of either Linn or DeFleur and Westie.

Criterion 3: Experimental Design.   The great power of LaPiere's design is that, unlike the other two, it permits the use of a nontreated sample for control purposes. A sample of establishments that had not been tested on the behavioral dimension, which was matched with the experimental sample by quality and geographic locale, received the same verbal inquiry. The distribution of responses from both treatment and control groups was nearly identical. This control of the effect of the treatment itself represents a methodological superiority over both of the later studies. If there is a moral to be drawn from this, it is that laboratories don't necessarily make experiments and field studies may be experimental.

Criterion 4: Assumptions Related to Scaling and Scalability.   Since LaPiere allows only an acceptance or a rejection—a dichotomous choice—on both the overt-action dimension and the verbal-attitude dimension, the problems of scaling, scalability, arbitrary assignments of the number of discrepancy units that are assumed to indicate an inconsistency, computations of means, grouping of data, use of only extreme scorers, and the many assumptions that must accompany these techniques are all eliminated from his pioneer work. This represents clear superiority over the later studies in assumptional parsimony.

Criterion 5: Statistical Treatment.   Assumptional parsimony is an impressive achievement since the fewer assumptions required, the greater the credibility of the conclusions. This assumptional parsimony is carried still further by LaPiere, where there are no unsubstantiated statistical assumptions or loss of degrees of freedom. Of the 251 establishments confronted with the acceptance-avoidance choice of action, *all but one chose to accept.* Of the 128 responding to the verbal test, *only one chose an unqualified acceptance* (over 90 percent of the establishments chose to reject on the verbal test, with the remaining providing qualified responses). The visible weight of this evidence regarding the inconsistency of attitude and behavior is so overwhelming that neither statistical approximations nor probability estimates are required to interpret the results. The ambiguity in conclusions of the two later studies, resulting largely from high frequencies of deviant cases, disappears in LaPiere's work. This time the data permit only one clear-cut conclusion regarding the hypothesis.

A Half-Century of "Progress"

We have demonstrated that the DeFleur and Westie study (1958), as judged by five broad criteria, appears methodologically superior to the later study by Linn (1965). But it is the oldest study, by LaPiere (1934), that uniformly has the highest credibility. To the extent that the analysis of these three studies is correct, we may have suffered a methodological regression during the thirty-one-year time lapse covered by them.

Linn's study is superior in some respects to that of DeFleur and Westie. For example, Linn relates attitude and behavior more directly to the same object and, by carrying the photography farce a step further, he confronts his subjects more directly with the overt action decision. Linn also introduces a different dimension into his analysis as a result of his attention to the direction of discrepancy between attitude and behavior— a question raised many years before by Merton (1940).

It is also true that Linn's design does not suffer from the use of extreme samples as does the DeFleur-Westie one. The modest chi-square that results from the earlier study would likely not have been significant had the total sample been included. Linn must also be credited for debriefing his subjects and presenting some of the rich comments obtained through that procedure. We are, however, unable to find the two later studies superior to the pioneer project in any respect. It is possible that another analyst could identify ways in which the LaPiere study suffers in comparison with the two later ones. Linn believes that his study is superior to the other two and states that "the DeFleur and Westie study is methodologically superior to its predecessors," including LaPiere (1965, p. 354).

Although they acknowledge the existence of the LaPiere study, DeFleur and Westie offer no criticism of it. Linn chooses to attack the validity of LaPiere's results on two fronts:

> First, the questionnaire which he used to measure attitudes toward the Chinese dealt with general prejudice indices and was *not* necessarily comparable to the behavior situation in the study. Secondly, LaPiere's presence with the couple probably had a considerable biasing effect. (p. 353)

We find these two criticisms of LaPiere's article difficult to understand. He reports that every establishment that had been confronted by the Chinese couple received the question: "Will you accept members of the Chinese race as guests in your establishment?" It seems to us that, if you are going to ask a question, that is about as close to the behavioral situation as you can get! The fact that half the subjects also were asked questions about other ethnic groups for comparative purposes does not alter the response distribution.

The influence of the investigator's role on the phenomena under study presents a persistent problem in social research. LaPiere was aware of this and made a deliberate effort to control for experimenter effect by remaining out of sight and forcing the Chinese to conduct negotiations alone whenever possible. His behavioral data are classified according to the presence or absence of the investigator and are so reported. There is no denying that this is an important problem and, despite LaPiere's valiant efforts to exercise control over it, it remains uncertain to what extent experimenter effects persist in his study. But the fact is that neither DeFleur and Westie nor Linn report an effort to control for this potential effect; Lapiere does.

Surely another analyst could, and probably would, come up with criteria of judgment different from the kind we employ. We have not attempted a balanced examination. We simply asked the extent to which an older study was as good or better than more recent ones. This seems to us the critical test of cumulative progress in the creation of knowledge. This one test—and we must acknowledge that it is limited—offers no evidence to confirm that assumption. In fact it suggests the possibility of regression. *Even those severest critics who sharply disagree with our 1969 analysis reach essentially the same conclusion:* "A thorough methodological analysis of the three case studies does not seem to indicate a regressive trend in methodology—although *there is no indication of a significant advance either*" (Ajzen et al. 1970, p. 272, emphasis added).

This was not a deliberate effort to select supporting studies after reviewing a mass of comparable articles. To the contrary, the best sequence available at the time was selected. At the beginning of the undertaking there was no assurance that the initial disturbing impression was correct. It makes little difference how one reaches the conclusion that we may not have been making much progress from the mid-1930s to the mid-1960s. However arrived at, it should be a matter of concern for social scientists. We submit, as one possible explanation for the lack of progress, that it may be a consequence of decisions made during earlier decades, largely in terms of scientific respectability. We may now be reaping the fruits of choices seeded out of the temper of those times (see Chapter 2).

In the early 1970s we had some indication that since the publication of Linn's study the situation might be improving (Deutscher 1973, p. 104). To update our analysis we will subject a comparable study done in the mid-1980s to our five criteria. By adding one more point in time to our methodological assessment we can see the progression of attitude-behavior literature over half a century.

A Fourth Study

Lord, Lepper, and Mackie

Scanning our post-1970 collection of attitude-behavior articles the article by Lord, Lepper, and Mackie (1984), which reports on two experiments, conforms most closely to the selection criteria for the other three studies. While the earlier studies focused upon race relations, Lord, Lepper, and Mackie examine attitudes and behavioral intentions toward a different minority, homosexuals, as well as members of fraternity- and sorority-like clubs. *It has the added advantage of appearing in print exactly fifty years after the publication of LaPiere's article.*

The experiments conducted by Lord, Lepper, and Mackie follow Linn's study by almost twenty years. These authors are responding to LaPiere, but fail to mention either Defleur and Westie or Linn. Lord, Lepper, and Mackie believe that they know why attitudes failed to correspond to behavior in LaPiere's study. They maintain that the stereotype of a Chinese person held by those who answered LaPiere's questionnaire did not correspond to the image presented by the Chinese couple accompanying LaPiere on his travels. Lord, Lepper, and Mackie suspect that, when answering LaPiere's questionnaire, correspondents were imagining the Chinese person as "a barefoot coolie tracking mud across their lobbies" (p. 1256). They argue that "if LaPiere had entered these establishments with such a 'prototypical Chinese' by his side, the proprietors' attitude-behavior consistency would have been nearly perfect" (p. 1256).

Lord, Lepper, and Mackie contend that better matches between attitude prototype [exemplars incorporating "the essential and most characteristic features of a class" of objects (p. 1256)] and behavioral object will result in greater attitude-behavior consistency. In other words, if bigoted people were confronted with their distorted stereotype of a minority, they would do as they say! The fact is that ordinary Chinese people do not go barefoot and wear pigtails, ordinary black people do not tap dance through life, and ordinary gay people are not limp-wristed. It is behavior in everyday encounters that is important, not behavior when confronting creatures of the imagination.

behavior in everyday encounters that is important, not behavior when confronting creatures of the imagination.

In their first experiment, their target group was members of three eating clubs on campus. These clubs are supposedly similar to fraternities and sororities at other universities. In the second experiment, the target group was homosexuals. Lord, Lepper, and Mackie maintain that the second study is "a more ecologically valid test" (p. 1260) than the first. We agree. Results from the study using homosexuals as the target group should be more generalizable and more comparable to results from LaPiere's study, than results based on eating clubs at Princeton. We will concentrate, therefore, on the second experiment in evaluating the credibility of Lord, Lepper, and Mackie's conclusions.

In the second experiment, male Princeton undergraduates completed a questionnaire about their impression of a number of groups, e.g., vegetarians, social activists, right-to-life supporters, and homosexuals, the only group in which the researchers were really interested. They provided profiles for a typical member of each of these groups. These thirty trait personality profiles were used to construct either a prototypical or nonprototypical description of a homosexual for each subject.

Two months after the initial questionnaire was completed, the students were recontacted and asked to participate in an experiment (subjects supposedly had no idea that this experiment was related to the questionnaire they filled out earlier). When they arrived for the experiment, subjects were told that Princeton was participating in a study to ease student transfers between Ivy League schools. The psychology department was assessing student willingness to participate in the program. They were asked to indicate their degree of willingness to participate by agreeing to one or more activities. The list of nine activities ranged in social intimacy from just being introduced to the prospective student to hosting the prospective student for a weekend visit.

After each subject had completed the baseline measure of willingness to participate he was asked to read some descriptions of prospective transfers. Subjects were asked to indicate how likable the described person seemed, how willing they were to interact with the person, and which of the nine previously described activities they would be willing to engage in with the person. The description of the target person, John B., included the statement that he had "on his wall a photograph of himself waving a placard" in a gay rights rally (p. 1261). Half of the subjects read a description of John B. that matched their initial prototype profile on homosexuals on the twelve most extreme points (prototypical). The other half read a description that matched six of the most extreme traits and mismatched the other six (nonprototypical). Subjects completed scales indicating how likable John B. was, how willing they were to interact with him, and which of the nine previously described activities they would agree to engage in with him. Finally, they completed a repeat of the 30-trait profile for both John B. and a typical male homosexual.

The intraindividual analysis showed mixed results. As the researchers suspected, the consistency between likability of homosexuals and intentions to interact with one was greater for the prototypical than the nonprototypical one. The relationship between consistency of attitudes on interacting with homosexuals and a subject's behavioral intentions was in the expected direction *but was not significant*.

For the interindividual analysis Lord, Lepper, and Mackie also examine the relationship between likability and behavioral intentions and between attitudes toward interacting with homosexuals and intentions. In addition, they examine differences between initial indications of willingness to engage in social activities with a prospective transfer student and willingness to do so after discovering that the target was a homosexual. Their results are in the direction they expected, but in order to get them, higher than usual significance levels were sometimes employed.

Based on their findings, Lord, Lepper, and Mackie conclude that "attitudes towards a social group will match behavior toward a member of that group only to the degree that the target person matches the prototype that served as the basis for the attitude in the first place" (p. 1263). As intended, they believe that they have provided empirical evidence for explaining why LaPiere did not find the attitude-behavior relationship he should have found. But have they? Let us now apply our five evaluation criteria for credibility to their study.

Criterion 1: Prediction. Lord and his collaborators (1984) are clearly interested in prediction. They begin the abstract of their article by stating that their paper "addresses the questions of when we can predict from an individual's attitude toward a social group to the individual's behavior toward a specific member of that group" (p. 1254). Observed discrepancies on the part of other researchers since LaPiere's time are attributed to measurement error—failure to accurately measure, or properly specify, the attitude prototype. Lord, Lepper, and Mackie maintain that more clearly specifying the attitude object will enhance prediction, or correspondence. They "expect consistency only when the stimulus matches the perceived stimulus in the verbal response situation" (p. 1255). On our criterion of prediction, Lord, Lepper, and Mackie are as primitive as Linn.

Criterion 2: The Sample. Compared to Lapiere's, DeFleur and Westie's, and Linn's, this article reports on the smallest, most homogeneous, and most unrepresentative sample yet! In their second experiment Lord,

Lepper, and Mackie studied twenty-four male students (presumably enrolled in an introductory psychology course) attending an elite, eastern university. As in Linn's study, the selectivity of the sample is compounded by the fact that only volunteers from among those who took the attitude test also took the behavioral test. (Forty students completed the first set of questions. Thirty-one were recontacted, seven of whom refused to participate.) Furthermore, the subjects apparently had little experience with the minority group upon which the study focuses and were, in fact, preferred because of this. Pretesting (no details of which are supplied) suggested that they would be unlikely to know "a significant number of homosexual men well enough to regard one target person as a small sample" (p. 1260). Finally, Lord, Lepper, and Mackie pay no attention to the expectations and obligations their student samples might feel as participants in an experiment. As we observed earlier in this chapter, since the early 1960s researchers have had no excuse for not being sensitive to this potential threat to validity.

Criterion 3: Experimental Design. Both studies conducted by Lord, Lepper, and Mackie are identified as experiments but the second experiment lacks experimental controls. Each group of twelve students is exposed to only one description, either the prototypical or atypical. This provides the basis for the comparison upon which the analysis is based. The researchers, however, have missed one crucially important control by not having a group of subjects take the behavioral test who had not been exposed to the attitude questionnaire. This failure means that, like Linn and DeFleur and Westie, they have no untreated control group for comparison. They are thus unable to determine what influence the initial set of questions (to determine attitudes) may have had on responses to the second wave of questions (to determine behavior).

The explanatory power of this study could have been strengthened by studying the effects of sex and sexual orientation on behavior. Male homosexuals and bisexuals should have been included in the experiment. The researchers should have also conducted the experiment with heterosexual, bisexual, and lesbian women. It would then be possible to explore effects due to sex, effects due to sexual orientation, and the interaction between sex and sexual orientation.

Criterion 4: Assumptions Related to Scaling and Scalability. The conclusions of Lord, Lepper, and Mackie are drawn from the results of differences among, and correlations between, attitude and behavioral intention scales. Before completing the 30 trait profiles when answering the initial set of questions, "students indicated on 10-point scales how likable they found a typical member of each group, and how willing they would be to interact socially with the typical member of each group"

(p. 1261). Upon their return the students read either a prototypical or nonprototypical description of John B. Then they "indicated on 13-point scales, labeled identically with the initial attitude question, how likeable they thought the person was and how willing they would be to interact with the person socially" (p. 1261). Why these scales are three items larger than the first set to which they are to be compared is not discussed. Subjects then chose which activities they would be willing to engage in and completed the two additional personality profiles we described earlier. The authors fail to provide a detailed description, or analysis, of their scale construction.

Since Lord, Lepper, and Mackie provide little information about the formation of their scales, it is impossible to evaluate them. This suggests that consideration of such issues was not important to these researchers. As in Linn's earlier study, there is no evidence whether or not, or to what degree, items form a scale. Scalability of items is simply assumed. Nor is it clear what exactly represents an inconsistency. Statistical significance of differences is substituted for an assessment of a substantive evaluation of the differences they found.

Criterion 5: Statistical Treatment.   Several features of the statistical analyses performed by Lord, Lepper, and Mackie are troublesome. Data were analyzed using *t*-tests for the difference between means on the attitude and behavioral scales for their intraindividual analysis and Pearson correlations between attitude and behavioral intention scales for their interindividual analysis and for changes in the social activities list. The difference between pairs of correlations [prototypical (completely matched subject's stereotype) versus nonprototypical (only partially matched subject's stereotype)] were tested for significance.

As in the Linn study, Lord, Lepper, and Mackie require numerous assumptions to perform their parametric analysis. There are assumptions about normality of the population, randomness of the sample, and interval measurement. There is no evidence that this study meets these assumptions any better than Linn's did.

The intraindividual analysis raises several questions. The behavioral intention scales are three items larger than their attitude scales. "This produced an increase in the variances of responses for students who read the 100% prototypical target person . . . but not for students who read about the 50% prototypical target person" (p. 1262). (In order to overcome this problem they standardized responses within conditions and computed the absolute difference in standard score units.) The authors neither discuss the interesting implications of this between-group difference, nor indicate how to account for it. Given their hypotheses we would have expected the opposite—an increase in variance for the nonprototypical group.

Also, as we noted earlier in our summary of this research, the findings on the statistical tests for intraindividual consistency are split. On the one hand, the researchers found that the mean absolute difference (in standard scores) between the likability attitude scale and the behavioral intentions scale was significantly less for the 100% prototypical target than for the 50% prototypical target. On the other hand, the absolute difference (in standard scores) between attitudes on interacting with homosexuals and behavioral intentions was *not* significantly different for the prototypical and nonprototypical groups. Lord and his colleagues observe that the difference of the differences for the two groups was in the expected direction but they neglect to discuss the fact that it was not significant.

There are problems with the interindividual analysis as well. First the researchers conduct six significance tests, examining the relationships of likability and preference for interacting with behavioral intentions. As expected, likability was significantly correlated with behavioral intentions for the prototypical target, which fulfilled subject's mental image of a homosexual, but not for the nonprototypical target, which only partially matched subject's stereotype of gays. Attitude on interacting with homosexuals was found to be "marginally correlated" with preference for interacting with a prototypical homosexual but not with a nonprototypical homosexual. In order to get this significant relationship for the prototypical group the researchers had to use a significance level of .10—twice the commonly used maximum level and the absolute largest level reasonably allowed. At the .10 level there is a one in ten chance of committing a type I error—rejecting the null hypothesis of no difference when it is in fact true.

The researchers next examined the relationship between the pairs of correlations for the two groups (prototypical versus nonprototypical target) on the likability-intentions relationship and on the preference for interacting-intentions relationship. The results were mixed. They found that "the difference between these pairs of correlations was statistically significant in the first case . . . but not in the second case" (p. 1262). Once again, there is no attempt to explain the nonsignificant finding.

Lord, Lepper, and Mackie then explored the correlations relevant to their list of social activities. They compared initial indications of willingness to engage in the nine activities to willingness to engage in the activities after reading the descriptions of the target person. The researchers found that students who were favorable toward homosexuals were willing to engage in more of the listed activities with the target than were students with unfavorable attitudes. As they expected, this relationship was strongly correlated for subjects reading about a prototypical target but weakly correlated for those who read about a nonprototypical target. The difference between the pairs of correlations was statistically significant.

The same results were found for changes in the average level of social intimacy of the acts to which subjects agreed. In this case, however, the difference between the pairs of correlations was found to be "marginally significant." For a second time the researchers raised the significance level above the standard maximum of .05 (in this case to .06) in order to obtain the result they desired.

The measures and statistical analysis employed by Lord, Lepper, and Mackie are the most complex of the four studies we are comparing. We have also shown in this section that their results are not as clear-cut as their conclusions would have us believe. Equally troubling is what they are actually testing.

Although Linn too used a measure of intention, rather than behavior, he realized that what subjects said they would do may differ from what they would actually do. In order to strengthen his case Linn incorporated a "validity check" by having his subjects actually appear for the supposed "picture taking" session. Like many other contemporary researchers (see Chapter 13) Lord, Lepper, and Mackie assume that behavioral intentions (asking respondents how they intend to act) are acceptable measures of behavior: "For each test, we considered that behavioral intentions as expressed on a measure of preference for working with a target person were functionally equivalent to behavior" (p. 1258). This common, albeit unwarranted assumption indicates further regression in methodology. One of the few things we can say with certainty about the words-deeds relationship is that sometimes people do not do what they say they will do.

Conclusion: What Validates What?

Like the other three studies, the Lord, Lepper, and Mackie study should be treated with the respect it deserves. This work was published in a reputable, referred journal in social psychology and meets contemporary standards for the state of theory and methodology. In addition, this work is superior to most on three points. First, the researchers conducted two studies, with the second experiment designed to overcome the weaknesses of the first. Second, they conduct both intra- and interindividual analyses. Third, and most important, they recognize that researchers must determine specifically what the subjects have in mind when indicating their attitudes. As their results showed, there were substantial individual differences in attitude prototype.

We noted above that another analyst, employing different criteria, could identify ways in which the latter studies we have examined are an improvement upon LaPiere's. Certainly Lord, Lepper, and Mackie believe that their work is superior to LaPiere's. By our criteria, however, their 1984 study is no better than, and in some critical ways inferior to, Linn's work. In 1969 we found stagnation, if not regression, in the study of attitudes and behavior over the previous thirty years (Deutscher 1969). Using the same criteria, we now reach the same conclusion for the past half-century—a "cumulative," although unwelcome, observation.

The relative amount of confidence we are able to have in the four studies we have evaluated raises questions about validity tests based upon independent verification (convergent validity) in contemporary social science. In Chapter 5, we will use this analysis as a launching pad for a consideration of the problem of validity and its cousin, reliability. As we shall see, the question of what validates what is a sticky one even under the best of conditions. In order to make optimal use of our credibility screen and to aid in properly discounting the evidence being considered, Part II will concentrate on methodological issues.

II

Methods:
The Credibility of Evidence

5

How Do We Know We Know?

The Validity Problem

The problem of validity has tended to receive short shrift in the social sciences. It is a neglect that holds for both quantitative and qualitative research (see Mishler 1990). At least this appears to be true when we compare it to the attention devoted to the problem of reliability. Following the customary distinction, the concept of validity addresses itself to the truth of an assertion made about something in the empirical world. The concept of reliability, on the other hand, focuses on the degree of consistency in observations obtained from the devices we employ: interviewers, schedules, tests, documents, observers, informants. The relationship between the two concepts is asymmetrical; i.e., measurement can be consistently in error as well as consistently correct, and therefore a high degree of reliability can be achieved anywhere along the continuum between absolute invalidity and absolute validity.

The notion of test-retest or any other reliability measure involving a time sequence is antithetical to social science since it requires the incorrect assumption that human thought and behavior are static, and therefore, that any change in response is a reflection of either instrument error or deception. Such recorded changes are, in fact, more likely to reflect shifts in sentiment or behavior on the part of the respondent. For this reason, we will restrict the concept of reliability to procedures that have no time component, e.g., interrater, interitem, interviewer, informant, or observer reliability.

The fuzziness in the distinction between validity and reliability derives largely from the fact that whether one is dealing with the idea of validity or with the idea of reliability depends on one's purpose and perspective (see Campbell and Fiske 1959). If, on the one hand, investigators are interested in the internal consistency of an instrument—a question of reliability—then they may randomly split the items into two sets and compare them for uniformity of results. If, on the other hand, they are interested in whether one half of the items on the same instrument can provide substantiating or confirmatory evidence that the other half are in fact getting at what is intended, then we have a test of validity. This is indeed an uncomfortable kind of relativity with which to live.

Appalled by the absurdity of it all, Weigert throws up his hands in disgust, describing the concept of validity as "an untenable naivete" (1970, p. 115). We cannot argue that he is incorrect, but although we may entertain the same conclusion, we are more hopeful than he. We believe that the ideas of validity and reliability taken together provide the basis for determining credibility. Unless we can cope in a satisfactory way with the question, How believable is the evidence? then we are permanently mired down. There can be no progress without consideration of that question and we view the concepts of reliability and validity, however fuzzy (or naive), to be the best available hooks on which to hang that essential question.

We have barely touched upon the confusion between these two concepts. For example, it must be allowed that every reliable indicator is a valid indicator of something! In other words, if a measure is highly consistent then it is reflecting a consistency in something in the empirical world. Here we identify the essentially subjective nature of the idea of validity: *When high reliability is coupled with low validity, validity is being defined in terms of what the investigator intends to observe.* Our observation is not valid unless it matches our intentions, unless it addresses that object in the empirical world about which we are curious. If it reflects some other object then, for all its reliability, it is valid only in relation to that other object. It has low validity for our purposes.

Having laid this definitional groundwork, let us return to our "obsession with reliability." Clearly, we believe that social scientists have tended to neglect validity and to be overattentive to problems of reliability. We are not alone in this belief. Kirk and Miller argue that "as a means to the truth, social science has relied almost entirely on techniques for assuring reliability. . . . Most nonqualitative research methodologies come complete with a variety of checks on reliability, and none on validity" (1986, p. 21).

The sources of our "enchantment with reliability," as Merton (1940) more graciously put it, can be at least partially identified. First, reliability is in fact an important issue meriting serious attention. We are indeed faced with serious problems not only of instability in our measuring instruments but of instability of the populations we are attempting to measure. This dual instability compounds our problems, since we cannot always be certain of the extent to which discrepant readings on our instruments are a result of instrument error and the extent to which they

are a result of the innate cussedness of our research subjects, who frequently insist on changing their minds—changing both their sentiments
and their actions—and therefore changing their responses to our deli-
cately balanced instruments. One reason, then, for our concentration on
problems of reliability is that they are central to our successful pursuit of
knowledge about human behavior.[1]

Clues to a second source of our concern with problems of reliability
can be found, we believe, in the sociology of knowledge. Recall that
during the 1930s sociologists who were most committed to objective
empirical research embarked upon a crusade to achieve scientific respectability for the discipline, which at that time suffered considerable contempt both within universities and outside. This crusade manifested
itself in an effort to purify sociology of its association with do-gooders,
on the one hand, and, on the other, in a self-conscious pursuit of methodological rigor along lines analogous to what was perceived as The
Scientific Method.

Problems of reliability were amenable to attack within this framework.
A body of technology already existed and could easily be developed
further. We know now how to measure reliability, we know how to
improve it, and, most important, we can obtain clear, convincing, and
reproducible evidence of the precise extent to which our methodological
refinements increase our confidence in the reliability of our data. We can
measure our improvements in measurement and we can measure them
well, and that is a very satisfying accomplishment—one upon which a
scientist in any discipline can look with pleasure and approval.

The most critical source of our obsession with reliability may be the
fact that we have been able to concentrate on it while simultaneously
neglecting validity because we have developed certain concepts that
encourage us to do so. The idea of the operational definition is a device
precisely designed to eliminate the problem of validity. When we define
the object of our interest to be the phenomenon our instrument is measuring, we need no longer worry about validity.

Conceptual innovations that achieve the same ends as the operational
definition are such notions as "intrinsic validity," "construct validity,"
and "face validity." There have been a variety of efforts to classify types
of validity, but such taxonomical games provide no solutions. Another
analyst has put it nicely: "The pretentiousness involved in such phrases
as 'face validity' for common sense, and 'group validity' for authoritative
opinion, and 'construct validity' for logical consistency is patently rhetorical" (Weigert 1970, p. 115).

We have suggested three possible explanations for our obsession with
reliability. Although they may be plausible in that they help us to understand why we have not concentrated on the problem of validity, they do

not obviate the need for an independent verification that our conclusions do in fact reflect the empirical phenomena we claim—i.e., that they are valid. We find the idea of convergent validity a useful one under some conditions. Webb and his colleagues (Webb, Campbell, Schwartz, and Sechrest 1966; Webb, Campbell, Schwartz, Sechrest, and Grove 1981) borrow the concept of triangulation from celestial navigation in order to argue that independent sources of information can confirm (validate) one another, even though each of those sources may have certain weaknesses:

> Once a proposition has been confirmed by two or more independent measurement processes, the uncertainty of its interpretation is greatly reduced. The most persuasive evidence comes through a triangulation of measurement processes. If a proposition can survive the onslaught of a series of imperfect measures, with all their irrelevant error, confidence should be placed in it. Of course, this confidence is increased by minimizing error in each instrument and by a reasonable belief in the different and divergent effects of the sources of error. (Webb et al. 1966, p. 3)

As we shall see when we consider the question of what validates what, the triangulation solution is only partial. That is, when our multiple sources agree, its usefulness is different from conditions under which those sources disagree. There are several criteria of validity, but much of the remainder of this chapter hinges on what we consider to be the relatively viable notion of convergent validity.

We have considerable respect for "common sense," and the notion of convergent validity is one we commonly employ in our everyday pursuit of confirmation of events in the world around us. We seek validation of questionable impressions by searching for an independent source— hopefully one that has a different set of defects from the original source. If we find several such witnesses, reports, or observations that are in accord and if we do not find independent observations that are contradictory, then we feel more secure in the truth of our impressions. That is convergent validation, and that is what Webb et al. mean by "triangulation." That is the kind of behavioral rule that we suspect ethnomethodologists seek in their efforts to tease out the methodology applied by the ordinary members of society in their own pursuit of successful interaction and in their own effort to make sense of the empirical world.

To the extent that different studies replicate each other's methods, concordance between their results must be viewed as evidence of reliability rather than of independent validation. In such a replication we have evidence only that the same methods obtain the same results when employed by different investigators. We have evidence of validity just to the extent that the investigators employ methods that are mutually independent.

One group of scholars appears to deny the possibility of comparing studies undertaken from widely different perspectives. In what may be a genteel avoidance of the issue, the members of a symposium attempting to relate field studies and laboratory experiments in social psychology have offered the following solution: Without denigrating either type of evidence, they conclude that the findings based on these two types of studies are simply not "commensurate" (Social Science Research Council 1954). We believe otherwise. In the attempt to analyze such different studies comparatively, the trick, it seems to us, is not to accept them on the terms of the original investigator; rather, it is necessary to provide one's own unifying perspective. When this is done such studies do become commensurate.

We noted in the previous chapter that the question of what validates what is a sticky one even under the best of conditions.[2] Let us pursue that comment. When two credible studies agree, there is evidence that they are valid. But what if they disagree? Which of the two is "invalid"? Campbell (1955), for example, is able to show a correlation of +.90 between the morale rankings of submarine crews as measured on an "expensive and extensive" questionnaire and as ranked by informants who knew all the crews. Since the two methods provide independent answers to the same question and those answers are nearly identical, we have evidence that our information is valid. But let us suppose that Campbell's comparative research had resulted in a low or negative correlation. What then? Perhaps one source of data is valid; perhaps the other one is; perhaps neither of them is. *It would appear that although we can achieve evidence of convergent validity when there is agreement, we are unable with this method to demonstrate where the source of invalidity lies when there is disagreement.*

It is possible that when the results of two independent tests disagree, neither is valid. Employing as their criterion the ultimate evidence of behavioral validity—direct observation of the behavior in question—Freeman and Ataöv (1960) find no correlation between direct and indirect indices of the behavior and no correlation between either index and the behavior itself. This study of student cheating also suggests the disturbing possibility that two independent observations may agree while both are in error. What if Freeman and Ataöv had found high correlation between their direct and indirect measures, and suppose they had no observation of the behavior itself? We would have assumed convergent validity and we would have been wrong. Their neat little validation study suggests one solution to the validity testing problem: The problem of validity is reduced when we have direct observation of the actual phenomenon we are attempting to approximate with our measuring instruments. Freeman and Ataöv have such a direct observation and so does LaPiere.

What are we to make of the contradictory conclusions we revealed in the previous chapter? Lord, Lepper, and Mackie argue that LaPiere is incorrect in concluding that attitudes and behaviors are unrelated. They suggest that attitudes and behaviors will be consistent when the "attitude prototype" matches the behavioral object. Do their findings invalidate LaPiere's? No! We have already noted the many shortcomings of the Lord, Lepper, and Mackie piece. Most importantly, LaPiere, you will remember, records direct observations of behavior under actual conditions of social interaction that are a real segment of the flow of everyday behavior of the actors. Statements such as this are not intended as denials of the "reality" of any observed behavior—including the behavior of students in experimental situations [such as those reported by DeFleur and Westie (1958), Linn (1965), and Lord, Lepper, and Mackie (1984)].

We have already conceded that any reliable observation must be a valid indicator of something. It may be possible to derive valid conclusions from experiments with students, but those conclusions would relate to the behavior of subjects under experimental conditions. Regardless of what Lord, Lepper, and Mackie may think by treating behavioral intentions as "functionally equivalent to behavior" (p. 1258) only LaPiere's work permits valid conclusions regarding the behavior of members of a dominant group toward members of a minority group.

Validity poses a serious problem when we use instruments designed to provide estimates of hypothetical behavior. If, instead, our data consist of direct behavioral observations, the problem of validity is reduced to the extent that fewer inferences are required. We then become free to concentrate on important problems of reliability. Thus, in the case of LaPiere, we know that he observed what he intended to observe, but we are not certain how accurately he observed it. It is not a difficult task to determine the extent to which different observers will make the same observations. Replication becomes an important and legitimate pursuit under these conditions, rather than the meaningless game it is under conditions where validity is indeterminate. As Ehrlich and Rinehart (1965) have demonstrated in their analysis of a highly reliable stereotype-measuring instrument that has been a standard tool since 1933, we can be consistently wrong and, as a consequence, consistently misunderstand human behavior.

Being misunderstood, especially when dealing with so muddled a problem as reliability and validity, is a perennial problem. In the process of developing the position on validity expressed in the last few paragraphs, we have frequently found our comments interpreted as supportive of a behavioristic stance. We hope that the following paragraphs will help clear this matter up.

Direct behavioral observations reduce and may even eliminate problems of validity, but only if the concern of the investigation is the behavior being observed. Thus, if one is evaluating a program designed to change behavior and if that behavior is directly observable, then behavioral indicators are required. But these qualifications are important since sometimes the behavior in question is not directly observable and, even more often, programs may be designed to do something other than have a direct effect on behavior. They may intend rather, to propagandize, to educate, to brainwash, to persuade, or to otherwise alter not so much what people do as what they think or believe or say. Such programs call for appropriate nonbehavioral indicators if they are to be properly evaluated. Furthermore, the relationship between attitudinal change and behavioral change remains elusive. It may be that under some conditions the most effective means of altering behavior is to first induce an attitudinal change.

Whether our observations are behavioral or attitudinal, we cannot afford, as scientists, to limit ourselves to input and output. As the discussion of prediction in Chapter 4 suggests, this is magical thinking. Regardless of the nature of our indicators, our primary concern is to build knowledge and this is done by focusing attention on the process of change—rather than focusing on the outcomes produced by certain stimuli.

In Chapter 2 we referred to the need for a new technology of behavioral observations—one that observed, recorded, and made sense out of the social process of which the act is a part. One example is the notion of "unobtrusive measures" introduced by Webb and his colleagues (1966, 1981). They argue that physical traces are nonreactive, i.e., not influenced by the process of being observed. Thus the differential wear of steps in a public building is a nonreactive indicator of differential use of that building or the presence of empty liquor bottles in trash is a nonreactive indicator of liquor consumption. This notion can be imaginatively applied to any number of areas of social research.

Sometimes the process of which the act is a part can be very simple. If we are concerned with student cheating on examinations, it is clear that the most valid indicator is the act itself: Freeman and Ataöv (1960) watch students cheat! When you remove yourself from direct knowledge of the phenomenon and attempt to obtain reports or estimates by indirection, you become vulnerable to a variety of distorting influences. Dealing with the more common and complicated social processes with which many social sciences are concerned, Becker and Geer insist that "participant observation can . . . provide us with a yardstick against which to measure the completeness of data gathered in other ways, a model which can serve to let us know what orders of information escape us when we use other methods" (1957, p. 28). What they are suggesting is a standard for gauging validity.

Criminologists have always been aware of the distortions that occur in statistics on crime as one moves from crimes committed, to crimes reported, to criminals apprehended, to criminals convicted, to prisoners. They speak of a funneling process that occurs as offenders move through the system. Each of these population samples represents an increasingly selective distortion in the residue. In the end, studies of prisoners are not valid bases for inferences about criminals. The moral is, stay close to where the action is, whether that action be lingual, attitudinal, or behavioral.

This reference to criminal statistics brings us back once more to the observation that any reliable data must be a valid reflection of something. At this point, however, we shift perspectives from small, independent studies to larger sets of data frequently gathered and reported for official or public purposes. The traditional problem with statistics in criminology is that there have been no reliable data available on criminals, in part because many crimes are not reported and many criminals are either never identified or never apprehended. Criminologists have therefore sometimes used data such as those provided by the FBI on crimes reported to the police or data on incarcerated criminals. When such data are used as indicators of crime, they are not valid. However, when such data are used as indicators of reported offenses or prison populations, they are indeed valid—to the extent that they are reliable. The classic case remains Emile Durkheim's use of nineteenth-century suicide statistics ([1897] 1951). Let us examine his interpretation of these data.

Durkheim's analysis suggests a remarkable stability in suicide rates within nations and within certain populations such as urban and rural or married and nonmarried or religious denominations. His data also suggest a high degree of stability through time. Furthermore, he observes that there are considerable differences in suicide rates among and between such populations and that these differences are relatively stable. The importance of these observations has been widely acknowledged among sociologists. There has also been considerable criticism.

One of the most common critiques is the argument that the data available to Durkheim were crude and unreliable and therefore the conclusions he draws from those data are questionable. But, as we have seen, reliability is essentially a matter of consistency or stability, and that is precisely what is most remarkable about Durkheim's data. They are, in fact, highly reliable. Since we are proceeding on the assumption that any reliable data provide a valid indicator of something, the important question about Durkheim's suicide data becomes, Of what are they a valid indicator?

In a highly critical vein, Jack Douglas (1967) suggests that what Durkheim is working with is the recording norms of officials who are reflecting nothing more or less than what they perceive to be the values of the community. This is the basis for his argument that all such official data are social constructions of reality. It is also the basis for suspicion of official data on the part of conscientious scientific analysts. Bernard Beck warns that "most of these officially and semiofficially generated statistics are untrustworthy and misleading" (1970, p. 27). There is, however, a more constructive note in Garfinkel's observation that there are "Good Organizational Reasons for 'Bad' Clinic Records" (1967, p. 186).

There are many examples of the validity of consistent data when their consistency is properly identified. Among the cases that sensitize us to the potential problems encountered, if official data are taken at face value, are surgery rates, juvenile detention rates, and grade distributions. There is evidence that rates of surgery in the United States are twice as high as those in England and Wales because there are proportionally twice as many surgeons in the United States, i.e., surgeries performed are a function of the number of surgeons (Brody 1976). It appears that adolescents are admitted to detention facilities based, in part, on availability of bed space (Bortner 1988, p. 119). And our own research shows that grades reflect the social processes that generate them (Pestello 1987).

The opportunity to conduct a participant observation study of grades assigned in a multiple-section course allowed us to witness the process of rate production in operation. We found that despite considerable differences in the ability and performance of the students between sections, and despite differences in the grading standards of the ten instructors, the grade distributions for the dozens of sections were similar. This held quarter after quarter because the grade-producing process served to produce a particular distribution for all sections of the course.

What these data suggest is that the question of how many people "really" are A students, or "really" kill themselves is essentially unanswerable, except within the limits of a collective judgment about grades or suicide. It may be that there was a dimension to Durkheim's notion of a "collective conscience" that even he did not recognize. Durkheim proceeded as if his data did indeed reflect the rates at which people took their own lives. He attributed differences in rates largely to differences in social constraints.

What is suggested by the ethnomethodological perspective (which is what we have been reviewing) is that the differences in rates are indeed a creature of the collective conscience—so much so that they may have little to do with the rates at which people "really" kill themselves. We believe that Douglas (1967), in his otherwise lucid critique of Durkheim, is essentially making this argument, although he fails to get it across in his eagerness to destroy the Master. Durkheim's data, we submit, provide valid information of official and public norms about how many people of what types ought to be killing themselves.

Many of the observations made in this and the preceding chapter are not likely to find common agreement among contemporary social scientists. It may be helpful to provide some exposure to contrary views. One of the best statements criticizing the viewpoint we have been presenting is by a group of psychologists who are among the most prolific writers on the attitude-behavior issue.

The Other Side

This chapter, like Chapter 4, is largely based on our 1969 article, "Looking Backward: Case Studies on the Progress of Methodology in Sociological Research." In "Looking Backward Revisited: A Reply to Deutscher," Icek Ajzen and his collaborators challenge us on four points:

> (1) the social sciences have been concerned with the validity problem, (2) Deutscher's treatment of "prediction" is inadequate, (3) there is no basis for the pessimistic evaluation of current methodology in the social sciences, and (4) there is a great deal of convergent validation, at least with respect to the area of discourse selected by Deutscher, namely the attitude-behavior relationship. (Ajzen et al. 1970, p. 267)

Their concern with our treatment of validity is twofold. After arguing that there is a vast body of literature on the validity problem, they charge us with cavalierly dismissing operational definitions as a useful device in creating valid indicators based on Bergman's (1951) outmoded formulation of operationalism. Second, and related to the first point, we are accused of confusing or misunderstanding various types of validity (test validity, construct validity, convergent validity, and the internal and external validity of experimental designs). The psychologists refer us to the classic works by Campbell on the difference between internal and external validity (Campbell 1957; Campbell and Stanley 1963).

Ajzen and his colleagues claim that our "objection to prediction is speculative, meta-theoretical, and based on a failure to distinguish between prediction and causal relationships" (1970, p. 268). They suggest that our concerns about validity would have been answered if we had been sensitive to this distinction: "It is only in the context of experimental or quasi-experimental designs (not correlational ones) that causal hypotheses can be investigated, and . . . we do have adequate guidelines for examining those factors that threaten internal and external validity" (p. 268).

These psychologists are most disturbed by our charge of methodological regression. They defend small, selective samples by arguing that homogeneous samples decrease variability due to extraneous factors and that small size requires a larger value of the test statistic for stated significance, thus providing more conservative tests of hypotheses. Furthermore, Ajzen and his coauthors argue that small, selective samples only threaten external validity or generalizability.

Our concern for having control groups is deemed inappropriate because the three studies we reviewed (LaPiere, DeFleur and Westie, and Linn) are correlational in design rather than experimental. Our argument for parsimony in statistical assumptions is considered irrelevant on the grounds that failing to use more powerful tests results in the loss of information. We are further chastised for overlooking many of the difficulties with LaPiere's study because we are enamored of field studies.

Among the shortcomings of LaPiere's study we are charged with missing is that:

> the description of the attitude object and the situation is sufficiently incomplete and ambiguous in the letter-questionnaire that it probably constituted a very different stimulus from the actual Chinese couple. The relationship LaPiere found might have been different if the question had been worded, "Would you accept a young, well-dressed, well-spoken, well-to-do Chinese couple accompanied by a mature, well-dressed, well-spoken . . . educated European gentleman as guests in your establishment?" (p. 270)

[This is exactly what Lord, Lepper, and Mackie (1984) argue.]

In addition, Ajzen et al. suggest that the persons answering LaPiere's questionnaire may have been seeking to avoid trouble and therefore answered dishonestly. (Their sensitivity to this possibility is not reflected in most of their publications.) They also speculate that respondents to the questionnaire may not have always been the same ones who served the Chinese couple—one of their arguments that we too view as troublesome.

Our critics also observe that the studies we critiqued use different measures, which may preclude meaningful comparisons between their results:

It seems that three, and not two, variables have been investigated, and it is useful to distinguish between them. The first variable is attitude toward an object (A_O) which is the amount of positive or negative affect toward the object. The second is behavioral intention (BI) which is the degree to which a person *intends to engage in* a particular behavior with respect to the attitude object. The third is the behavior (B) that a person *actually engages in* with respect to the given attitude object. (p. 271, emphasis in original)

Each of the studies we compared employed a different subset of these variables. Furthermore, different norms may have been appropriate for each of the different studies. Differences in findings may be due to this fact since evidence exists showing that norms and attitudes are codeterminants of behavior.

The Last Word

It is tempting to exploit the opportunity to get in the last word by dwelling on many of the details of the above critique. We have done our best to resist that temptation and to touch here on only a few points. Some of those points are extremely important. For example, in the psychologists' critique there appears, for the first time, a clear indication of the nature of the conceptual problem. It comes not, as one might expect, from the use of different verbal dimensions, but from the use of different behavioral ones.

In their critique, Ajzen and his fellows point out a distinction between "behavioral intention" and "actual behavior." This is a distinction that one encounters in the empirical world: People frequently intend to do things that they never actually do, just as they do not intend to do certain things they later find themselves doing. We first learned the importance of this kind of distinction from LaPiere.

In reflecting on his earlier comparative study of prejudice in France and England, LaPiere comments in "Attitudes vs. Actions" that "at that time I overlooked the fact that what I was obtaining from the hotel proprietors was still a 'verbalized' reaction to a symbolic situation" (1934, p. 231). The Illinois psychologists and LaPiere are clear on this distinction. It is curious that neither Lord, Lepper, and Mackie, nor Linn, nor DeFleur and Westie take note of it. Until we understand better the conditions under which behavioral intention is related to actual behavior, we cannot assume that studies dealing with these two perspectives are equivalent or comparable. Thus, the studies we chose to compare might have reached different conclusions because they were studying different relationships.

Our critics object to the assertion that validity has been a neglected issue. Actually, our statement is a relative one, suggesting only that validity has been neglected as compared to reliability, but that is a minor point. They do cite a number of references (and there are others) that wrestle with the logic of validity and sometimes suggest methodological devices for dealing with it. In considering their comments, it occurred to us that the problem is not so much that social scientists have been inattentive to validity (as we suggested) as that they have not done much about it. The literature they cite is largely hortatory, urging colleagues to be more attentive to the problem. We submit that there was practically no concern in the social sciences for validity issues prior to the mid-1950s and that there has been little since that time.

Our observation is derived from our reading of empirical studies. But of greatest importance is our impression that the vast literature on reliability has exerted considerable influence on the design and reporting of research. The vast literature on validity, if there be such, has not to any large degree found its way into the design and reporting of research.

All of this has to do with an important phenomenon that the critique amply illustrates but the critics ignore: *What people say may not always be related to what they do.* The rhetoric of science and the behavior of scientists do not seem to coincide when it comes to matters of validity. It is also true rhetoric that Bergman's (1951) formulation of the operational definition is acknowledged to be outmoded. Most reputable social scientists would accept this. It is equally true, however, that Bergman's formulation of the operational definition is still widely used.

While we will allow that it is rhetorically correct that prediction is unrelated to cause and effect, our reading of the products of social scientists, however, suggests otherwise. For the moment we will concede that, rhetorically, none of the studies reviewed in 1969 "could have had . . . an objective of confirming or disconfirming a causal relationship since all . . . were correlational in nature" (Ajzen et al. 1970, p. 268). Ajzen et al. fail to compare their true rhetoric with the fact that *all of the studies clearly imply exactly that objective.* Perhaps our critics and we sometimes talk past each other because they are attentive to what is *said* about research, while we are attentive to what is *done* in research.

The psychologists conclude that our objection to prediction is "speculative, meta-theoretical, and based on a failure to distinguish between prediction and causal relationships" (p. 268). All of this is correct! We are speculating (perhaps the most important and the most useful procedure in that chain of activities that make up science); our objective is in part meta-theoretical; finally, it is precisely in the confusion of prediction with causal relations that we find our argument. Although we don't believe it correct to suggest that we confuse them, they are indeed frequently confused.

Correlation analysis, in the sense that Ajzen and his coauthors use that term, has nothing to do with explanation and is atheoretical. Because it only describes, it cannot make any cumulative or abstract contribution to knowledge. In taking such a position, they completely discount a great deal of what we believe is very important evidence. Clearly, there are many kinds of research that they would call correlational, but that we find useful—as useful and as credible as some experimental analyses.

Actually, the distinction made by the critics between correlational studies and those with the objective of confirming a causal relationship seems to us neither clear nor useful. Correlation techniques are employed in theoretically grounded research to provide a partial test of causal or directional hypotheses. When we correlate cigarette smoking with lung cancer, it is in order to accumulate evidence of the extent to which smoking may cause cancer. Very few of the studies finding a relationship between attitude and behavior fail to state or imply a causal relationship between the two—sometimes one way and sometimes the other. It would be difficult to find any study dealing with attitudinal and behavioral change that fails to suggest causality. This being the state of affairs, it is unwise to suggest that one need not be concerned with (external) validity in correlation studies. If they can tell us nothing beyond themselves, then they can tell us nothing.

We do, nevertheless, find sound experimental evidence to be the most credible of all. The fact that LaPiere did introduce some controls into his work adds immensely to its credibility, and the fact that neither Linn nor DeFleur and Westie did so (although both might have and should have) detracts immensely from theirs. Surely it is inappropriate to excuse them from such rigor (as our critics do) by tacking the appellation *correlational* to their work.

The desirability of controls is further documented by the comments of one of the critics who is a photographer. He suggests that there may be a sizable proportion of people who resist having their photograph taken under any conditions. Thus it is impossible to determine how many refusals are a result of racial bias and how many are generalized reactions to the camera. This is an important point that had not occurred to us.

It follows that the closer the observation to the empirical phenomenon, the greater the probability of validity (other things being equal). Each step away from that direct observation requires an assumption about the relationship between the indirect indicator or estimate and the phenomenon itself. Sometimes our assumptions are technical ones required to rationalize statistical procedures. Sometimes they are logical assumptions required in order to make inferential jumps. Statistical devices provide estimates of and confidence limits to what we would find in the empirical world *if we could approach it directly.* Thus, the fewer statistics required to substantiate the findings, the fewer assumptions, and the greater parsimony.

For these reasons we fail to understand the critics' argument that researchers are remiss if they do not use every statistical technique whose assumptions the data appear to meet. It seems to us that if it is not essential that we make innumerable statistical assumptions, we ought to abide by the rule of parsimony. Incidentally, one assumption that usually must be made in dealing with someone else's analysis is that there are no computational errors. If there are no computations this assumption is unnecessary. Ajzen and his colleagues did discover such an error in the DeFleur-Westie chi-square.

It is true that we are "enamored" of field studies, especially (but not exclusively) those which incorporate elements of experimental design. It is equally true that we are skeptical of most laboratory experiments with human subjects (regardless of their so-called internal validity). The grounds for this skepticism will be spelled out later. Our critics, on the other hand, seem quite taken with evidence derived from laboratory experiments with students (homogeneous groups reduce unwanted variation). It seems to us more important to discover how people behave in everyday life and at least one psychologist agrees with us. In an address to the annual meeting of the American Psychological Society, Robyn Dawes suggests that relying upon college students for subjects may lead to a flawed view of human nature. Students, he argues, live in a unique environment, which causes them to act differently from people in other social worlds (Raymond 1991).

What concerns us is their failure to recognize that conclusions regarding the relationship between attitude and behavior may be related to the setting in which the research takes place. For documentation, the reader and the critics are referred to the two sets of studies cited in the opening paragraph of Ajzen's concluding section—those which show a relationship between sentiments and acts and those which do not. Note that the set that suggests a relationship consists for the most part of laboratory experiments, while their set suggesting no relationship is nearly all field studies. It makes a difference how the study is done; methods (not "good" or "bad," but "different") may explain some of the lack of convergent validity.

There is nothing wrong with evidence from the laboratory (much of the argument in this book is based on such evidence) as long as it passes the double screen. The test of credibility holds, of course, for any source of evidence, as does the conceptual test. We should admit as evidence almost anything that has an empirical base and makes sense: field studies, surveys, experiments, novels, ethnographies, biographies, histories, philosophies, and well-grounded polemics. Independent convergence among such various data is, in fact, independent, while if one restricts legitimacy to only one of these sources of evidence, identical sources of errors (sources derived from the method) occur in all of the studies. This is hardly independent convergence.

Our critics assert that small samples are not necessarily bad. This is true. An informed analysis of a single case can provide highly credible evidence. Of course, it is generally better if there are two cases, since we then have a basis for comparison. But it is probably best to have three, because this provides the points necessary to establish the type of curve (if any) with which we are dealing. As a matter of fact, the selection of a probability sample is an irrelevant ritual in theoretical research (Zetterberg 1965; Glaser and Strauss 1967; Etzioni 1968a). We do suspect, however, that our basis for this position is quite different from that of Ajzen and his coauthors.

They argue that a small sample may be superior, since "it may actually provide a more conservative test of the investigator's hypotheses because it demands a stronger relationship in order to obtain a standard level of significance" (1970, p. 289). Knowingly treading on the dangerous grounds of the Type I–Type II error bind—making an arbitrary decision as to whether the investigator wishes to risk either falsifying a true null hypothesis or accepting a false one (we are not certain that it is necessary to risk either)—we nevertheless translate this to mean that a small sample is likely to encourage conclusions that are contrary to what is found in the empirical world. The English word *conservative* is, in our opinion, inappropriately used by social psychologists in this context.

In effect, since the demands are more stringent for us to reach any given level of significance, and since conclusions are frequently based upon that level, conclusions based upon excessively small samples may be in error in that they do not represent what is found in the universe from which the sample is drawn. *Linn acknowledges that he would have reached opposite conclusions with a larger sample.* It does not take a very great inflation of sample size for the same thing to occur with the DeFleur-Westie data. In this sense, their samples seem to us to be too small. What kind of knowledge do we have when conclusions are reversible depending on the size of the sample?

The critics do find serious flaws in these studies, which we overlooked in 1969, and their conclusion, which seems something of an understatement, is acceptable to us: "Thorough methodological analysis of these three . . . studies does not seem to indicate a regressive trend in meth-

three . . . studies does not seem to indicate a regressive trend in methodology." But, they continue, "there is no indication of a significant advance either" (Ajzen et al. 1970, p. 271). Although we are not dissuaded of the impression that we may have been in reverse, we are satisfied with their conclusion. It should be of interest to social scientists that there are two independent empirical analyses that suggest that we did not improve methodologically over the thirty-year period from the mid-1930s to the mid-1960s. (If we include the last point on our time line, the same truth holds to the mid-1980s.) That is convergent validity!

Notes

1.   How can one explain the radically different images of the same Mexican village portrayed by Robert Redfield (1930) and Oscar Lewis (1951) or of life in Samoa by Margaret Mead (1928) and Derek Freeman (1983)? Are the discrepancies attributable to lack of reliability on the part of the earlier observers or to the validity of a changing world?

2.   It follows from the evidence presented so far in this book that the present state of knowledge provides no basis for confidence in a time sequence test of validity. We cannot assume that a later study either validates or fails to validate an earlier one on the sole grounds of its later occurrence.

6

Anyone May Lie a Bit, Cheat a Bit, and Try to Be Helpful

Getting in Our Own Way

The need to discount evidence as part of our screening process was mentioned in the first chapter of this book. To what extent can we accept different kinds of evidence as credible? Although C. Wright Mills has dressed it up in contemporary language, this is not a new problem. It dates back to the origins of modern sociology. It was Herbert Spencer's 1874 statement that appears to have fed Mills's concern: "From the intrinsic natures of its facts, from our own natures as observers of its facts, and from the peculiar relation in which we stand towards the facts to be observed, there arise impediments in the way of Sociology greater than those in the way of any other science" (1874, p. 72). Spencer proceeds to wrestle with such contemporary issues as "objectivity" and "reactivity" in the social sciences. It is precisely such issues that we continue to address over a hundred years later in this and the following two chapters.

Although we have allowed almost any source legitimacy as "evidence," we do lean most heavily on survey research findings, laboratory experimental reports, and the results of participant-observational field studies. Chapters 6, 7, and 8 are designed to sensitize us to some of the credibility problems typical of those three sources. Martin Trow (1958), meanwhile, reminds us in his critique of Becker and Geer's advocacy of participant observation that every cobbler thinks leather is the only thing. We have already confessed to being "enamored of" field studies and to being "taken with" the quality of evidence derived from experimental design. We also have reservations about the validity of much of what is reported on the basis of large-scale surveys. But the fact is that leather is not the only thing and for certain purposes it may be a very poor material; we have referred to the possibility that we sometimes try to chop down trees with shovels because we have no axes and our shovels are very good.

Common to all of these methods is the problem of reactivity. Interviewers and respondents are human beings engaged in an interactive encounter. The resulting protocol is a product of that interaction. This is sometimes called *interviewer effect* and, as we shall see, efforts are made to minimize it. Participant observers are present in the situations that they observe, and their very presence alters the social nature of that situation. This is sometimes called *observer effect* and efforts are made to deal with it too. Finally, the fact that subjects in an experiment know that they are taking part in an experiment and usually know who the experimenter is introduces those kinds of reactivity sometimes referred to as *experimental effect* and *experimenter effect*. This is the central problem that Webb and his colleagues (1981) address in their essays on "unobtrusive measures." Their solution is two-pronged.

First, Webb and his coauthors suggest that, when possible, certain nonreactive indicators be used, such as empty liquor bottles in the trash, worn steps in the library, or nose prints on the museum exhibit. Such indicators are not created in interaction with the researcher, but it is also true that they are not always available. The clever methodologist must begin by first asking, What objective traces are left by such behavior?— as the heavy use of a stairway can be verified by the wearing of the steps. Of course, we must be careful even of the conclusions we draw from nonreactive measures.

The second prong to their solution lies in the process of triangulation, which we discussed in relation to validity. If, for example, we have convergence in the conclusions from a survey, an experiment, and a field study—each with its own peculiar form of reactivity—then they become collectively more credible. Reactivity seems to us endemic in social research. Precisely how much it distorts our findings and under what conditions remains debatable, and there are indeed many social scientists who deny that it deserves any serious attention. Nevertheless, we will adopt the position that as long as reasonable doubt exists, reactivity must be seriously considered.

Earlier in this volume, we quoted Benney and Hughes's observation that "the interview, as itself, a form of social rhetoric, is not merely a tool of sociology but a part of its very subject matter" (1956, p. 138). The same can, of course, be said of experimental or observational studies. Their point is that there are some things social scientists do understand about human interaction and that those things pertain as well to interaction between interviewer and respondent as they do to any other kind of interaction. That the psychological experiment can be viewed in the same manner is clearly reflected in the subtitle employed by an experimenter in reporting his experiment with experiments, "The Psychological Experiment as a Social Interaction" (Friedman 1967), and the title of Wuebben, Straits, and Schulman's (1974) edited work, *The Experiment as a Social Occasion*. It is this simple suggestion—that the few things we think we do know as social scientists ought to be applied to our own activities as social scientists—that lies at the heart of Julius Roth's (1965) piece, "Hired Hand Research."

Roth presents three telling cases in which research assistants responded to the social situation of the research by altering the coding to make their work easier and keep their jobs. He argues that cheating, carelessness, and distortion on the part of hired research assistants are "exactly the kind of behavior we should expect from people with their position in a production unit" (p. 191). Roth reminds us that we know from studies in industry, as well as in other kinds of organizations, that workers tend to develop their own set of norms regarding production—independent of whatever norms may be set by management. If this process of informal norm-setting occurs among other kinds of hired help, then surely it must also occur among the hired help we employ on our large-scale research projects.

Roth spells out a solution to the problem of the fraud he identified: If we treat co-workers as colleagues and fellow "pros," then they will act that way; if we treat them like employees, then they will act that way. He suggests three factors that would improve the quality of the research product. Based on his reading of social science principles, the first is the problem of size. Although the problems of hired hand researchers can be encountered in any size research group, it is more evident in larger research organizations: "The larger the group, the more difficult [colleagueship] becomes until the point is probably reached where it is virtually impossible, and the organization must be run on the basis of hierarchical staff relations with the lower echelons almost inevitably becoming hired hands" (p. 195). This leads to the second problem, subordination. Subordination of some research members hampers collegial relations and thwarts the interchange of ideas. Finally, Roth believes that the adherence to a rigid plan constrains research results, rather than producing the most accurate information: "Sticking to a pre-formed plan means that others cannot openly introduce variations which may make the study more meaningful" (p. 195). Assistants can only have an impact on the design covertly. Roth concludes that standard practices in most research organizations threaten the validity of the data collected.

It would seem that in spite of our obsession with reliability over the past few decades, we still are far from solving the problem. The hired hand thesis applies to any kind of large-scale research project that employs assistants in any capacity—as interviewers, coders, bibliographers, technicians, statistical clerks, etc. Aside from the distance this kind of organized research creates between investigator and data, it also curtails intellectual independence. No longer can one (as Mills advised) be both theorist and methodologist.

Roth demonstrates how deceitful data collectors fail to follow instructions. On the other side of the coin, Peneff (1988) documents how dedicated data collectors also fail to follow the rules of the survey. In his study of a French survey research organization, Peneff finds that the actual behavior of interviewers strays from the instructions they are given in order to *save* the survey. Interviewers

> try to interest respondents in the interview and get them to take it seriously by letting their own personalities show and interacting in nonneutral ways. No question is asked exactly as worded. Not only were personal comments added and various introductions used to explain the phrasing of questions, the original questions were often altered to avoid evident misunderstandings or too many refusals. (p. 522)

Peneff concludes that deviations from the research design are not so much cheating, as is often assumed, but a response to the definition of the situation. By looking at the interviewers who were most valued and experienced, he found that they were "the most likely to disregard their instructions and least likely to conform to the ideal of anonymous inquisitor" (p. 522). The best interviewers adopted flexible techniques similar to those used by field-workers in collecting qualitative data.

A recent exchange in the *Journal of the American Statistical Association* reveals that statisticians, whom we tend to think of as lacking interest in such issues, are becoming concerned about interview data being the product of a "linguistic and interactional event." The exchange featured an article by two anthropologists, Suchman and Jordan (1990), five comments on the article from a diverse group of scholars, and a rejoinder by the anthropologists. Suchman and Jordan analyzed videotapes of five interviews and, sounding much like Peneff, find that

> the validity of survey data is potentially undermined by the same prohibition against interaction that is intended to insure reliability. As a remedy, we recommend a collaborative approach that would allow the kinds of interactional exchanges between interviewer and respondent necessary to ensure standardized interpretations, without introducing interviewer bias. (p. 233)

It is to survey research that Roth, Peneff, and Suchman and Jordan primarily speak. Roth suggests that by doing things "right" researchers can get hired hands to do surveys as they should be done. Peneff and Suchman and Jordan reveal that the problem is more fundamental. Interviewers must bend the rules in order to get the job done at all. We (the younger two of us) observed this in our own work as graduate student telephone interviewers.

As we witnessed the social psychology of the data collection process we were particularly struck with the negotiation that sometimes occurred with closed-choice attitude questions, where there is no room for interviewees to relay the complexity of their thoughts and feelings. It was apparent to us that such questions forced many subjects to respond in ways foreign to how they thought and expressed themselves. Some examples we faced in asking Likert and semantic differential questions were: Sometimes people would only agree to select one of the allowable answers if they could qualify it, wanted to select two of the possible answers, could not make up their mind, or insisted on responding in terms that would not fit one of the answer options.

The fact that many answers were negotiated between interviewer and interviewee was made most apparent when working with "troublesome" subjects. We were often able to finesse the subject into deciding upon a single allowable choice, but it was clearly the product of negotiation. As responses were coded, cleaned, and analyzed, the natural complexity, imprecision, inconsistency, and indecision in the way subjects first expressed their thoughts and feelings were eliminated. Proponents of survey research would maintain that one is left with neat indirect indicators. The important question, however, is: Indicators of what? Like Phillips (1971), we found answers to be artifacts of the interview process. Let us consider the peculiar vulnerability of this and other kinds of research that depend on conversations for their data.

The Problem with Talking to People: Surveys and Interviews

We know from our everyday experiences that different opinions on the same subject can be elicited from the same people in different situations. Such opinions may at times be inconsistent with each other, but regardless of such apparent inconsistency, all such opinions may be valid. All of them may be real opinions. An attitude that is likely to be expressed under conditions of actual social interaction is real and becomes a public opinion when it is expressed. As for our private opinions—basic, consistent, internalized orientations toward objects—they rarely have an opportunity to find expression as public opinions or as actions.

In a sense, then, such private opinions are rarely "real." Exceptions occur in situations where people can express themselves collectively with anonymity or in confidence among intimates. This public opinion then may be congruent with the private opinion. Thus, in 1964 when the United States Congress was considering a sizable increase in salary for its members, a Republican attempt to eliminate the pay increase was thwarted by a vote of 125 to 37. Minutes later, when the bill was voted on, a demand for a roll call succeeded, and the pay increase was overwhelmingly defeated (*Congressional Record* 1964). Consistency in this inconsistent pattern was observed as Congress considered another pay issue in January 1989. When it comes to pay increases, congressional voting behavior reflects one opinion as long as behavior remains anonymous. But politicians reverse their votes when they know they will be held individually accountable for them.

If exceptions to the reality of private opinions occur in anonymous collective situations, they also can occur when people have the opportunity to express themselves individually with anonymity as in such cases as nose picking, voting, masturbating, the purchase of certain items of consumer goods, cheating one's self at solitary games—like solitaire or in self-deprivational games such as those involving smoking, drinking, or dieting—or responding to a survey interview. As the case of Congress suggests, private acts and opinions cannot be assumed to have any relationship to public acts or opinions.

Paradoxically, then, one of the few instances in which an attitude is unlikely to be translated into an opinion or an act in any social context is when it is elicited in a rigorously controlled interview situation by highly trained interviewers employing a technically high quality instrument. This is not to deny the "reality" of interaction in an interview situation. We suggest only that the situation is so meticulously constructed and carefully managed by one party in pursuit of a clear goal (to obtain a completed interview) that it is difficult to imagine any routine social situation that resembles the formal interview. In short, responses to formal interviews inform us about behavior in a formal interviewing situation and little else. The conditions where such data may be otherwise informative are considered later in this chapter.

So brash a statement demands explanation! Current research-interviewing technology assumes the desirability of sterile conditions in the interview situation: Neither the interviewer nor the instrument should act in any way upon the situation. The question, ideally, should be so put and so worded as to be unaffected by contextual contaminations. The interviewer must be an inert agent who exerts no influence on response by tone, expression, stance, or statement. Consistency is crucial. The question must be unloaded in that it does not hint in any way that one response is more desirable or more correct than any other response. It must be placed in the sequence of the instrument in such a way that the subject's response is not affected by previous responses. The respondent is provided with maximum assurances of anonymity and the implied guarantees of protection from sanctions. *In effect, the respondent is urged to reveal the most private of opinions on an object without relating it to any other objects, or placing it in any context, with the assurance that the interviewer doesn't care what is said and no one else will ever know what is said.* We are confronted then with the paradoxical argument that we obtain an "unreal" opinion when people are provided with the opportunity to state what they "really" think.

The interview is structured in such a way as to maximize the opportunity to elicit a private opinion. The facts of social life are that real utterances of opinion are always public in the sense that they occur in the presence of others. They never occur in isolation and one must always consider the consequences of having uttered them. In real life, there is neither anonymity nor guarantee against possible sanctions. Public opinions are always uttered in a particular context, both in the sense of assessing the impact they are likely to have on others who are present and in the sense of resulting in part from, and being influenced by, what has immediately preceded their utterance in the flow of the action. Consequent overt behavior toward the object of the opinion also takes place in a social context and is as much constrained by others and by the actor's interpretation of the situation at the time as is the utterance of an opinion. Real expressions of attitude and overt behavior rarely occur under the conditions of sterility that are deliberately structured for the interview situation.

Survey methodologists view their instruments, their interviewers, and the interview situation as potentially contaminating elements. Efforts are made to elicit opinions that are more purely private by using knowledge about situational effects for the purpose of removing or reducing those effects. In contrast to the approach of the social psychologist, this is a strangely negative role of knowledge: The student of public opinion seeks to learn how people express their opinions and their behavior under real (public) conditions in order to alter those conditions in such a way that they become unreal and thus facilitate the elicitation of private opinions.

It follows from the discussion so far that in more *gemeinschaft*, folk type societies there is less likelihood of divergence between public and private opinions. These societies are hospitable to fewer publics, encompassing a limited variety of perspectives, and thus contain a narrower range of public opinions. Again we are confronted with a paradox: It is precisely in those societies where rigorous efforts to assess public opinions are most likely to be perceived as necessary and most likely to occur that the opinions they elicit are least likely to be real.

Our consideration of survey and interview data has been focused on validity issues: To what extent do we get what we intend when we ask people questions and record their answers? Roth (1965) does not contend with the validity or the appropriateness of the methods. To the contrary, he raises questions about reliability and suggests solutions in order to improve our confidence in such research. Survey researchers constantly seek ways to reduce response variance attributable to such phenomena as interviewer effect and the ambience of the interview, including the external features in the setting in which it takes place. As Hyman (1949, p. 38) put it, the general aim of modern opinion and attitude research has been to provide a situation in which the respondent's "true" attitude can come out unhindered by any social barriers.

Survey researchers have learned that the type of pairing of interviewer and respondent can strongly influence the data obtained. Methodological studies by survey organizations suggest that people express different opinions to different kinds of interviewers (in terms of age, sex, and race) in different kinds of situations (alone vs. with others, at home vs. in the office, etc.). Such variation is seen as technical interference with reliability; it messes up consistency. From this perspective, the survey researcher finds such situational effects on interview outcome utterly abhorrent. The purpose in studying them is to find ways of eliminating or at least reducing them. But studies of this kind of "distortion" can provide a wealth of information if they are interpreted as providing opportunities for reclamation rather than opportunities for garbage disposal.

We located three examples of efforts in this direction. Each utilizes knowledge of interviewer effect and deals with surveys of black communities. During World War II, it was suspected that there might be some underlying discontent with the Roosevelt administration among blacks. This discontent, it was felt, could affect the 1944 elections in ways not revealed by the polls. On the basis of earlier National Opinion Research Center studies, Williams and Cantril (1945) knew that blacks respond differently to black and white interviewers. They reasoned that blacks were likely to hide race-sensitive opinions from white interviewers. Their study was designed to measure the extent of such opinions. Race-sensitive responses were to be identified by differences obtained when one half of the Harlem sample was interviewed by whites and the other half by blacks. They concluded from this survey that the suspected underlying discontent did not exist and therefore would not distort predictions based on the polls.

The second study attempting to make use of interviewer effect took place in an Illinois college town in the 1960s. Bindman (1965) reports a wide range of discrepancies when black respondents previously interviewed by whites were reinterviewed by blacks. He is aware that such data are ordinarily interpreted as reflections of low reliability, but he recognizes that this interpretation is based on the assumption that there is only one "correct" answer. Bindman sees the discrepancies for what they are: different kinds of responses to different kinds of interviewers. As a result of both his reinterviews and the cross-interviewing similar to that of Williams and Cantril, Bindman is able to add new dimensions to his analysis.

Anderson, Silver, and Abramson (1988) look at the impact of interviewer's race on electoral participation in election studies. They discovered interesting anomalies created by racial variation in interviewers. Black nonvoters were more likely to tell black interviewers that they voted, when they did not. They also found that blacks interviewed by blacks were more likely to vote and endorse civic norms. Thus, who asks the questions may not only alter answers on attitudinal surveys, but also induce changes in behavior.

Using knowledge of interviewer effect and controlling it in order to obtain new knowledge is only one of several means of obtaining "real" opinions. We (Deutscher 1958) have argued for the employment of popular stereotypes in the deliberate creation of loaded questions. In a survey of public images of the nurse, four independent tests of validity provided convergent evidence that the opinions elicited by stereotyped—i.e., loaded—questions were real. At that time we observed that some of the better methodology texts grudgingly acknowledged—parenthetically, in footnotes, or as an afterthought—that "loaded" questions are not *necessarily* undesirable. In this chapter, we are suggesting the obverse: "Unloaded" or objective questions are not *necessarily* undesirable. In describing the nurse survey, we wrote:

> We asked "leading" questions and we asked "loaded" questions, because we were seeking neither superficial information nor testing the respondent's knowledge. We literally desired to "lead" the respondent into revealing his [or her] "loaded" feelings, rather than to obtain simpering cliches. (Deutscher 1958, p. 57)

Marquis (1970) displays the kind of ingenuity that recognizes that what are traditionally viewed as dangerous biasing tactics can provide useful hints for the improvement of interviews. Marquis is dealing with what he calls "facts" (presumably in distinction from attitudes or opinions or beliefs). Even when seeking to obtain the most straightforward kind of health information, it becomes clear that "interviewing persons about facts is not necessarily similar to interrogating computer memories or retrieving data from written record sources. One essential difference is that the personal interview relies heavily on verbal transactions between human beings" (Marquis 1970, p. 203; see also Sacks, Krushat, and Newman 1980). Marquis's point of departure is the observation of gross underreporting when interview reports of sickness and medical service utilization are compared to information contained in medical records. In a controlled survey experiment, Marquis finds that the application of operant conditioning in the form of gentle reinforcement (anathema to the traditional survey interviewer) significantly increases the amount of accurate health information obtained. Most importantly, he recognizes the broader implications of his relatively small finding: "The presence or absence of the kind of social reinforcement used in this research is only one small part of a wide variety of interviewer behaviors which can be systematically varied in the household interview setting" (Marquis 1970, p. 213).

This chapter would be incomplete without reference to the fact that even if survey research and polling were to begin to elicit real *individual opinions*, the major problem of reality in *collective opinions* would remain (in terms of the likelihood of collective action following their expression). This issue was raised by Blumer in 1947 and remains unanswered. At that time Blumer argued that "if public opinion is to be studied in any realistic sense its depiction must be faithful to its empirical character" (1948, p. 543). Blumer's analysis rests essentially on the observation that, although everyone may carry equal weight in the voting booth, everyone does not carry equal weight in collective actions undertaken in a society. The opinions of the president of the United States may carry weight at the ballot box equal to that of any other citizen; there is, however, considerable disparity in the weight carried in the formation of national policy.

Blumer argues that

> current sampling procedure forces a treatment of society as if society were only an aggregation of disparate individuals. . . . Certainly the mere fact that the interviewee either gives or does not give an opinion does not tell you whether he is participating in the formation of public opinion in the society. (1948, p. 543)

Eighteen years later, Angus Campbell writes that "it is curious that Blumer's hopes for the functional analysis of public opinion have been so little realized" (1965, p. 633). In Chapter 2 we considered the comments of Blumer's discussants. It appeared that in 1947 we social scientists were unable to cope with his carefully developed argument, largely because we were so defensive about our scientific reputation (Newcomb 1948; Woodward 1948). Smith and Carter's (1989) response to Peneff suggests that we are still defensive about our scientific reputation.

In this chapter we are not attempting to argue that current public opinion polling and survey methods are never valid. In our discussion of loaded questions and, earlier, of essentially private acts, we have suggested that, on occasion, current methods are appropriate. Sometimes private opinions may have real consequences. Blumer points out that there are conditions under which everyone's opinion does have equal weight:

> Many actions of human beings in a society are of this nature—such as casting ballots, purchasing toothpaste, going to motion picture shows, and reading newspapers. Such actions, which I like to think of as mass actions of individuals, in contrast to organized actions of groups, lend themselves readily to the type of sampling that we have in current public opinion polling. In fact, it is the existence of such mass actions of individuals which explains, in my judgment, the successful use in consumer research of sampling such as is employed in public opinion polling. (1948, p. 547)

Blumer provides a rationale for the use under certain conditions of the sterile, anonymous, unloaded, individual-oriented questionnaire. In a critique of public opinion research Nehemiah Jordan makes the same observation: "This is why the concrete act of voting is closely related to behavior evoked in public opinion research—the psychological field of the polling booth is obviously very similar to the psychological field evoked by the public opinion poll" (1963, p. 4). In our efforts to understand the frequent lack of concordance between attitude and behavior, we have been struck by the fact that there is congruence in the very areas where Blumer suggests there should be: "Consumers sometimes do change their buying habits in ways that they say they will [and] people frequently do vote as they tell pollsters they will" (Deutscher 1966, p. 247).

In the preceding chapter, the Illinois psychologists provided us with one clue to understanding the discrepancy that is sometimes reported between attitudes and acts: There are different kinds of sentiments and different kinds of acts. Studies that use these same terms may, in fact, be referring to very different phenomena. A second explanation appears for the first time in this book in the preceding paragraphs. Blumer points out that we can expect behavior to relate to sentiments when both are elicited under the same conditions—in the same kind of situation. It follows that when a verbalization is elicited in one situation (e.g., private) and a behavior is elicited in another (e.g., public), we may expect them to be different.

In this discussion of credibility issues related to surveys and interviews, we have barely touched on the psychological literature dealing with such phenomena as "acquiescence response sets" (the inclination to go along with anything) and "social desirability" (the inclination to answer "right"). These are problem areas that bridge the research of survey sociologists, psychological testers, and attitude researchers. It is our impression that many psychologists engaged in experimental work do not share the survey interviewers' abhorrence of such "interference." Nor do they study such things in order to learn how to eliminate them. The psychologist seems rather more curious about how such phenomena enter into the behavior of subjects.

Problems of credibility in experimental research will be considered in Chapter 8. In the following chapter, however, we will consider the role of language in the verbal exchanges we call surveys and interviews. It is possible to consider language as a source of distortion that must be eliminated, but it is also possible to consider language as a most revealing and helpful tool—if we can grasp its nuances. Although language may get in the way when we conduct formal interviews or administer questionnaires, advocates of participant observation suggest that it becomes most useful when it is considered in the context of whatever action is occurring.

7

Speaking in Tongues

Language and Social Research

Although social scientists do not always recognize it, it is impossible to deal with survey and interview situations without considering language. These are situations that by definition require linguistic exchanges. In this chapter we will consider the survey and the interview from a linguistic perspective, first exploring the problems that arise with language when it is lifted out of its conventional social context (as in the survey or interview). We will then consider the extent to which participant observation resolves our problems by being attentive to language within its conventional contexts. Finally, we will consider the weaknesses and limitations in seeking solutions in this direction. Let us begin pursuing the problem of reactivity from a somewhat different angle.

262185

Speaking Out of Context:
Questionnaires and Formal Interviews

One type of reactivity is found outside the relationship between the investigator and the objects of investigation. It lies in what G. H. Mead would call the conversation between the "I" and the "me" as it occurs in the investigator. By interacting with the data in a variety of ways, subtle changes are produced in the outcome. We think of this as a reactivity of the scientist qua scientist, and some aspects of it transcend social science to include all scientific endeavors [see Gould (1977, 1981) on the occurrence of this in the natural sciences]. Aaron Cicourel (1969–1970) articulates this problem in terms of language, either oral or written, which he sees as the instrument through which nearly all of our data are filtered. We devise things to say to our subjects or respondents and we listen to what they say in return (either to us or to each other or to our confederates). In privately considering such linguistic exchanges and making sense out of them, we pass our data through a filter, being attentive to some of them and inattentive to others.

This is not, however, the only linguistic filter that permits some data to pass through and strains out others. Usually our data are forced through a second and finer filter: the coding process. That is, in our efforts to make sense out of the data, we translate them into a more manageable form involving sets of categories. The choices we make in creating those categories and the further decisions we make when we place data in categories are another kind of linguistic filter. Our data then require translation both in their reception and in their classification. And this is not the end of it. Cicourel (1969–1970) suggests that in the reporting of research findings we need to consider—here we encounter yet a third filter—language as a critical variable in producing research results. Cicourel also raises the disturbing question of what does not pass through these three filters and how such information can be recovered.

Sociolinguists such as Cicourel (1969–1970) and Anderson (1967, 1969–1970) point out that translation problems exist even when the investigator is a native speaker of the language in which research is conducted. This is a consequence of the existence of various dialects or speech variations within any society. Becker contends that

> there are plenty of reasons, based on thinking from a great variety of sociological and social psychological positions, to suppose that even people who share a language will make a different kind of sense out of questions whose wording seems simple and clear. (1989, p. 315)

How else can we account for the fact that "when the 1990 census asked people for their race, it got a quarter-million different write-in responses?" (Dayton Daily News 1991).

Unless both participants to an interaction are fluent in the same specific speech variation, it becomes difficult for them to fill in the meanings they would consider "obvious" in interacting with their own kind. This is the issue that Anderson (1967, 1969–1970) addresses in a series of papers. Translation problems arise whenever different kinds of people are required to deal with the same question. Both Anderson, from a more positivistic perspective, and Cicourel, from a more phenomenological perspective, identify the same issue as critical and frequently overlooked in sociological methodology. Such convergence is one bit of evidence of the importance of the issue: Increased sensitivity to the relevance of language in domestic research is seen as urgent regardless of the theoretical orientation of the sociologist.

In their plea for researchers to pay greater attention to language, Potter and Wetherell provide some insight into why we have ignored it: "Language is so central to all social activities it is easy to take for granted. Its very familiarity sometimes makes it transparent to us" (1987, p. 7).

If reactivity is ubiquitous in social research, so too is the definitional problem of a research encounter (Emerson 1987). This is actually a variety of reactivity since it involves the researcher as an active agent, but it is a more social variety than the kinds usually considered. Whenever a person is in a social situation it becomes imperative to muster some reasonable definition of what is happening so that the encounter may be appropriately enacted. Investigators may define themselves as engaging in an encounter with a "subject" or a "respondent" and the situation as one that advances knowledge of self. But the other person also needs to be satisfied as to what is happening.

It can by no means be assumed that the investigator's definition of the situation is automatically shared. Subjects may see themselves as the victim (e.g., "I'm not telling any white interviewer anything that can be used to put down black children"). On the other hand, they may see themselves as the beneficiary (e.g., "It's about time you people got around to finding out what us middle Americans think"). Or the situation could be defined as one requiring courtesy to an uninvited guest (e.g., "I don't understand what you want, but do come in and have a cup of tea"). Obviously there are any number of possible definitions. The discussion that follows focuses on the interview, but these linguistic problems are encountered in any kind of research that requires that an account be given by the researcher to the objects of research.

Benney and Hughes (1956) define an interview, in part, as a relationship between two people where both parties behave as though they are of equal status for its duration, whether or not this is actually so. This kind of fiction is obviously going to come off better in some cultures than in others, among some segments of a society than others, and among some mixes of individuals than others. The kind of cultural climate that tolerates a situation like an interview is "a fairly new thing in the history of the human race" (p. 142). The interview is most generally seen as an encounter with a stranger. There are wide variations in prescribed forms of interaction and language with a stranger. As we shall see below, there are equally wide variations in such particular concepts as privacy, security, and those matters considered to be intimate or personal in nature.

The Southeast Asian cultural value of courtesy has been described in detail by Emily Jones (1963). This "important and pervasive value" defines the interview situation in a manner that has a large potential for distorting supposedly comparable data. It can act as a deterrent to obtaining reliable information—either in response to formal questions or in an interviewing situation that is more open. From the perspective of the respondent, it is a cultural obligation to see to it that the interviewer is not distressed, disappointed, or offended in any way.

To further complicate matters, should the interviewer be a product of this same culture, then the obligation not to distress, disappoint, or offend respondents is reciprocated. This amiable definition, however, has its advantages as well as its drawbacks. For example, "To ask personal questions is well within the bounds of courteous behavior" (Jones 1963, p. 71).

Many different definitions of the interview situation may be subsumed under the gross cultural value that leads to a courtesy bias. Mitchell suggests that a courtesy or hospitality bias is common in Asia everywhere from Japan to Turkey:

> The direction of the courtesy bias is different in different countries. For example, the humility of the Japanese is said to lead them to under-evaluate their own achievements, class positions, and the like. On the other hand, some researchers in the Middle East claim that respondents there tend to exaggerate their achievements, class position, knowledge of the world, and extent to which they are modern rather than traditional. (1965, p. 681)

If courtesy is highly valued in some parts of the world, one might anticipate that the opposite would be true in other parts. There are certainly ethnocentric societies (and ethnic groups within societies), where all outsiders—including interviewers—are considered fair game for deception. Such a "sucker" bias is described by the Keesings (1956; cited by Mitchell 1965, pp. 681–82) in a study of elite communications in Samoa. The sucker bias can be viewed as a put-on: The respondent defrauds the interviewer by acting, for example, as someone the interviewer might imagine him or her to be (Robert Weiss, personal communication, April 15, 1972). This observation can be extended to include the courtesy bias as well, since it, too, is a form of put-on.

Although it may well be within the bounds of courtesy to ask personal questions in Southeast Asia, most other peoples set limits. Hunt, Crane, and Wahlke report that "even native French persons asked to help in translating interview questions could think of no discreet way to ask respondents their religious views" (1964, p. 66). Lerner (1956, p. 193) remarks on the basis of interviews that the French equate security with privacy. It follows that if they permit a breach of their privacy for interviewing purposes, they view this as a self-breach—a violation of their personal security. Lerner's problem was not a matter of the validity of

data obtained but a matter of obtaining it in the first place: "Most refusals were based squarely upon the feeling that such an interview was
an unwarranted intrusion into their personal affairs" (pp. 187–88).

Both Lerner and Hunt et al. report types of resistance among the
French that differ from the typical American survey experience. The
traditional survey checklist of yes-no type questions was regarded with
suspicion by both Austrians and French: "A relatively high proportion
could not be persuaded to answer in the customary and familiar form
used in almost all American surveys" (Hunt et al. 1964, p. 65).

Europeans described such questions as "too brutal" and suggested
that they smacked of American gimmickry. This differential definition is
further confounded by the observation that the French regard as silly,
frivolous, and unworthy of attention any question that requires a respondent to play a role (e.g., "What would you do if . . . ?"). Lerner
interprets this within a culture-personality framework:

> Such questions are handled with greater facility by people . . . who are
> closer than the French are to other-directed personalities, and who, having
> a less stable or less rigid conception of themselves and their proper con-
> duct in the world, show a more supple capacity for rearranging their self-
> system upon short notice. (1956, p. 191)

Lerner relates this observation to an earlier experience interviewing in
the Middle East, where he found that the "traditionalists" were unable
to answer such questions as, What would you do if you were president
of Syria? The "moderns," on the other hand, had no difficulty responding to questions that required them to take the role of a newspaper editor, the leader of their country, or a resident of another country (Lerner
1956, p. 191). *There are then cultural differences in both those things people are
able to talk about and those things they are willing to talk about.* We have already noted the inability to make discreet inquiries about religion among
the French. This is also the case in Muslim Pakistan but not so in Hindu
India.

The Almond-Verba (1963) five-nation study reports that Italians seem
reticent about political topics. Middle-class Americans prefer not to be
too specific about their incomes. And there are people who consider sex
talk taboo:

> In some African areas, as well as in other parts of the world, there is
> reluctance to talk about dead children and the number of people in a
> household. . . . In the Middle East there is a reluctance to discuss ordinary
> household events, and Chinese businessmen in any country are reported
> to be especially secretive about any and all facets of their work and person-
> al lives. In many countries, respondents are reticent about political topics

in general and party preference in particular. On the other hand, it is by no means clear that family planning is nearly as sensitive an issue in the developing countries as might be expected. (Mitchell 1965, p. 675)

But the overriding cross-cultural problem remains that of differences in definitions of what must be perceived as an alien social situation by most people of the world—certainly by the less cosmopolitan and more poorly educated. Americans have had sufficient routine exposure to polls and surveys, both as consumer and respondent, to feel that they know what they are. The same assumption cannot be made regarding other peoples in other societies. The study of the evolving social relationship between interviewer and respondent in various cultures is in itself an important sociological undertaking. It is, of course, not directly to problems of cross-cultural research that this book addresses itself. Let us consider the implications of our discussion so far for the kinds of talking research we do at home. If sentiments are expressed, it is usually a verbal process.

When Benney and Hughes (1956) suggest that the interviews are a part of sociology's very subject matter, they are reminding us that the peculiar thing about human interaction is its symbolic nature and, in large part, the symbols employed are linguistic ones. It is possible that many of the kinds of errors in translation and interpretation—the semantic slip-ups—that occur in cross-lingual situations also occur between interviewer and interviewee within our own society. In his unique analysis of the interviewing process in a domestic survey, Riesman (1958) identifies many of the communication problems we have reviewed above.

Like some European legislators and Middle East traditionalists, some American academicians appear to reject role-playing questions: they are "too 'iffy' to make sense" (Riesman 1958, p. 275). Yet these very types of questions that met resistance in one kind of college proved to be "just what the doctor ordered" in another kind (p. 316). What we referred to in Chapter 3 as Riesman's discovery of a bit of the Arab in American professors, suggests not only that yes may mean no, but also that there may be degrees of "yesness" and "noness." If this is true, then one cannot assume a simple dichotomy and, furthermore, one cannot assume a symmetrical scale with no and yes at points equidistant from the center. Asymmetry in scale distributions points up the fact that what appears to be a strong no is not necessarily as strong as a strong yes (Jordan 1965).

Critics of surveys in developing countries have argued that there may be no "public opinion" in those countries or that "opinion" may be restricted only to certain areas (Mitchell 1965; Wuelker 1963). This is the logic that Herbert Blumer applied to the domestic scene so many years ago and that we reviewed in the previous chapter. It has been empirically verified for one "developing country" by Converse (1964), who found that even issues considered to be salient to wide segments of the American population had relatively small publics. The Blumer thesis on public opinion is further documented by Riesman: "We see here one of the problems of a national survey, namely, that coverage and comparability mean that the same questions will be asked of those who are virtually 'know nothings' and those who could write a book on each theme" (1958, p. 360). He concludes that "on a national survey there is always danger in the assumption that we are in fact one country, and that issues relevant to one part of the population are or could become meaningful to another" (p. 365).

Throughout his analysis of an American national survey, Riesman is sensitive to the role of politeness as it enters into the interview situation—a phenomenon reminiscent of the Southeast Asia courtesy bias discussed earlier. Finally, he provides us with an illustration of the manner in which "cultural" differences between an English-speaking interviewer and respondent can impinge upon the interview situation on the domestic scene. The case in point is the inability of the northern faculty member in a southern college to accurately take the role of his southern interviewer:

> "Southern charm" is . . . a two-way street. Interviewers who might, in old Southern fashion, emphasize their kin connections to gain entree, might also evoke the gallantry of otherwise fearful administrators and respondents; this was perhaps especially likely where an apparently well-born interviewer could talk to the intellectual elite with freedom from demagogic cliches on the race question: class pride, in the South especially, can link Jeffersonian traditions of academic freedom to good manners in expressing such traditions. Obviously enough, such nuances of communication might well be lost on a City College graduate teaching his first year of anthropology at a state-controlled institution in the Deep South. (Riesman 1958, p. 322)

This example provides an instance of what are essentially social-structural interferences with communication in a presumably monolinguistic situation. It appears, then, that it is possible that there are types of lingual interference that operate not only cross culturally, but that also derive from social-structural differences within a given society. Furthermore, there may be microscopic interferences resulting from the particular situations in which people find themselves. Definitions from all of these levels can enter into the construction of the interaction between interviewer and interviewee.

The meaning of the interview for middle-class respondents is posed like this:

> Although the interviewer is a stranger, an outsider, he is a well spoken, educated person. He is seeking information on behalf of some organization, hence his questioning not only has sanction but sets the stage for both a certain freedom of speech and an obligation to give fairly full information. . . . At the very least he has had some experience in talking to educated strangers. . . . So he becomes relatively sensitive to communication per se and to communication with others who may not exactly share his viewpoints or frames of reference. (Schatzman and Strauss 1955, pp. 336–37)

In contrast, the lower-class person infrequently meets a middle-class person in a situation anything like the interview:

> Here he must talk at great length to a stranger about personal experiences, as well as recall for his listener a tremendous number of details. Presumably he is accustomed to talking about such matters and in such detail only to listeners with whom he shares a great deal of experience and symbolism, so that he need not be very self-conscious about communicative technique. He can, as a rule, safely assume that words, phrases, and gestures are assigned approximately similar meanings by his listeners. But this is not so in the interview or, indeed, in any situation where class converses with class in non-traditional modes. (pp. 336–37)

Cicourel (1967) sees the interview situation in Goffmanesque terms as a managed performance on the part of both actors, where, regardless of social class or other structural differences, a bargain is implicitly struck concerning what will be tolerated, how both present themselves, interest in each other, and so forth. His sensitivity to linguistic and paralinguistic nuances of interaction and the manner in which they enter into the interview "findings" provokes him into designing an alternative strategy to conventional survey interviewing. This strategy, derived from the phenomenology of Alfred Schutz, leads to a concentration on the routine grounds for making sense of communication. What is not said becomes as important as what is said. Linguistic codes and their switching become data. Standard techniques such as the "probe" (e.g., What do you mean by that?) are prohibited since they strip respondents of vague, taken-for-granted expressions that they characteristically use (Cicourel 1967).

Although primitive, this approach provides a refreshing glimpse of language and its use in the interview as a central datum. From Cicourel's perspective, formal precoded instruments become anathema, imposing a role of passive compliance upon the respondent—compliance to the preconceived categories of those who write the questions. Although the problems of measurement reactivity are clearly present in the interview, their very recognition as such reduces their problematic aspects. Recall that one of the major solutions offered by the authors of *Unobtrusive Measures* was to avoid verbal indicators. Cicourel and the ethno-methodologists are committed to treating conversations as data in themselves. It becomes possible, then, to view the interview as an exchange in which one or another variety of reality is negotiated or socially constructed by the interviewer and the respondent.

Evidence concerning the great varieties of classification and categories employed in different languages alerts us to the possibility that problems of the same order may arise within a language community (Deutscher 1968). It is possible, as Schatzman and Strauss suggest, that the lower-class respondent "cannot talk about categories of people or acts because, apparently, he does not think readily in terms of classes" (1955, p. 333). On the other hand these same scholars are aware that, as middle-class observers, they may be unable to recognize lower-class classifications. The latter explanation seems more credible.

Jordan's (1965) secondary analysis of previously published scales does suggest that sometimes the categories imposed by an investigator are unlike those in the minds of the subjects. In order to detect the scales people may carry around in their heads, Hamblin (1966, 1971a, 1971b) has followed a lead from psychophysics. He suggests that social scientists employ ratio measures that are based on whatever ranges or intervals are used by respondents. Hammersley (1989) observes that Blumer (1931) makes a similar point with his advocacy of "common-sensism."

Researchers need to keep in mind the fact that communication styles do vary, as, for example, among the social classes. Schatzman and Strauss are convinced, on the basis of transcripts of interviews, that lower-class respondents are interpersonally incompetent—relatively unable to take the role of the other. Cohen and Hodges appear to verify this position and conclude that "interview and questionnaire techniques are more likely, when applied to lower class respondents than when applied to respondents in the other strata, to produce caricatures" (1963, p. 333). In commenting on the lack of any visible signs of role-taking ability in the interviews of lower-class people, Cohen and Hodges concede that this does not deny its existence and remind us of the "peasant shrewdness" of the lower classes as, for example, in their "conning" ability (p. 332).

A solution to this field communication problem is suggested by Basil Bernstein (1964), who also suspects a class link between verbal fluency and role-taking ability. The middle class switches easily between an "elaborated" coding of English and a "restricted" code, while the lower classes are limited to the restricted code. Bernstein provides a clue to methods of tapping lower-class communication channels when he observes that "in restricted codes, to varying degrees, the extraverbal channels become objects of special perceptual activity; in elaborated codes it is the verbal channel" (p. 63).

It would seem to follow, then, that in order to successfully interview users of restricted codes the field-worker must shift detection devices from verbal indicators to nonverbal indicators. The semantics of the situation, which is what the field-worker seeks to grasp, are revealed through communication channels other than those based on vocabulary or syntax. One survey expert masterfully understates the issue: "Since those who prepare questionnaires are typically from the middle and upper classes, the instruments they produce are likely to be somewhat inappropriate for large segments of the population" (Mitchell 1965, pp. 678–79).

It should be clear by now that the interview is in fact a peculiar situation. Possibilities of distortion arising out of differential definitions of that situation have been discussed. This section took Aaron Cicourel's work as its point of departure. An earlier statement of his seems helpful as we bring our discussion of language to a close. Cicourel (1967) is interested in the ways in which conversational materials and their properties are changed as they become written reports, surveys, and interviews. Interviews and questionnaires are frequently removed from the social situation in which the conversation occurs. Therefore, the correspondence between interview and questionnaire answers and the actual activities to which they refer (seldom empirically established) is doubtful. That doubtful correspondence between verbal statements and overt actions is, of course, what we are all about in this book.

What specifically concerns Cicourel is the variation in degree of management of verbalizations under various conditions. And if there is any doubt about the ability and inclination of ordinary people to shift their style of speaking along with the context in which the speech occurs, Labov's (1966) data on New Yorkers should dispel it. His data show a consistent shift among all social classes toward more phonetic "correctness" as the context shifts from informal conversation ("casual speech") to the interview ("careful speech") and finally to highly formalized contexts (reading style and word lists).

It would appear that a great deal remains to be learned about how to communicate with those we seek to understand. In our interviews and questionnaires we may more frequently talk at them than talk with them. Certainly the nonverbal dimensions of language require considerably more attentiveness than they have received so far (for an application of paralinguistics to social research see Grimshaw 1969–1970, 1981;

Scheff 1990). It is remarkable that social scientists have managed to so great a degree to avoid consideration of the methodological implications of language. Some comfort can be taken from the growing attention to language in the social sciences as a consequence of the emergence of ethnomethodology, phenomenology, discourse analysis, and sociolinguistics. Researchers are also beginning to examine the problematic use of language in ethnographic studies (see the works in Van Maanen 1990). Unfortunately, these promising developments seem to have little impact on the study of the relationship between attitudes and behavior (see Chapters 12 and 13).

The unique quality of human conduct is its symbolic mediation through language, and our basic research tools are lingual. Sociologists generally understand that this is the heart of George Herbert Mead's imagery of human nature. This discussion assumes that the language cannot be divorced from behavior, "for language, in the full, is nothing less than an inventory of all the ideas, interests, and occupations that take up the attention of the community" (Brown 1958, p. 60). As Kenneth Burke would have it, "the names for things and operations smuggle in connotations of good and bad—a noun tends to carry with it a kind of invisible adjective, and a verb an invisible adverb" (1954, p. 244). The Hugheses sum it up this way: "There is generally a great deal in a name, as Juliet plainly knew. Often it is more than a pointer; it points with pride, or with the finger of scorn" (1952, p. 130).

The alternative proposed by some sociologists to the transitory verbal exchange known as an interview is participant observation. This technique provides an opportunity to interview in context—such that the invisible adjectives and adverbs become visible—where things are happening and the interview is a part of them. It also presents us with a world in which what people say is intimately related to what they are doing, although perhaps not consistently so from the perspective of the naive outsider.

Becker and Geer (1957) draw on their participant observation of medical students to examine the differences between participant observation and conversational interviews (unstructured or undirected interviews) as methods. Their intent is to identify shortcomings in the latter without denigrating it. These co-workers identify factors likely to cause interviewers to miss important data that would probably be revealed to participant observers. Their comparison is limited to interviews about situations and events unobserved by the researcher and for which the behavior of the subject during the interview itself is not the object of study. (Most interviews do not fall into these categories.)

Becker and Geer's advocacy of participant observation as the preferred method is based on its completeness as a form of observation. It is "an observation of some social event, the events which precede and follow it, and explanations of its meaning by participants and spectators, before, during, and after its occurrence" (p. 28). No other method provides as much information about the phenomenon of interest.

Participant observation and interviewing are shown to differ in their ability to deal with three concrete methodological problems. The first problem results from language differences across groups. Any distinct social group has common understandings organizing action and expressed in a language with nuances fully understood only by members of the group. Interviewers are likely to make errors in interpretation because they mistakenly assume that they understand the interviewee. "In contrast, participant observation provides a situation in which the meaning of words can be learned with great precision through study of their use in context, exploration through continuous interviewing of their implications and nuances, and the use of them oneself under the scrutiny of capable speakers of the language" (p. 29).

A second advantage of participant observation that Becker and Geer note is that it reveals important matters that might be omitted during an interview. Because participant observers spend so much time with their subjects, it is difficult for crucial matters to be either intentionally or unintentionally hidden from them. The third critical difference between the two methods is revealed in the ability to detect distortions. Individuals' perceptions are colored by the positions they hold. Differences in perception affect what an interviewer is told. "Participant observation makes it possible to check description against fact and, noting discrepancies, become more aware of systematic distortions made by the person under study; such distortions are less likely to be discovered by interviewing alone" (p. 31).

Of greatest importance to the issues addressed in this volume is their explanation for differences between what people say and what they do:

Changes in the social environment and in the self produce transformations of perspective and it is characteristic of such transformations that the person finds it difficult or impossible to remember his former actions, outlook, or feelings. Reinterpreting things from his new perspective he cannot give an accurate account of the past, for the concepts in which he thinks about it have changed and with them his perceptions and memories. (p. 32)

Speaking in Context: Participant Observation

Perhaps because, as Ajzen and his colleagues (1970) suggest, we are "enamored of" it, we are inclined to emphasize the more advantageous attributes of participant observation in this volume. It is also true that its weaknesses are more easily recognizable than the subtler flaws of more conventional methods. Nevertheless, let us consider some of the problems inherent in participant observation—problems that must be brought to the surface if we are to manage our discounting effectively. In some quarters participant observation is viewed as an extension of ancient ethnographic techniques that have long since been replaced by more reliable scientific methods. Although we believe this position absurd, no method can be accepted without proper discounting and judgments of credibility.

There is little question of validity in field studies since they occur where the action is. There is, however, a very real problem with reliability. They are observations of unique events, usually by a single observer, and not subject to replication. How do we know that the observer observed what is reported? Furthermore, how do we know that what one observer honestly reports is the same as what another equally honest observer might report? Selective perception resulting from preconceptions or other blinding perspectives can affect what we see and hear as well as how much we see and hear (Hanson 1990).

When this problem is taken to the extreme, observers run the risk of "going native," that is, becoming a group member rather than an observer. Their observations are then grossly tainted as subjects are glorified or romanticized. How great a threat is this? We side with Irwin, who contends that

> this is a small danger compared to its opposite, that of developing ideas about people without having understood them. Understanding them requires studying them closely in their natural contexts. (1987, p. 47)

It may be argued that, as a protective corrective, the field-worker ought to embark on the enterprise without preconceptions—without even reading the relevant literature until immersion in "reality" has occurred. This is the position taken by Glaser and Strauss (1967) but it seems to us self-deluding. We cannot erase our background and preconceptions on command. We must and will carry them with us into whatever situation we set out to study. Furthermore, we like to think they are useful—that we needn't start from scratch every time we seek to learn something. We doubt that this procedure is worth trying even if it is thought possible.

Becker and his colleagues used small teams working closely together, primarily to permit collection of more and different sorts of data, but also as checks on each other. Although this may enhance reliability a bit, the fact is that in their study of a medical school Becker, Geer, Hughes, and

Strauss (1961) rarely observed the same events. Advocates of team research include among its strengths the division of labor for which it allows (see Douglas 1976, Chapter 9; Whyte 1984, Chapter 8).

If other techniques are open to the criticism that the method itself is permitted to select out and guide the kinds of problems studied, so, too, is participant observation. Surely there are big and important problems that are simply inaccessible through participant observation. It is also true that nature does not always provide us with an ongoing act of the type about which we are curious. There may be nothing available in which to participate or observe. Does this mean that we simply avoid the problem? Furthermore, some kinds of activity are socially defined as private and thus may never be available for observation even though we know they occur frequently.

Ralph LaRossa points out:

[W]hile it is not impossible to get permission to watch families in their homes and while some of the best qualitative family studies are observational studies, it is a lot more difficult—practically, methodologically, and ethically—to carry out a participant observation study of family life than, say, a participant observation study of a friendship group or a religious cult. (1988, pp. 252–53)

Hochschild (1989), however, advises that home life can be studied through participant observation by simply playing the role of the "family dog." Laud Humphreys's (1975) study of outhouse homosexuals demonstrates that even groups struggling to keep their lives and activities hidden are not immune to observation.

As with the interview or the laboratory experiment, reactivity remains a problem in this type of fieldwork. To the extent that the field-worker participates in the process observed, becoming a part of the action, his or her presence alters the outcome. Field-workers do not simply watch reality unfold in front of them. They are also in the process of creating reality (Emerson 1987). Things might not be the same if the field-worker were not around—even if he or she is the "family dog." This is as true of the unobtrusive observer who "fades into the woodwork" as it is of the observer who assumes some routine role in the situation.

There are, in participant-observational procedures, ethical problems that are potentially more dangerous than their counterparts in other kinds of research (see Filstead 1970; Punch 1986). Although the experimental subjects may be deceived about the nature of the experiment, they know that they are involved in an experiment (and that, as we shall see in Chapter 8, is part of the problem with experiments). But sometimes the subjects in participant-observational studies do not know they are involved in research and therein lies deception of a different order.

Humphreys (1975), in particular, has been severely criticized for the deceptions he used to gain access to his tearoom subjects. Although their identities were not revealed, he took great risks with their lives, as the tragedies noted by Desroches (1990) demonstrate. It is certainly doubtful that the subjects would have willingly cooperated with him had they known who he was and what he was doing.

In many cases this kind of deception is unnecessary. In their study of drug dealing, the Adlers (Adler 1985) demonstrate that even those with much to lose if exposed can be coaxed into participation. As they indicate, however, researchers of such subjects must be very careful in establishing and maintaining their field relationships. One of the factors working in the researcher's favor is that individuals are usually flattered by the attention and seeming importance that comes with being studied (Taylor and Bogdan 1984, Chapters 2 and 3).

At another level is the problem posed by the intensity of participant-observational work. It is extremely demanding of the observer, usually requiring everything a normal participant would do during the course of a day and, in addition, requiring observation, remembrance, recording, and analysis—sometimes well into the night. This procedure requires not only a high level of technical skill, but also a certain amount of talent (see Goffman 1989).

Furthermore, as mentioned above, participant observation is practical only within limited settings. The action must be localized in an establishment or some other specific social context. As Trow (1958, p. 34) observes, this method is useless in dealing with important problems involving dispersed publics. Trow also raises a point that is rarely understood by advocates of participant observation. Because the method provides access to the inside, it is assumed that all of the inside dope and inner feelings of participants will become exposed. But as ethnomethodologists understand so well, there are many important things that insiders act on but take for granted. There are other important things that are simply taboo for insiders to discuss with one another, although a stranger on a bus or an interviewer might have access to such data: "Participant observation is a relatively weak instrument for gathering data on sentiments, behaviors, relationships which are normatively proscribed by the group under observation" (p. 34).

Although we have concentrated in this and the preceding chapter on interviews, questionnaires, and participant observation, much talking also happens in the doing of a laboratory experiment. In many respects our discussion of language can be extended to cover the experimental procedures discussed in the chapter that follows.

8

What Can You Believe Nowadays?

In this chapter, we consider the value of data derived from laboratory experiments. We start by reviewing Stanley Milgram's obedience experiments, primarily as reported in "Group Pressure and Action Against a Person" (1964). Then we will consider a principal challenge to the generalizability of data obtained in experiments put forth by Martin Orne (1962) in "On the Social Psychology of the Psychological Experiment: With Particular Reference to Demand Characteristics and Their Implications." The barbaric hell devised for experimental purposes by Milgram represents one of the most credible experiments in the literature. Orne, on the other hand, raises questions about the credibility of any laboratory experiment because of the very nature of the enterprise. We will let the reader decide.

In the early 1950s Solomon Asch (1951) demonstrated that individuals' public *judgments* are influenced by the others in a setting. Milgram wanted to know if *acts* are also influenced by pressures to conform. Results of his cleverly crafted "study of memory and learning" deeply disturbed him (1965, postscript). In the experimental variation reported in the 1964 article, eighty male subjects of diverse age and occupational status were divided between experimental and control conditions. The experimental condition teamed two research confederates (adult actors) with a naive subject—the three "teachers"—to test a fourth person. This "learner," who was also a confederate, was quizzed on a list of paired words.

When the learner made a mistake, as he did in a predetermined fashion, the subject punished him by depressing one of thirty switches, which supposedly administered an electrical shock. The thirty dummy switches were labeled from 15 to 450 volts with each successive switch 15 volts higher than its predecessor and the higher voltage switches labeled extremely intense, severe, and dangerous. The two teacher confederates began by recommending the mildest shock and advocated increasingly severe shocks for each mistake made. Since the lowest level recommended by any of the three teachers was the one to be administered, the naive subject could determine the actual shock level as long as it was not higher than the level recommended by the others. It was also up to the subject to actually depress the shock switches. The learner's response to the increasingly severe shock levels ranged from grunts to demands to be released from the experiment.

In the control condition, there was no group influence. A naive subject teacher and a confederate learner were paired in each session. The procedure was the same as the experimental condition, except that the naive subject was solely responsible for determining and administering the shock punishment for errors in the learning task. The results of this experiment are quite dramatic.

When plotted on a graph, the mean shock levels administered to the learner by the naive subject for each trial in the control condition form an almost flat line between the third and fourth voltage levels (45 and 60 volts, or a slight shock as designated on the shock box). In the experimental condition, when shock levels are plotted across trials, mean shock levels successively and rapidly increase. Milgram finds that subjects in the experimental condition "were substantially influenced by group pressure" (1964, p. 141). He concludes:

> [T]he substantive contribution of the present study lies in the demonstration that group influence can shape behavior in a domain that might have been thought highly resistant to such effects. Subjects are induced by the group to inflict pain on another person at a level that goes well beyond levels chosen in the absence of social pressure. (p. 141)

A note of caution in the interpretation of the results is provided by Milgram. He observes that the tacit approval of punishment by the experimenter complicates conclusions that can be drawn. The implied assent of the experimenter to the use of all shock levels produces an authoritative sanction in the experimental condition. Without such a sanction subjects might behave differently, as they did in later experiments in which one independent variable was the closeness of the experimenter (see Milgram 1965).

The possibility that Milgram's subjects were responding to the presence of the experimenter raises the issue of demand characteristics that Orne (1962) so insightfully developed. The central point of Orne's work is that experimental subjects are active participants in a special form of interaction. "Experimental subject" is an established social role with which most people are familiar. In agreeing to play that role individuals understand that they are implicitly agreeing to follow any request the investigator makes. They become remarkably compliant. Orne empirically demonstrates that subjects will endure psychologically noxious tasks assuming that the researcher must know what he or she is doing.

Subjects believe that they are furthering science and thus have a stake in the outcome of the experiment. So that their efforts will make a contribution, they want to be "good subjects." To be a good subject is *"to validate the experimental hypothesis"* (p. 778, emphasis in original). Orne suggests that for subjects the experiment becomes a problem to solve. They try to guess the experimental hypothesis in order to know how to behave. Subjects draw on all sorts of cues to ascertain the researcher's hypothesis and, on that basis, what "proper" behavior should be. As we shall see below, there is also evidence that they *assume* the presence of a confederate and make decisions as to who that person is (Martin 1970). Their behavior then is affected not only by the experimental variables, but also by their definition of the experimental situation, including any cues that convey an hypothesis, whether accurate or not. The latter are called *demand characteristics* of the experimental situation.

Demand characteristics are endemic to the experimental situation. Subjects will *always* attribute meaning to what transpires around them and form an hypothesis about the purpose of the experiment. They will then act on their hypothesis. If researchers want to be able to apply their results beyond the laboratory setting, demand characteristics cannot be ignored.

Rather than abandoning laboratory experiments, however, Orne proposes empirical solutions to factor out the effects of demand characteristics. We lack Orne's confidence in the solutions he suggests. Nonetheless, Orne has raised a thorny problem, which researchers cannot afford to disregard.

Subjects Are People Too

The survey methodologist uses knowledge of situational effects on interaction primarily as an emetic for decontaminating instruments and purifying the situation. Many social-psychology laboratory experiments reflect interest in essentially the same problem, but the psychologists assume a more positive stance toward their subject. Rather than attempting to remove contaminating effects in order to create private behavior, the psychologists attempt to *add* contaminations under controlled conditions in order to achieve a better understanding of public behavior. Like sociological field studies and survey research, this body of literature is nevertheless severely circumscribed as a source of evidence. But its limitations are not all of the same order.

Some psychologists are themselves aware of the artificiality of the situations and the contrived nature of the interaction typical of experiments in social psychology. Apparently psychology, too, had its voices in the wilderness during the thirties (see Rosensweig 1933). Irwin Silverman and Arthur D. Shulman (1970) suggest that much the same thing was happening in psychology that we have described in Chapter 2 [for a similar assessment of changes that took place in small-groups research, see Couch, Katovich, and Miller (1988)]. Milgram insists that "eventually social psychology must come to grips with significant behavior contents that are of interest in their own right and not simply trivial substitutes for psychologically meaningful forms of behavior" (1964, p. 138). He deplores the use of such tasks as sorting IBM cards, making paper dolls, or eating crackers—all of which have been employed in experiments conducted by his colleagues.

When we refer to the artificiality of many experimental situations, we mean that they are inauthentic or simulated: Such experiments do not deal with what they intend, but with an approximation of some element of the intended phenomenon. It is the difference between what Haney (1976) calls *functional* and *literal* replication. In this sense experiments are artificial—in the same sense in which the interview frequently obtains "unreal" or private opinions. In both cases, our results may be largely artifacts of our procedures. But it is also true that, just as the interview is a "real" form of interaction in its own right, so, too, is the experiment.

If one intends to study the behavior of students in situations that they themselves define as experimental, there is no better place to do it than in an experiment. The work of Friedman (1967) and Rosenthal (1966) is of this order as is Orne's report. Drabeck and Haas (1967) have made a particularly constructive effort to reconsider the issue of realism versus artificiality. Their approach is to consider the question, What is it that makes an experiment "realistic"?

Even more basic to the social-psychological experiment is the underlying determination to perceive the research subject as an object. Unfortunately people are not simply inert reactors to external pressures; they are actors who frequently enter into the construction of the act and sometimes even initiate action of their own. It is possible to find an occasional psychologist pleading with colleagues as Orne does. In describing his efforts to identify samples of more or less suggestible experimental subjects, Orne reports that he was unable to find a task boring enough to make subjects give it up in a reasonable length of time. In a thoughtful discussion, he concludes that

> the experimental situation is one which takes place within the context of an explicit agreement of the subject to participate in a special form of social interaction known as "taking part in an experiment." . . . Once a subject has agreed to participate in a psychological experiment, he implicitly

agrees to perform a very wide range of actions on request without inquiring as to their purpose and frequently without inquiring as to their duration. (1962, p. 777)

It is precisely this concern for the subject as an active agent from which Campbell's (1957, pp. 298–99) long history of interest in reactivity derives. "Any measurement procedure," he states, "which makes the subject self-conscious or aware of the fact of the experiment can be suspected of being reactive measurement" (pp. 298–99). In spite of such admonitions, it does not appear that most social psychologists are aware of the need to view the experiment itself as a form of interaction. Even though persuasive experimental evidence is added to the earlier admonition, resistance based on counterevidence persists (see Hanson 1969; R. A. Gordon 1969; Wuebben et al. 1974).

In spite of such serious shortcomings, the experiment has, nevertheless, superior credibility to survey research in several respects. First, there is usually some theoretical framework to guide it and to make it coherent. It, as opposed to many survey reports, is unlikely to result in a random assortment of "facts," which presumably speak for themselves. Second, through experimental controls, the experiment, by definition, must create loaded situations for study rather than sterile ones. This permits us to determine more precisely the effect of specified interventions. We have some estimate of what things would have been like had there been no intervention. Clearly not everything that happens in a laboratory is an experiment and sometimes experimental design is implemented through survey research [despite the concerns Lieberson (1985) presents in his strong case against using experimental design for nonexperimental data]. Finally, as we have indicated before, methodological conclusions drawn from experiments are more likely to be interpreted in terms of a positive contribution to understanding human behavior than are methodological discoveries in survey research.

As is also true of surveys and field studies, the experimental literature provides hundreds of reports from which one can pick and choose. The experiments with which we are concerned deal mostly with interpersonal influence. It is important to note that some of these have been designed to study the consequences of group pressures on overt behavior or action as well as on opinion or attitude. Among these, there are a few that have managed to create experimental situations involving relatively meaningful behavior. Some of the best examples of this type of experiment are found in the work that takes Helson's (1947) notion of adaptation level as a point of departure.

Helson considers the various components of the situation, including the actor's personality, social constraints, and the meaning of the object toward which the attitude or behavior is directed. The experimental setup employed by Helson and others is such that the actual experiment is viewed by the subject as an extraneous incident occurring during the course of what is believed to be the experiment. Himmelstein and Moore's work (1963) discussed in Chapter 10 provides an example. Milgram's work also fits this model and seems to us to be uniformly credible. But not everyone agrees—especially Martin Orne.

Milgram has published a number of reports, in addition to the one discussed in detail earlier in this chapter. Some of these employ his terrible electrical shocking machine and some of these do not. In a 1968 paper (Milgram 1968a) he describes an experiment that is less subtle than the one we have concentrated upon. In the later study, the naive subject is actively supported by the experimenter in administering increasing voltage to the "learner." The question addressed in this study is that of obedience to authority. He does find that subjects—this time adult working males in New Haven—throw excessive voltage into learners, in spite of personal qualms, as long as the experimenter keeps supporting their actions. In order to assure himself that it is the authority of the person rather than the authority of Yale University to which his subjects are responding, Milgram repeats the experiment in a rather shabby downtown office in Bridgeport. The results, although somewhat less impressive, are sustained.

This article is followed by four critiques and a rejoinder (Erickson 1968; Etzioni 1968b; Masserman 1968; Orne and Holland 1968; Milgram 1968b). For the most part, the critics find Milgram's work enchanting. But this is not the case for Orne and Holland. [In later works Orne's (1969, 1970) thinking is further clarified in what he considers to be more adequate statements of his position.] Although Masserman is also critical—largely on the grounds that after all this is only an experiment and it doesn't really tell us much about what happens in everyday life— neither his logic nor his evidence is as persuasive as that presented by Orne and Holland. Let us consider what they find problematic with what is probably one of the most credible sets of experiments available.

Orne and Holland argue that it is not possible to generalize Milgram's results beyond the laboratory; they question the success of the deception required in this and other experiments that con naive subjects; they say that in an experiment people will do whatever they are told to do by the experimenter; they do not believe that anything can be learned about the outside world from an experiment as long as the subjects know that they are participating in an experiment regardless of whether they know its purpose or anything else about it. The essential argument is summed up as follows:

[T]he agreement to participate in an experiment gives the E *carte blanche* about what may legitimately be requested. In asking the S to participate in an experiment, the E implicitly says, "Will you do whatever I ask for a specified period of time? By so doing you may earn a fee, contribute to science, and perhaps even learn something of value to yourself. In return I promise that no harm will befall you. At the completion of the experiment you will be no better or worse off than you are now and though you may experience temporary inconvenience, this is justified by the importance of the undertaking." A corollary to this agreement is that the S may not ask why certain things are required of him. He must assume that these actions are legitimate and appropriate for the needs of the experiment. (Orne and Holland 1968, p. 291)

All of this is an extension and application to Milgram of the argument presented by Orne in "On the Social Psychology of the Psychology Experiment." Holland (1967) replicated Milgram's work and, in interviewing his subjects during a debriefing, found that "three quarters of the Ss run in the analog of Milgram's situation indicated that they did not really believe the deception when carefully questioned after the experiment" (Orne and Holland 1968, p. 291). The dilemma for the analyst is that both Milgram and Orne inspire a high degree of confidence in their work and the problem of discounting therefore becomes knotty. In the end it is a matter of judgment. Were Holland's respondents simply afraid to appear foolish and gullible? We cannot be certain, but on this point we will continue to assign high credibility to Milgram's work. Others must make their own decisions. [Miller (1986), criticizing Milgram's narrow focus on his subjects' behavior, raises a very different issue—missed opportunities to observe the social construction of behavior.]

The Asch model (see Chapter 11), which we suppose is the ancestor of Milgram's design, is clever and innovative and has been widely employed in experimental social psychology. But the use of confederates as a standard component of such experiments must inevitably create problems, especially when the subjects tend to be sophisticated undergraduates. Surely, if subjects suspect the presence of a confederate when they participate in an experiment, then the very purpose of the experiment must be sabotaged. This is as true when there is in fact no confederate or when the subject suspects the wrong person as it is when subjects are correct in their suspicions. Just as the respondent's definition of the interview situation impinges on the interaction that takes place, so too does the subject's definition of the experimental situation. And there is evidence that deceived subjects do not behave in the same way as undeceived subjects (Stricker, Messick, and Jackson 1969). Martin (1970) has pursued this problem by staging various "experiments" before a class and then determining who, in the experimental situation, is likely to arouse suspicion by participants in experiments. The fact that 79 to 98 percent of the members of his classes suspected the presence of a stooge in the four experiments they viewed is worth considering.

Even Sherif's classic discovery of the autokinetic effect in the early thirties—endlessly replicated, duplicated, varied, and extended since that time—is questioned as a consequence of the new sensitivity to reactivity. Sherif (1958) discovered that when no point of reference is provided, subjects tend to establish norms—their judgments converge—as to the direction and extent of movement of a spot of light in a darkened room. In two experiments reported in 1970, Alexander and his colleagues provide evidence that the autokinetic effect may be largely a consequence of expectations created by the laboratory situation. They point out that "the laboratory setting itself generates expectations for patterned and orderly stimulus experiences," and that "stability, regularity, and logical purpose are associated with [Sherif's] design and conduct of the experiment and presentation of experimental stimuli" (Alexander, Zucker, and Brody 1970, p. 112). Their experiments, in which they deliberately redefine the situation for subjects, tend to support their contention.

There is another serious weakness of experimental work that tends to impugn the credibility of the kinds of conclusions we will begin to draw from it in Chapter 10. It is a weakness that is at least partly shared by field studies that tend to reach the same conclusions. The observation that is most important in all of these studies is something other than personality, social structure, and culture appears to account for a large segment of the variance in human behavior: It is the actor's perception of the situation—which appears to provide much of the material from which lines of action are constructed. To paraphrase Erving Goffman (1964), Where else but in a social situation does action take place? But it is the central concept of David Riesman's *The Lonely Crowd*, which suggests the serious weakness we are addressing (Riesman and Denny 1950).

Riesman delineated societies and eras that he described as other-directed, inner-directed, and tradition-directed. Societies may vary in the extent to which members' thoughts and actions are guided by their contemporaries (rather than by internalized constraints). There is also the suggestion that generations may vary in this respect, and the implication that in a mass society some segments may be more or less other-directed than other segments or strata. Riesman's thesis generally follows the tradition of the national character or personality and culture schools. Most of the literature we will review as evidence of the extent to which the company one keeps is related to the behavioral choices one makes is based on experiments and observations of Americans, nearly all middle class, and frequently youthful college students. Do people in other parts of the world behave like Americans? Do lower- or upper-class Americans behave like middle-class ones? Do middle-aged and older people behave like youngsters? There is considerable evidence that, at least in some respects, the answer to all of these questions is no! It is not safe, then, to conclude that the tendency of others is to conform their behavior to their perceptions of what others around them approve of in the same way that middle-class American college students do (see Raymond 1991). We will consider the evidence related to this issue in Chapter 10.

Systematic Distortion: The Ubiquitous Type I Error

It has been suggested that laboratory experiments are simulated substitutes for reality, frequently dealing with trivia and generally lacking any real consequences for the actors. The likelihood of subjects playing a game called "being in an experiment" seems high. Clearly these experiments tend to be isolated fragments unrelated to anything that is otherwise happening in the flow of everyday activity of the subjects. Finally, there are many population biases in these studies, including nationality, social class, and age.

But that is not the end of it. We cannot properly discount research that we have not seen, and editors of professional journals are the gatekeepers of most of what we see. It is in this respect that an observation documented by David Bakan and others becomes troublesome (Bakan 1968; see also Gold 1969). Some editors of psychology journals have in fact used a specific confidence level at which the null hypothesis must be rejected as a criterion of eligibility for publication. This not only assumes that a null hypothesis is a necessary prerequisite to knowledge, but that the rejection of that hypothesis at, say, the $p < .05$ level is a predeterminant of what is and is not good research. For at least one editor that level was not considered adequate. Bakan cites an editorial by Arthur W. Melton, written as he stepped down after twelve years as editor of the *Journal of Experimental Psychology*:

> In editing the Journal there has been a strong reluctance to accept and publish results related to the principal concern of the research when those results were significant at the .05 level, whether by one- or two-tailed test. This has not implied a slavish worship of the .01 level, as some critics may have implied. Rather, it reflects a belief that it is the responsibility of the investigator in a science to reveal his effect in such a way that no reason-

able [person] would be in a position to discredit the results by saying that
they were the product of the way the ball bounces. (1962, pp. 553–54)

An unanticipated consequence of such an editorial policy is that it
provides a rationale for precisely the kind of discrediting it was designed
to avoid. One research team, for example, argued in the midsixties that
the frequently observed significant differences between attitude and behavior were a spurious artifact of that editorial policy. They believed that
investigators finding a relationship between the two variables are unlikely to get their results published because journal editors consider such
findings "unexciting" and "not worthy of publication" (see Insko and
Schopler 1967). Although such journal editors may still exist, the evidence of the eighties suggests a contrary conclusion. Nearly all research
currently being published reports a relationship between the two (see
F. P. Pestello and F. G. Pestello 1991).

Although Bakan appears to recognize the consequences of such a
policy, he makes it clear that he considers it neither necessary nor desirable to change it: "It is important to point out that I am not advocating a
change in policy in this connection" (1968, p. 9). But let us consider the
implications of such an editorial policy. If one hundred investigators test
the hypothesis that there is no relationship between, say, group pressure and the actions of an individual and ninety-nine of these investigators find no difference at the .01 level, while one of them does find
differences large enough to permit rejection of the hypothesis, it is the
lone investigator whose research is eligible for publication. The ninety-
nine need not bother to send their papers to the journal. It is then the
findings of a minority of investigators that get into print even though all
of the one hundred studies may have been conducted in identical ways.
This suggests something more than the lack of publication of certain
important studies or the occasional publication of results that are, in
fact, in error. It suggests a systematic distortion of knowledge since, in
our example, the adoption of the .01 level of confidence means that out
of every one hundred experimental trials, differences as large as those
observed can be expected to occur once *as a result of chance alone*. We need
not even consider the likelihood that in these "publish or perish" times
a young experimenter, itching for a promotion, may run his or her experiment until the desired results are obtained and the paper gets
published—even if one hundred trials must be run. [Such disturbing
practices, and much more fraudulent ones, are well documented by
Broad and Wade (1982).]

In short, the disturbing conclusion we must reach is that such an
editorial policy systematically selects out conclusions that are in error;
when a null hypothesis is true it publishes the one chance finding and

deliberately rejects the ninety-nine correct ones. But what of verification? The answer is clear. Of the one hundred studies that attempt to replicate the study, ninety-nine fail to verify while one does so at the .01 confidence level. Again it is only this last one that is eligible for publication. The incorrect conclusion is confirmed, and we move ahead with greater confidence in our knowledge. All of this does not mean that research published in journals with such a policy must all be rejected out of hand. In fact, *if we carefully follow the dictates of probability theory, we can safely assume a high level of confidence in the reverse of many findings published under such an editorial policy.*

However, even if we depended exclusively upon such journals for our sources of information, we could not apply this principle of reciprocal conclusions, since authentic and inauthentic findings are randomly mixed, Fortunately, we are not that dependent upon any one source of data and thus are free to consider each article as a case in itself, without the need to apply probability theory to a large sampling of articles.

All of this is, nevertheless, of serious concern to us since much of the evidence on which we base the arguments in Chapter 10 is derived from psychology journals, some of which did have such an editorial policy. Fortunately, it seems to us that there is enough evidence from other sources (with their own peculiar kinds of weaknesses) to provide a degree of convergent validity. We remain confident in our tentative conclusions in spite of this great weakness in one source of evidence.

Can the Weakness of One Be the Strength of the Other?

The criticisms in Chapters 6, 7, and 8 are not meant to discourage or to induce a cynical "to-hell-with-all-of-their-data" reaction. It is important that we understand the potential weaknesses and limitations of data derived from any source, so that we may use them in a sensible manner. In other words, very little is so useless that it should be thrown away, but most is so circumscribed that it must be appropriately discounted. There is also a useful device for treating data so that they become part of a cumulative, credible body, rather than having to stand on their own weak two feet. This chapter closes with an illustration of how different sources of error (different weaknesses) may, taken together, enhance our confidence in their conclusions. What we hope to demonstrate is that two wrongs *can* make a right. This is one version of what Webb et al. have called triangulation. Let us see if the strengths of one may be the weaknesses of the other.

This illustration consists of a comparison of a study conducted in the laboratory by a psychologist and one conducted in the field by a sociologist. Raven (1959), the psychologist, employs the Asch design in an experiment with undergraduate subjects aimed at determining the effects of group pressure in changing attitudes. His subjects are volunteers who express an interest in the subject of racial attitudes. With the use of confederates Raven creates a number of situations that lead him to conclude that (1) a member of the group who has deviant attitudes tends to select and distort the content of what is communicated so as not to be rejected by the group and then (2) to select and distort what is perceived so that it tends to be more and more in line with group norms and (3) seeing more evidence to support the group norm, brings attitudes into conformity with those of the group.

There are striking parallels between this laboratory simulation and Gorden's (1952) field study of a cooperative rooming house. Gorden, a member of the co-op, administered a political questionnaire to fellow members on the pretext that he needed to try it out. Later, in the presence of other co-op members, parallel political questions were informally raised by Gorden. In both of these studies "private opinions" are first elicited and the subjects are later confronted with the need to express themselves publicly. Gorden notes

> an acute awareness of the presence of the other members of the group when they are asked to express their opinion. Confused efforts to appear nonchalant, efforts to escape the situation, and attempts to prevent others from hearing one's response are all telltale signs of the awareness of pressure. (p. 57)

Raven and Gorden are both interested in the way in which members of a group who are aware of their own deviant attitudes alter those attitudes to preserve their group affiliation. Pursuing the problem independently and employing very different methods, they reach identical conclusions. Taken by itself, either study has enough weaknesses to leave its conclusions in doubt. But, because the weaknesses of one are the strengths of the other, they provide, in combination, highly credible evidence in support of the hypothesis they share. What we have is something like an error-canceling process. For example, Raven's laboratory work contains all of the kinds of potential reactivity that occurs when students define themselves as "participating in an experiment." They know what an experiment is and they know who the experimenter is. Gorden's field study, on the other hand, takes place in a natural setting where people are going about their everyday routines. He not only observes subjects relating to their fellows, but he employs interviewing techniques. He is part of the scene; the subjects know him in other contexts. The kinds of reactivity likely to occur under these conditions are problematic in equal measure to Raven's, but *they are very different*. There is a difference in the types of discounting that must take place in considering the credibility of these two studies.

Raven's subjects are homogeneous and they are selective in the sense that he deliberately removes those subjects who are suspected of being "suspicious." Gorden's population is heterogeneous; it is also selective but in different ways. What kinds of relatively isolated (and mobile?) people are found living in boarding houses? At any rate his subjects are varied in age, occupation, and race. Raven has a segmented experience to observe—one of no great import to the participants either before or after. In contrast, Gorden's study involves an affect-laden issue that transcends the research situation and has real consequences for the participants. Although Raven's study is clearly more reliable (reproducible, objective, standardized in its technique), Gorden's is clearly more valid, dealing with a live issue among an ongoing social entity rather than simulating both the issue and the group. In general, Gorden has a relatively loose study while Raven remains in tight control of the situation and of his subjects.

There is, of course, a residue of problems that both studies share, such as the lack of experimental controls or the imposition of arbitrary scales created by investigators but not necessarily reflecting the categories employed by subjects. What this residue means is that these studies must still be discounted to a degree. But what is most important is that taken together they become far more credible than either of them standing alone. This, we submit, is because the strengths of one are in large part the weaknesses of the other. Both of these studies conclude that when opinion becomes public rather than private, it is likely to change radically. Furthermore, they both note that the change is in the direction of conformity to the perceived group norms. In Chapter 10 we will consider other evidence pointing in the same direction, but our point for the moment is that we find these studies taken together highly credible.

Many such instances of convergence lie buried in the literature. We have only to seek them out. Hovland, although he identifies seven specific methodological artifacts that tend to bring about opposite results, nevertheless concludes that it is "quite apparent . . . that a genuine understanding . . . requires both the survey and the experimental methodologies. At the same time there appear to be certain inherent limitations of each method" (1959, p. 14). In 1954 the participants in a summer seminar discussing the possibility of narrowing the gap between field studies and laboratory experiments in social psychology arrived at some pessimistic conclusions. They suggest that a different orientation toward theory results in "noncorrespondence" between field and laboratory findings: "Conclusions reached through the two methods will not necessarily agree nor even be related. Field-workers tend to talk a different dialect from that used in laboratories, and field and laboratory results are less often contradictory than incommensurable" (Social Science Research Council 1954, pp. 38–39).

In the past three chapters, we have made no effort to be exhaustive in enumerating the types of vulnerability to which different methods are susceptible. It should be clear that any approach has certain built-in deficiencies. It should be equally clear that any approach has certain built-in advantages. Some problems are better addressed with some approaches than with others and some investigators are happier when working in one medium than in others. It is also true that the categories we have chosen are based on commonsense usage of such terms as field studies, experiments, surveys, and interviewing. Such commonsense categories lack a certain precision when we begin working seriously with them. It is not only possible, but desirable to impose the logic of experimental design on survey or participant-observational work. That being the case, they cannot be and, in fact, are not logically distinct categories. They have nevertheless proved useful hooks on which to hang our discussion. In Chapter 9, our final venture into the methodological dimension, we shall turn to a series of arguments that suggest, with considerable merit, that much of what we see as discrepancies between sentiments and acts is more apparent than real.

9

The Logic of Our Procedures

What Is an Inconsistency?

Our text in this concluding note on methods concentrates on a fragment of Donald Campbell's "Social Attitudes and Other Acquired Dispositions." In this article, Campbell submits that the logic of literature suggesting an inconsistency is faulty. There is, in fact, no inconsistency between attitude and behavior if one will just look at the discrepancy from the proper perspective. Instead of conceptualizing the relationship in terms of a dichotomy, consistent-inconsistent, he suggests that the relationship is better represented as a continuum. As he says, "by and large, this literature has confused correlational inconsistency with situational threshold differences, and thus exaggerated the inconsistency present" (1964, pp. 159–60).

Campbell draws on the analogy of hurdles to clarify his logic. Using LaPiere's study of discrimination toward the Chinese as an example, he demonstrates that people who reject Chinese in a mailed survey but accept them in a face-to-face encounter are not inconsistent. These two situations have different situational thresholds. Although it may be difficult to reject nice, well-mannered, civilized patrons, it is apparently much easier to reject anonymous, generic Chinese patrons on paper. This, however, is not inconsistency. Campbell argues that inconsistency would be evident only if the Chinese were rejected in the face-to-face situation, but accepted on the questionnaire. There is no evidence that this occurred.

Campbell tenders a literally "methodological" solution to the relationship between sentiments and acts—one that addresses itself to the logic of our procedures and to the manner in which we think about our data. There is a certain elegance about this and it does provide a partial explanation. On the other hand, it by no means resolves all or even most of the problematic aspects of the relationship between what people say and what they otherwise do. After considering Campbell's (and related) arguments, we will turn to some of the more technical explanations suggesting that observed discrepancies between sentiments and acts are more apparent than real.

Late in World War II, Louis Guttman invented a new way of thinking about the relationship between items on a test or questionnaire, or what had previously been referred to by the noun *a scale*. Guttman converted the noun into the verb *to scale* and in so doing converted an arbitrary set of presumably related items into a process, one that not only determines more precisely their empirical relationship, but that tests that precision through predicting responses on each item in the given set from responses to other items. He called this process "scale analysis" and its logic is the logic employed by Campbell in his metaphor of high hurdles and low hurdles (see Guttman 1947, 1950).

Campbell reasons that "apparently, it is very hard to refuse a well-dressed Chinese couple traveling with a European in a face-to-face setting, and very easy to refuse the Chinese as a race in a mailed questionnaire" (1964, p. 160). Note, and store away, that Campbell is dealing with two factors here: (1) the personal confrontation vs. the impersonal mailed questionnaire, and (2) the specific Chinese couple vs. the abstract or generalized "Chinese race." Campbell does not develop the second factor. It is the first factor on which Campbell concentrates his analytic skills.

It seems to us that the explanation quoted from Campbell above is not unlike that tendered by LaPiere. The only difference lies with the example, LaPiere suggesting that it is considerably different to find oneself face-to-face with a flesh and blood Armenian woman than it is to respond to items on a social distance scale about Armenians. There is a difference between those two examples and their shared explanation, on the one hand, and another example proffered by LaPiere. He suggests that a male university professor when questioned about the likelihood of his visiting a French whorehouse during a Parisian tour would undoubtedly offer an honest and emphatic demurral (and we imagine that was true in the thirties if not in the nineties). But, LaPiere asks, how is anyone including the professor himself able to determine how he would in fact behave in Paris (presumably after a few bottles of champagne) when actually confronted with the opportunity? This example poses a problem and suggests an explanation very different from the two ethnic illustrations. It is a kind of situation that suggests that discrepancies or inconsistencies, although they may sometimes be more apparent than real, can also be very real.

Both Campbell and LaPiere explain the inconsistency in terms of different definitions of different situations. Then they part company. LaPiere is willing to settle for the word *different* in describing the discrepancy. Campbell, however, adds a value dimension, suggesting that observed differences fall on a continuum that is the result of some choices being "harder" than others. Campbell converts the apparent discrepancy into a *harder* to *easier* scale. Life is full of thresholds: questions that are too hard to answer, situations that are too difficult to face, hurdles that are too high to jump. There is nothing inconsistent about failing to pass these thresholds while simultaneously answering easy questions, facing routine situations, or jumping low hurdles. By this criterion, LaPiere has no evidence of inconsistency. In Campbell's terms,

> The fact that 92 percent of the cases were mediocre in their Sinophilia, having enough to get over the low hurdle but not enough to get over the high hurdle, is irrelevant to the problem of inconsistency, but rather speaks only as to the heights of the hurdles. (1964, p. 160)

What is very likely to attract the attention of scientists is the observation of a departure from normal expectations: an inconsistency, an anomaly, an irregularity, an incongruity. These are the kinds of discoveries that create questions worth pursuing. This is the kind of impetus that drove LaPiere through a series of studies to his classic "Attitudes vs. Actions." Consider, in this light, Campbell's charge that LaPiere is *wrong* to conclude that his subjects' behavior does not provide a clue as to their attitudes. What Campbell has done is to carry LaPiere's explanation far enough with the logic of scale analysis that he no longer needs to view the situation as anomalous.

Campbell has done his scientific work in clarifying an apparent inconsistency. But those who provided him with his point of departure were in no sense wrong. They were merely antecedent to Campbell, in one of those rare cumulative sequences in building social science knowledge. Campbell has not removed from the empirical realm the fact observed by his predecessors: People frequently do not act in accord with their sentiments! That empirical fact remains. What is different is that we are now beginning to understand it.

Although the inconsistency has been removed in the mind of the scientist (as a result of the new understanding), that same observable inconsistency remains in the empirical world. These two facts are hardly incongruent, although a bit of verbal exorcism might illuminate their compatibility: Perhaps we should reserve the term *inconsistency* for our preliminary observations of a discrepancy and, upon discovering reasonable explanations, magically alter the reference so that, at that point in the development of knowledge, it becomes, not a pumpkin, but a *difference*. Students, including ourselves, are inclined to see behaviorists and phenomenologists at opposite poles. But this is not always a correct perception. Two self-styled behaviorists provide the same phenomeno-logical interpretation of an inconsistency as we have. Kendler and Kendler remark that the terms *consistent* and *inconsistent* "are judgments made by the scientist about the social behavior he observes. . . . They refer to the responses the psychologist makes to the behavior he is observing" (1949, p. 27). The question then becomes, Whose social real-ity are we talking about?

Part of the vulnerability of Campbell's argument lies in the fact that it is often difficult and sometimes impossible to objectively determine what is hard and what is easy. Although there may be a degree of shared intersubjectivity in the definition of these matters, that consensus can vary from group to group. In short, what is hard and what is easy is not always as clearly defined as it is, say, among questions on a school test. And even there not all students would agree as to which questions are harder than others. In the instance of racial attitudes and behaviors, the hurdles might in fact be reversed! For example, we can easily imagine that at the time Campbell wrote his article there were southern restau-rateurs (or northern school superintendents) who sincerely held egalitarian ideology but were being governed in their behavior by fear of losing their customers (or their jobs) if they practiced what they preached. It would have been "hard" for such functionaries to voice prejudice, but "easy" for them to turn blacks away from their restaurants or schools.

The possibility of interchangeability of hurdles is also illustrated by Minard's (1952) study of Appalachian miners (referred to by Campbell) and Lohman and Reitzes's (1954) study of Chicago union men. Although both of these studies describe white men who work under egalitarian conditions while living in discriminatory communities (with norms of the situation governing their relationships with blacks), it is also conceiv-able that white people may live in an egalitarian community while work-ing under discriminatory conditions (with the norms of the situation still governing their relationship with blacks). In the latter case, the white workers would more likely reject blacks at work and accept them at home in contrast to the finding of those two studies. The hurdles be-come reversed.

All of this is not to say that Campbell's logic does not reflect what sometimes happens empirically. One of Linn's subjects tried to explain how such hurdles occurred in his study. Speaking of having her picture taken with a black man, she says, "On the questionnaire it seemed all right but when it came to the real thing, it seemed 'scary'" (1965, p. 362). The high and low hurdles are clearly identified. Louis Guttman (1959) published empirical verification of Campbell's argument four years be-fore that argument was made. Guttman suggests that each different orientation to a given social object (belief, norms, anticipatory behavior, overt action) can be regarded as a subuniverse and that the different facets of this subuniverse need to be examined in terms of their interrelationships. To demonstrate his reasoning, Guttman reorders a set of correlation coefficients reported in a study of interracial behavior in Brazil (see Bastide and van den Berghe 1957). The nearly perfect scales that emerge from Guttman's (1959, pp. 320–21) analysis provided empirical verification of Campbell's argument.

The scaling thesis is not the only important point made by Campbell in his brief analysis. Campbell is explicitly concerned with the sorting out of two different types of inconsistency, only one of which he would allow as a real inconsistency. If we know the order of the hurdles as a result of our scale analysis, then certainly we no longer can think of those who jump low hurdles and miss high ones as inconsistent. We can, however, take note of the inconsistency of those who jump the high ones while missing the low ones—those who do the hard thing while failing to accomplish the easy one or, in Guttman's terms, those who betray the strongest subuniverse while remaining loyal to the weakest. The matrix that illuminates these two kinds of differences between sentiments and acts, in any area of human behavior, looks like this:

		Expresses sentiment?	
		Yes	No
Performs	Yes	X_1	Y_2
act?	No	Y_1	X_2

The two X cells are easily recognizable as consistent ones. In X_1, people who express an affirmative sentiment ("I think white people are neat") can be observed performing concordant acts (hanging out with white people). In X_2, people who express a negative sentiment ("I think white people are dangerous") can be observed performing concordant acts (avoiding white people). Although these two cells share the virtue of concordance or consistency, we recognize that they represent radically different empirical phenomena. What we sometimes fail to recognize is that the same is true of the two Y cells. In the case of Y_1, we have Merton's (1940) example from Chapter 2 of the northerner who talks a good line about racial equality while practicing discrimination. In the case of Y_2, we have his example of the southerner who mouths prejudice while practicing less discrimination than his or her northern counterpart. We choose this example from Merton's discussion deliberately because it illustrates again that there are limits to the application of

Campbell's logic (there is nothing wrong with the logic itself). When we have our hurdles properly ordered, we may comfortably discard one of the Y cells as involving no inconsistency. But, in other cases we must stop by simply recognizing that the two Y cells represent very different kinds of inconsistency. Which of Merton's two Y cases is a real inconsistency and which is spurious?

The identification of different kinds of orientations to a social object and their clear delineation from one another is a first essential step in the solution of our conceptual problem. The extent to which and the manner in which those orientations relate to one another is the next step. This is the problem addressed in Chapter 13. It was first broached by Ajzen et al. in Chapter 5. They sort out attitude toward an object from behavior and both of these from "behavioral intention." They suggest that differences in the findings of the three studies they considered may be attributable to differences among these three types of orientations since they are not uniformly tapped by all studies. Such a question must remain unanswered until we know something about the relationship among these three orientations. If any two of them are highly correlated, then we may assume that they are interchangeable for analytic purposes. If they are not correlated or if they are negatively correlated then we can assume no such thing. If they scale, as Campbell and Guttman suggest they may, then we can determine one from the others within reasonable limits.

Before leaving Campbell's illuminating suggestion that apparent inconsistencies may dissolve if we examine them properly, it may be equally illuminating to consider the reverse of that situation. If some *apparent inconsistencies* can be explained in this manner, we ought to be sensitive to the possibility that some *apparent consistencies* may obscure real, underlying inconsistencies. That we can sometimes be deceived by apparent uniformity is illustrated by Cohn, Barkan, and Halteman's (1991) study of punitive attitudes toward criminals and by Donald Roy's (1952) study of a machine shop.

Cohn, Barkan, and Halteman note that there is a large body of literature documenting agreement among racial groups on punitive attitudes toward criminals. By examining correlates of punitiveness for blacks and whites, however, they find that punitive attitudes are held for different reasons by the different groups. Attitudes of whites are based partly on prejudice and those of blacks stem from their fear of crime. The authors conclude that "both within sociological theory and the formulation of public policy . . . it would be unwise to assume the existence of a public consensus on punitive attitudes and, perhaps crime seriousness as well" (p. 294).

Donald Roy's study is the same research that Julius Roth puts to work in our discussion in Chapter 6. A naive observer (perhaps a time-and-motion-study researcher) examining the behavior of Roy's machine shop workers would note that frequently they do not appear to be doing anything. They smoke, they horse around, they hang out in the lavatory, they gossip around their machines, etc. A somewhat more sophisticated observer might note that the men refer to the jobs they are doing at such times as "stinkers" or as "gravy." An even more meticulous observer would consider that these two words, referring to jobs that the men appear to neglect in the same manner, are not synonyms, but antonyms.

It takes a participant observer like Roy to come to recognize how these names are used to designate different kinds of jobs and how those designations, in turn, have different consequences—in spite of the apparent similarity of the workers' behavior. They do indeed loaf on a stinker job. They do so because the job is so difficult that no matter how hard they work, they figure they cannot exceed their minimum day's wages anyway: So, why bother to work at all? The consequence of such a definition is that the day's production quota is not nearly met. A gravy job, on the other hand, is one where the men do not work most of the day because it is so easy that they can make what they consider to be a reasonable day's maximum in a few hours. These two different definitions, resulting in apparently similar behavior, have two very different consequences for production. The lesson is that we ought to suspect apparent consistency as much as we suspect apparent inconsistency.

This is a lesson brought home to us during fieldwork we conducted (Pestello 1985). The members of the "natural food" co-op we observed sought to exemplify the ideals of community. Members were usually very warm toward each other; there was a lot of touching and hugging when they gathered. Significant events in each others' lives were noted and appropriately acknowledged. Birthdays were one of the occasions calling for special honoring of an individual.

We witnessed one celebration where nothing inconsistent was seemingly occurring. The members sang "Happy Birthday" and ate cake. The cake they ate was homemade and, it was announced, contained sugar. We knew that they all thought sugar was bad to consume; some believed it to be poison. Several of the members had told us that they never knowingly eat goods containing refined sugar.

Were the co-op members consistent or inconsistent? They were both with the same act! Members were consistent with their deeply held attitudes of community and the honoring of each other. At the same time, they were acting blatantly inconsistent with their deeply held attitudes toward unnatural food. The world is a complex place, more complex than our most common research methods usually allow.

Methodology as Theory: Are Observed Inconsistencies More Apparent Than Real?

There are other, somewhat less methodological and more technical efforts to explain observed inconsistencies between sentiments and acts as artifacts of how we do our research. Since these do in fact explain some of what, up to this point, we have thought of as discrepancy, they are actually partial *theories*. They illuminate in part our understanding of the relationship between what people say and what they do. It is in this sense that methodology becomes theory. In attempting to order the observations made by contributors to a collection of papers he has edited, Chein makes a distinction between "surface" and "real" inconsistency. The former, which at the beginning "looks like an inconsistency no longer seems to be one when we get to know enough about what is going on; the inconsistency vanishes under adequate inspection" (1949, pp. 53–54). We take Campbell's analysis to be an example of how to dissolve such apparent inconsistency. Chein's point in making the distinction is that in properly identifying a surface inconsistency as such, "we have in the very process of doing so, resolved it" (p. 54). This argument encompasses not only the pure methodological reasoning of Campbell and Guttman, but also, and at the other extreme, the process of doing badly what we ought to know how to do well. In its most candid form, this suggests that some research is simply incompetent technically, and thus its findings need to be completely discounted. Observed differences may be more apparent than real then, because they are spurious artifacts of improper research technique: The "surface" inconsistency, having been explained, dissolves!

Tittle and Hill (1967) provide a comparative analysis of fifteen studies of attitude and behavior, many of which have been mentioned in this volume. One of the bases for their classification is the type of attitude measure used. Their analysis shows a clear relationship between the kind of measure and the kind of resulting relationship between attitudes and behaviors (see, in particular, their Table 1, p. 203). They then proceed to report their own study of voting attitudes and behaviors, which incorporates four different types of attitude measure (Likert, Guttman, Thurstone, and Semantic Differential):

> The degree of interrelationships of the several attitude measures varied considerably. . . . This points up the fact that various methods of measuring the same characteristic may result in the ordering of individuals quite differently. Presumably the variation is accounted for by error factors intrinsic to the measurement techniques. (p. 208)

They believe that their data show that the degree of correspondence observed between attitude and behavior is partly a function of the techniques employed. Howard Ehrlich (1969) carries this argument from the measurement of attitudes to the measurement of behaviors.

Ehrlich argues that one of the technical difficulties lies in an inconsistency in the developmental stage of our measurement techniques: "While the operations for attitude scale construction are relatively well standardized, the operations for observing and recording behavior, particularly in natural settings, are generally unstandardized" (p. 29). As we observed in Chapter 4, DeFleur and Westie (1958) make the same point. Ehrlich continues with the observation that "while the items of attitude scales are presumably a representative set of statements from the attitude domain studies, most behavioral units selected for study have been chosen on a nonsystematic or *ad hoc* basis" (1969, p. 29). Ehrlich concludes that at least some of the observed discrepancies can be attributed to the differential rigor in measurement of the two dimensions. It would, however, seem a reasonable extension of this logic to suggest that some of the research that reports consistency between sentiments and acts needs also to be discounted on the same grounds. Actually, Ehrlich believes that the attitude dimension is also sorely wanting in that it "has been demonstrated to be seriously imprecise and unreliable" (p. 29). His conclusion on methodological grounds is that we need to suspend judgment regarding the relationship between attitudes and acts. When he completes the double screen, by considering the conceptual problem, he concludes that our knowledge in this area is "untenable." Ehrlich screens out everything, but does leave us with some hopeful suggestions for new directions in research. Most of his paper focuses on the problem of what's in between attitudes and behaviors. We shall return to that subject and to Ehrlich's recommendations in Chapter 11.

The state of the art, technical incompetence, or other method-related factors can be used to discredit any research of which one may disapprove or with which one may disagree. A capable critic can find serious flaws in even the best research, and this is not an uncommon device in efforts to support the contention that there is or is not a certain kind of prevailing relationship between sentiments and acts. Clearly, such criticism is necessary and appropriate, and much of Part II of this volume has concentrated on alerting the student to certain bases for judging the procedural soundness of research in this area. But the argument that research findings are methodological artifacts can also be a cop-out. It is true that those reports that are utterly incredible do not tell us anything. It is equally true that few studies fall in that category. In the closing section of Chapter 8, we suggested that there is a peculiar mathematics involved in adding the results of weak studies. Rather than a simple addition of weakness piled on weakness, the mathematics is more near-ly analogous to the logic of the solution of simultaneous equations, where unknown variables are identified by using sets of equations, none of which permits the identification by itself. The coupling of different kinds of incredibility may provide credible conclusions, for the strengths of one may indeed be the weakness of the other.

Campbell is right. Some kinds of observed discrepancies between sentiments and acts can be understood as matters of degree in terms of the logic of scaling. It would be a mistake, however, to assume that this represents a complete or satisfactory solution to the problem. In Part III we shall learn not only that many discrepancies of the type noted in Chapter 3 may be very real, but we shall also consider why this is so.

III

Theory:
A Hatful of Explanations

10

The Social Situation: Does Bad Company Cause Naughty Behavior?

Public and Private Opinion

It seems clear that people express different opinions depending on whom they are talking to and under what conditions. We have opinions we express in private and they are not necessarily the same as those we express in public. Furthermore, the opinion we express in one public is not necessarily the same as that we express in a different public. In fact, what we sometimes refer to as private opinion is no more than an opinion expressed in a more restricted public. Although we will continue to employ the term *private opinion* for rhetorical purposes, these are actually opinions expressed in those publics that members of a society define as "in private." An authentic private opinion would be one never shared—never spoken or acted upon—and therefore of no social consequence. This usage is consistent with those employed by other researchers (see Chapter 13). Investigators make the distinction between private and public on the grounds of threatened "disclosure" of the opinion to significant others.

When we examine field and laboratory observations of overt behavior, this same kind of variation persists. Our discussion in Part II serves as a springboard for the thesis developed here. In this chapter we will document some of the polemical aspects of the earlier methodological discussions and pursue further the differences between sentiments and acts displayed under different conditions.

While working as a part-time juvenile probation officer, one of us was impressed by the frequency with which parents insisted that their children were really good children, but had gotten in with the wrong crowd; other children—bad ones—had led their youngsters astray. Juvenile judges shared the premise of evil companions. Conditions of probation and parole inevitably prohibit association with certain categories of people. Contact with known criminals is sufficient grounds for the revocation of adult parole. Most impressive was the juvenile judge's great reluctance to use an important legal correction option always available. Delinquents would be institutionalized only as a last resort *because* of the kinds of naughty children with whom this would throw them into close and continuing contact.

The actions of the juvenile justices are consistent with one sociological theory of crime. With their theory of differential association, Sutherland and Cressey (1978) argue that bad behavior is learned through interaction with others who advocate bad behavior. It is one of the all too rare frameworks for explaining behavior that has at its center the observation that what a person does is influenced by what others around the person accept and endorse.

We suspect that most of us have experienced the application of this kind of conventional wisdom at the hands of "understanding" parents, friends, or associates. Such popular notions seem to suggest an ignorance of the importance attributed by psychologists, sociologists, and anthropologists to the behavioral constraints imposed by "personality," "social structure," and "culture." Such concepts suggest relatively stable forces built up over a long period of time, which constrain people to talk, think, and act in certain ways. Except for a few "deviants," these same forces compel us not to talk, think, or act in other ways.

Conventional wisdom, then, does not seem in accord with most social-scientific knowledge. Our interest in the folk knowledge of parents and judges is derived from the general concern of this book: How come people talk or act one way at one time and then talk or act another way at another time? Could it be that they find themselves thrust among evil companions at one time, while being immersed in good company at another? Let us consider the evidence.

Evidence can be derived from a variety of independent sources. If there is one common feature in all of the American community studies—from Middletown, to Yankee City, to Elmtown—it is the finding that people vary their opinions and their actions with the context in which they are observed. It is important to note, in view of our earlier discussion of methodology as theory, a reminder provided by Warriner: "In most studies such an inconsistency is explained away by searching for some bias in the observational technique or by looking for some coercive, 'distorting' factor in the milieu" (1958, p. 165).

Warriner's insistence that inconsistencies are not a methodological artifact is crucial. He is suggesting that the findings are not distorted by the instruments. Instead, people's views are distorted by their interpretation of the situation in which those views are called forth. People can publicly support public morality by advocating prohibition and at the same time approve of drinking in their limited circle of friends. Both of these sentiments are real. The same person can vote for prohibition and consume alcohol at home. Although these two acts appear inconsistent with each other, they are perfectly consistent with that person's public opinions vis-à-vis two different publics to which they refer: a circle of close acquaintances and "people in general." The only way we ever learn this person's private opinion is through the response to a perfect interviewer, with a perfect questionnaire, in a perfect interviewing situation. But for what purpose would we want to elicit this private opinion? Respondents' real opinions are those which are manifested in the real situations in which they find themselves.

The irrelevance of private attitudes for conduct is documented in Stanton Wheeler's 1961 study at a reformatory for male felons. His data suggest considerable private support among inmates for conventional values. But this support is not revealed. In like manner, custodial officers reveal private opinions that are more like those of inmates than the inmates perceive them to be. Inmates are in constant contact with one another and feel the need to conform to what they believe the expectations of others to be. Thus, the inmates' public behavior is conspicuously hostile toward the staff (Wheeler 1961). The degree of influence persons in an interaction situation will be able to exercise is subtly altered by the actor's definitions of those other persons. Miller, Butler, and McMartin (1960) report a study suggesting that perceived ability of others to reward has a greater effect on the actor's behavior than comparative perceptions of the ability of others to punish. It is little wonder then, that prisoners should be more influenced by their comrades than by guards.

The volatility of sentiments—their vulnerability to external influences— is also documented in an illustration from an attitude experiment conducted by a pair of psychologists. Everything in their two trials is exactly the same, except the designation of the sponsor. In one case, subjects are informed that the sponsor is "The Institute for Propaganda Effects"; in the other, the sponsor is identified as "The Institute for the Study of Communication and Information Processing." Silverman and Shulman (1970) report "highly significant differences in attitude change scores" resulting from the change in sponsor designation.

Salancik (1982) provides a similar demonstration of the power of context. In a series of course evaluation studies, he found that the correlation between enjoying a course and recommending the course to a fellow student varied from a low of .19 to a high of .73, depending upon the definition surrounding the request for information. When respondents thought that the information requested was part of a sociology project, low correlations between course enjoyment and recommendation were observed. When the context was changed to practical advice solicited by a potential acquaintance, the correlation rose dramatically. Respondents changed the way they answered questions depending upon how they perceived the situation.

Although less dramatic, Milgram (1968a) finds a similar effect when he shifts sponsorship from Yale University to the deliberately shabby surroundings of the "Research Associates of Bridgeport." Full obedience to the experimenter's commands drops from 65 to 48 percent of subjects under this condition.

Compartmentalization

The ease with which people in a complex society can hold contradictory sentiments in insulated compartments, with no manifestation of dissonance or anomie, has been observed by field researchers among widely diverse publics. Robert Coles (1971) combines longitudinal observation with informal interviewing. One person candidly observed that "sometimes I'd like to tell every colored person I see to go back to Africa. Half of them are on welfare. They don't want to work. Their kids steal." In a seeming reversal of what he first said, he then adds

> I'll tell you, I feel sorry for the colored person. They've had an awful time in this country. Sometimes I wonder how I'd feel if I was colored. Sometimes I stop and think: They do the dirty work in this country—just like I do. (p. 4)

So much for race and poverty, but as Coles shows, those who called themselves hawks on the Vietnam War can be as tormented by that war as any dove. He reports a conversation with a factory worker a few days after the funeral of his son who had been killed in the war:

> I hate this war. The sooner it ends, the better. But I hate the people who spit at the flag and insult the country. I ask you: how can a man believe that his son's life was wasted? The people I see on television knocking this country don't have to ask themselves a question like that. (p. 4)

Lest one think that this phenomenon is unique to the Vietnam War, a particularly unpopular war, similar inconsistencies were expressed in the face of 1991 hostilities with Iraq, a military engagement receiving general public support.

Kriesberg (1956) describes such compartmentalization among steel distributors who participated in the gray market during the Korean War. "All of the men in the gray market agreed with the government that national security was a prime consideration and the nation faced a dangerous threat to its security" (p. 274). According to Kriesberg, some of these men neatly sort their evaluations into one compartment and their conduct into another:

> Inconsistencies are not perceived, and if they are pointed out, the rejoinder is, "that's too deep for me." However, this shifting of perspectives from context to context cannot be regarded only as a way of escaping from the strain of conflicting obligations. The same inconsistencies, vagaries, and compartmentalizations are to be found among those who did not engage in activities they felt were condemned by the government. (p. 274)

Both Coles and Kriesberg imply that compartmentalization occurs all of the time. People compartmentalize consistent as well as inconsistent fragments of their social lives. It is a normal process to hold diverse opinions about an object—some of which may be contradictory. Student nurses too are impressive in their ability to simultaneously assimilate the cold, impersonal, professional orientation and the warm, personal, helping orientation. Compartmentalization on their part was found to be more common than accepting one set of institutional values over the other (Deutscher and Montague 1956).

In an abortive attempt to measure the extent of opposition to fair housing legislation, Rose (1961) found so much inconsistency in response that he was forced to abandon the effort. He found that he could not measure the extent of the opposition, because there were almost as many different results as there were approaches to the question. He observes that an individual may hold several attitudes toward an object that are logically incompatible if confronted with each other in the same setting. The most significant finding that emerged from this study, according to Rose, was that most of the expressed attitudes were contradicted by other expressed attitudes or by reports of behavior. Westie (1965), in a piece we will discuss at greater length in Chapter 13, reports considerable inconsistency among Americans who voice agreement with the values of the American creed but are inclined to devalue blacks when situations are specified.

Among the types of resolutions to this contradiction is compartmentalization. Westie's interviewers took special note of inconsistent responses and probed respondents unmercifully about them: "Of the 293 inconsistencies noted, respondents admitted approximately 42 percent . . . and recognized but denied about the same number. . . . Nearly 16 percent of the inconsistencies remained unseen even after extensive probing" (Westie 1965, p. 535). Perhaps of even greater importance is the fact that about a quarter of the explanations elicited in this manner were *explanations of consistencies!* The compartmentalization observed by Westie involves a conscious disconnection of apparently inconsistent sentiments; like Kriesberg's gray marketeers, people are aware of them but see no relationship. "Repression," which Westie distinguishes from compartmentalization on the basis of awareness, is, for our purposes, just another type of compartmentalization.

One of the classic field studies of compartmentalization is by Lohman and Reitzes (1954). They demonstrate empirically the manner in which the situation is defined differently for the same individuals in different settings—at home and at work. This conclusion is based on a study of white laborers. Their subjects were members of a union with a policy of granting blacks job equality, but they lived in a neighborhood that strongly endorsed residential segregation.

The workers were consistently inconsistent. This paradox becomes intelligible when "seen against the background of the organizational structuring of the individuals as members of the neighborhood group and on the other hand as members of an organized work group" (p. 342). The results show a significant association between community involvement and rejection of blacks in the neighborhood; a significant association between union involvement and acceptance of blacks at work; and no association between neighborhood rejection and work acceptance. White union members can be egalitarian and accepting of blacks at work while simultaneously exhibiting prejudice and rejection of blacks in their neighborhood. Those who persist in ignoring the locale in which an interview takes place or a questionnaire is filled out ought to consider these findings.

Toward a Situational Sociology

At the end of Part II, we pointed out the apparently anomalous perspective of two rather extreme behaviorists who remind us that consistency is a creature of scientists and has no relation to how people perceive situations (Kendler and Kendler 1949). The evidence does suggest that this is frequently the case. This is also a central theme of the ethnomethodological argument. On this issue the extremes of positivism and phenomenology seem to meet (and that is convergence worth noting!). Jack Douglas, for example, builds on Harold Garfinkel's position that

> sociologists and other outsiders often see social actions as involving moral conflict because they assume the actors are (or *should* be) attending to

certain abstract morals in a "rational" way, whereas there are generally understood, situated meanings or common-sense criteria of rationality specifying the appropriate processes of inference. However, it is also most important to note that most of us live highly compartmentalized moral lives: we have *situated moral and other meanings* for many different types of situations and feel relatively little need to relate the situations to each other via abstract meanings. (1970, p. 385, emphasis in original)

Although the behaviorists say it more clearly and succinctly, the argument is the same and, more important, it is made on the same grounds. Such inconsistencies are not to be easily dismissed as reflecting deception on the part of respondents or technical inefficiency on the part of our instruments. Anticipating both the behaviorists and the ethnomethodologists by several decades, Robert Merton observed that internal tests of consistency assume rationality—that people never really hold inconsistent attitudes—and he concludes that "in making this assumption, the investigator is using *norms* of logic, not *facts* of sociology" (1940, p. 20, emphasis in original).

We do not mean to imply that people holding discordant views or behaving in ways other than their verbalizations indicate are always able to mobilize so neat a psychological separator as compartmentalization. To the contrary, this situation, when the person is confronted with it, can create considerable stress. Gorden's study of members of a cooperative rooming house reveals the stress that people undergo when they feel constrained to modify private opinions (i.e., previously elicited in an anonymous interview) in the presence of their fellow co-op members. Gorden notes

an acute awareness of the presence of the other members of the group when they are asked to express their opinion. Confused efforts to appear nonchalant, efforts to escape the situation, and attempts to prevent others from hearing one's response are all telltale signs of the awareness of pressure. (1952, p. 57)

Nevertheless, these individuals did tend to alter their private opinions to conform to their conception of the group norm when giving their public opinion.

Milgram reports much the same kind of reaction when his laboratory subjects find themselves behaving in ways contrary to their beliefs: "Persons were observed to sweat, tremble, stutter, bite their lips, and groan as they found themselves increasingly implicated in the experimental conflict" (1964, p. 268). Milgram describes the "obedient" subject who insists that he will not continue to hurt the victim, yet while talking in this manner proceeds to the highest shock level on the generator: "He displayed a curious dissociation between word and action" (p. 269). In their own way, these studies parallel the findings of Wheeler (1961) in his work on committed felons. The major difference is that the former set of investigators induce stress by entrapment of their subjects. Wheeler, on the other hand, demonstrates how stress is avoided by conformity to perceived expectations and suppression of private opinions.

Even under the deliberately designed conditions of fantasy characteristic of controlled experiments, there is no evidence that attitude, or opinion, or behavior remains stable through time or under changing conditions. As we discussed in Chapter 8, the bias resulting from publication policies in some journals, as well as prevailing norms in psychology, militate against publication of findings of "no difference." These experiments are so designed that their results can be interpreted as evidence that people react almost immediately to adapt themselves to perceived social constraints. The only conclusion we can draw from this body of literature is that, like the sociological field studies and the methodological investigations in survey research, actors can harbor real attitudes that can be contravened in such a way that within a short period of time they become different—although still "real"—as a consequence of redefinitions of the situation by the actor.

Much of this psychological research is concerned with the concept of *compliance* and is designed to investigate compliant behavior. Some of Kelman's earlier work and later investigations by Goldstein and McGinnies provide examples (Kelman 1958; Goldstein and McGinnies 1964). The rapid erosion effect of group pressure toward conformity in the experimental situation—presumably as a consequence of exposure to other groups and other pressures—has also been documented (Watts and McGuire 1964). This provides convergence of experimental observations with field observations such as those by Lohman and Reitzes.

Some laboratory experiments have been designed to study the consequences of group pressures on behavior as well as on opinion change. Among these a few have even managed to create experimental situations involving relatively meaningful behavior. Such studies clearly demonstrate that private opinion has nothing to do with overt behavior in a real situation, i.e., one that involves other people and that has meaning to the subject.

The evidence from the field studies, like the evidence from the laboratory, suggests that one's private opinion is not likely to be the same as public opinion, that one can hold a number of public opinions simultaneously, and, incidentally, that there is no necessary relationship between any kind of opinion about an object and subsequent behavior toward that object. And that is one answer to the key question addressed by this book. Referring to only a single area of interaction, Kohn and Williams suggest:

> [T]here is now abundant research evidence of situational variability in intergroup behavior: an ever-accumulating body of research demonstrates that allegedly prejudiced persons act in a thoroughly egalitarian manner in situations where that is the socially prescribed mode of behavior, and that allegedly unprejudiced persons discriminate in situations where they feel it is socially appropriate to do so. (1956, p. 164)

We suppose we might have taken their word for it in 1956 and saved ourselves a great deal of trouble. But then, we do not expect many social scientists to simply take our word for it even with an additional thirty-odd years accumulation of evidence including much from fields other than race and ethnic relations. We will continue to bring critical evidence to bear in the closing section of this chapter after we try to spell out the implications of this remarkable convergence of some highly credible evidence.

Implications: Take Care of the Company You Keep!

In 1961 Dennis Wrong challenged "The Over-Socialized Conception of Man in Modern Society." Reacting to determinism, which pervaded the social sciences and which seemed to be seeping into popular currency, Wrong asked if in fact people were as constrained by a monolithic culture, as social scientists would have us believe. A few years later Harold Garfinkel referred more bluntly to the models of social actors constructed by the various social sciences: He called them "judgmental dopes." The cultural dope and psychological dope are, respectively, the person in the sociologist's society and the person in the psychologist's society (see Garfinkel 1964). Although both Wrong and Garfinkel have, in our opinion, properly identified one of the most critical issues in contemporary social science, their solutions are not so clear.

Wrong appears to have opted hopefully for a human image free to construct lines of action at will. Garfinkel, on the other hand, worked his way toward an imagery of people constrained in their most microscopic relationships by an indelibly imprinted set of taken-for-granted rules. The evidence we have been sampling, converging from a variety of sources, suggests to us a somewhat different solution to the problem posed by Wrong and Garfinkel.

As we have suggested above, laboratory experiments have been designed to study the consequences of group pressures on behavior as well as opinion change. Some of the best examples of this type of experi-ment are found in the work that takes Helson's (1947) notion of adapta-tion level as a point of departure. These experiments illustrate a wide range of the phenomena we are discussing. Helson considers the vari-ous components of the situation, including aspects of the actor's person-ality, social constraints, and the meaning of the object toward which the attitude or behavior is directed.

Himmelstein and Moore (1963) employ the typical experimental setup used in laboratory studies designed to study the consequences of group pressures on behavior and opinion change. The actual field experiment is viewed by subjects as an extraneous incident occurring during the course of what they believe to be the actual experiment. The device is to have a student (confederate) wander into the experimental setting dur-ing an interlude and solicit the subject's signature on a petition in the presence of another confederate who has been instructed either to agree or refuse to sign the petition. Although Orne would question the kind of atmosphere created by "being in an experiment" (whether or not the subject is wise to precisely which set of activities comprise that experi-ment), there is no reason for the subject to suspect that the petition is anything but real.

In the design of Himmelstein and Moore the petition is unloaded (designed not to elicit strong feelings), the race of the confederate is varied, and prejudice is the dimension of personality that is tapped. What is remarkable about the experiment is that when the bystander signs the petition, the naive victim is also more likely to sign. When the bystander refuses to sign the petition, the naive victim is less likely to sign than otherwise. What is even more remarkable is that the influence of this stranger on our victim persists regardless of the race of the stranger, the extent of prejudice of the victim, certain pretested "person-ality" traits of the victim, or *the content of the petition itself.*

In sum, it did not seem to make any difference to a lot of people who the petitioner was, or what kind of people they themselves were, or even what the petition had to say. Significant numbers appear to have been influenced by the action of the stranger. This is the kind of observa-tion that has been made in hundreds of experiments under controlled conditions, with varying degrees of credibility, since Sherif discovered the autokinetic effect in the early thirties. It led Himmelstein and Moore to conclude that petition signing does not represent the inner conviction of the individual (what we refer to as private opinion) but rather the situational factors brought to bear upon the individual.

Milgram's research also provides clear experimental evidence that the kind of private opinion sometimes sought by the survey researcher has little bearing on public behavior. It is, in fact, clear that the subject's *public* opinion may be unrelated to action. In some of his later experiments, Milgram (1968a) had the experimenter take a deliberately aggressive authoritarian role in order to test the "obedience" of subjects. Transcripts reveal that some subjects unfailingly obeyed the experimenter while publicly protesting against their own actions.

Milgram (1968a) provides several examples from his later experiments in which subjects persist in behaving contrary to their opinions, clearly at some psychological discomfort. Yet, in some ways, Milgram's 1964 article is even more persuasive since there is no apparent pressure on the subject to administer the shock. The decision is made by the experimental subject alone. Recall that the "teacher" is "in charge" of making the decisions about how much voltage to administer when the "learner" makes a mistake. In effect, Milgram's diabolical experiments provide evidence in support of the thesis that sometimes people do naughty (or good) things because of bad (or good) company.

It might be argued that, as in the case of many laboratory experiments, students see through the game. But Milgram's later experiment was with adult males, not students, although it was still an experimental situation. There are, however, field experiments in which controls are imposed upon people engaged in their normal everyday routines—without their knowledge. Lionel Dannick, for example, has demonstrated the extent to which pedestrians will disregard a stoplight when a stranger does (Dannick 1969, 1973). He found people much more likely to follow a stranger's lead whether the stranger chose to cross against a light or wait for the light to change. The decision to act or not to act appears in large part to be determined by the actor's assessment of the immediate situation and only in small part by any inner proclivity or private attitude. Although sex differences are observed by Dannick, they are not great. His controls for age and social class reflect little variation.

Dannick's situation is a trivial one, but it does occur during the course of everyday routines for a heterogeneous population who cannot know they are in an experiment. It provides some confirmation that what is observed in the laboratory can also be seen outside. If Milgram's strength lies in the terrible potential consequences of the subject's actions while its weakness lies in the artificiality of the laboratory situation, then Dannick's strength lies in the reality of the situation while his weakness is in the superficiality of the action. Clearly the strengths of the one are the weaknesses of the other and we have another instance of convergent evidence.

Is all of this merely verification of that defect in the American character David Riesman described as "other directedness"? Perhaps, but there is some evidence, albeit scanty, to the contrary. In a study that preceded both of his previously mentioned experiments, Milgram found evidence of social conformity among students in France and Norway (Milgram 1961). Although Norwegians were considerably more conforming than the French, both showed a strong tendency to conform to erroneous judgments provided by confederates. Unfortunately, Milgram provides no comparisons with American students under the same experimental conditions. Nevertheless, he does conclude that social conformity is not exclusively a U.S. phenomenon.

Several years later and in a very different land, Shanab and Yahya (1977) replicated Milgram's test on Jordanian children (age six to eight), preteens (age ten to twelve), and teenagers (age 14 to 16). Their findings were similar to Milgram's work with Europeans, with neither age nor sex differences in compliance. The researchers observe "that this study has revealed not only that obedience and overobedience are culture free but that such behavior is observed very early in life" (p. 535). Others have also found that foreign students, including Asians, behave just like American students when they are subjects in American experiments (Zajonc and Waki 1961). The other-directed person may be less a product of national character, as Riesman would have it, than of human nature.

An earlier generation of American sociologists noted a herdlike behavior among crowds under certain conditions. They referred to these conditions generally as "collective behavior" and tended to restrict their observations of human milling, contagious actions, and other cattlelike acts, to situations in which there were no traditional standardized rules for behavior (Blumer 1946). It appears now that their observation may hold for a far wider range of behavior than they suspected—including such obviously rule-governed situations as pedestrian behavior at street intersections controlled by traffic lights.

If the implications we have drawn from these studies are correct, then it becomes easier to understand not only why people may not always demonstrate consistency between their sentiments and their acts, but also how normal everyday citizens can slaughter other normal everyday citizens—whether on the basis of religion (as is the inclination of the Irish in Northern Ireland, Vietnamese in Vietnam, and Hindus, Sikhs, and Muslims in India), or language (as with the French and English in Quebec or the Flemish and French in Belgium), or ethnicity (for example, East and West Pakistanis prior to the creation of Bangladesh, blacks and Cape Colored in South Africa, or Indians and blacks in Guiana), or something called "national interests." This last provides the basis for solid German burghers, too old or otherwise unfit for combat duty, to do their patriotic thing to Jews in death camps.

Such things need not be matters of life and death. They can be as trivial as crossing a street or crumbling crackers in one's soup. What they share in common is that they are strongly influenced by the actor's definition of the immediate situation—the way things are sized up. That definition, in turn, seems to be affected in large part by perceptions of what others expect and what others do. During the early sixties, when television quiz shows were the rage in the United States, the great hero of them all was a charming, brilliant, young scholar named Charles Van Doren. The shocking discovery that he, in collaboration with those managing the show, was "cheating" led to the demise of the TV quiz show for a while.

With the kind of situational explanation proposed here, we can better understand the public cheating in which an otherwise honest scholar found himself gradually entwined on a television quiz program. We can understand it just as we can understand (while simultaneously being appalled) how ordinary American soldiers could murder Vietnamese civilians. Evidence from the laboratory and from field studies (Raven 1959; Gorden 1952; Kreiger 1979; Pestello 1991) suggests that once a line of action is initiated, a certain amount of momentum is built up and one action seems to call for the next until the actors find themselves well along a path never anticipated. Furthermore, it is likely that people also find themselves believing that that is the proper place for them to be.

It is likely that readers can find in their own experience an example of this type of behavioral and attitudinal inertia. Unless there is a radical revision of the situation, we find that, having been set in motion, we continue to move. It seems to us that we have an explanatory framework evolving that is based on empirical evidence. It helps us understand such varied phenomena as collective murder, jaywalking, and cheating. More to our point, it helps us understand why sentiments and acts are frequently unrelated. This is the beginning of a general theory of human behavior that is of some importance and of some use.

The credibility of the folk hypothesis that evil companions cause naughty behavior tends to be confirmed by the available evidence. Both the field studies and the experiments reviewed here provide evidence that a considerable proportion of the variance in human behavior can be explained by efforts (conscious or unconscious) on the part of people to bring their sentiments and acts into line, not with each other, but with what they perceive to be the sentiments and acts of others in the immediate situation. If it is properly reinterpreted, further confirmation can be found in the methodological literature of survey research, which was discussed in Chapter 6. It is not our intention to argue that situational constraints explain all, or even most, of the variance found in human behavior. Such constraints do, however, appear to explain significant and frequently large amounts of that variance. The residue can probably be explained by such phenomena as cultural differences, social-structural differences (differential location and participation in the society), personality differences (relatively enduring predispositions, and values resulting from effective socialization), biological or genetic differences; by interactions among these sources (see Acock and DeFleur 1972); and by idiosyncratic, whimsical, or "accidental" factors.

Surely one cannot hope to understand human behavior or social processes without considering how certain types of situations become available for people to define at one time rather than another, in one culture rather than another, among some segments of society rather than among others, and how some individuals manage to resist involvement while others do not. Social scientists have vigorously explored such historical, cultural, social structural, and personality dimensions. In contrast, little attention has been paid to the situational constraints that confront people in the world they never made. This chapter aims to redress that imbalance—to draw attention to social content as well as social context.

We think that the social situation is a notion that is different in kind from the constructs culture, social structure, and personality. It is different in that it is an ethnoconcept—one that views behavior from the perspective of the people who are subjects of study. The other concepts are objective or scientific in that they are devices for viewing the behavior of people from the perspective of outsiders (scientists). From this objective perspective the subjects of study become literally objects of study. It seems to us that such abstract forces as culture, social structure, and personality provide little understanding of why people behave as they do in everyday life. Furthermore, unlike the social situation, those concepts are fictions created by the social scientist. None of them exist—except for the social scientist who finds them useful. Unlike the social situation, such concepts are, as some sociologists like to put it, heuristic devices.

There is no culture out there that imposes upon us an imperative to act like one another and differently from those located on other patches of geography; there is no culture other than what the anthropologist has chosen to subsume under that rubric. It is not even clear that culture is an objective concept. It may be viewed as inherently ethnocentric in the sense that it is constructed by an outsider out of what appear to be all the odd and funny things that foreigners possess, say, and do. Urban anthropologists sometimes find data compelling them to recognize the limitations of their concept. Elliot Liebow, for example, denies that lower-class life in black ghettos can be understood as mute compliance with cultural imperatives (Liebow 1967).

The argument regarding personality and social structure is a parallel one. There is no personality in one's head (or wherever it may be) that drives one to act along certain consistent lines different from those chosen by one's neighbors because they have a different personality. As was true of culture, there is no personality other than what the psychologist has chosen to subsume under that rubric. Nor is there a social structure in which one is located and that coercively leads one to assume so-called roles and statuses that differentiate one socially from others in the society. There is no social structure other than what the sociologist has chosen to subsume under that rubric.

All of these concepts are then inventions, myths, and fantasies, which, although sometimes useful, may blind the analyst to the very real constraints imposed by the immediate situation in which the actor is involved. This is not to deny that such concepts should continue to be used. As we have said, they are heuristic devices. We do not mean to be playful. It is true that when the immediate social situation is controlled experimentally, large amounts of the variance in human behavior remain unexplained. An examination of the data in any social science study reveals substantial minorities of stubborn, inner-directed, culturally entrapped (or whatever) subjects. One reason why the so-called ecological fallacy is a fallacy is that even in the areas and among the populations where such phenomena as delinquency or suicide are at their highest rates, most people are neither delinquents nor suicides.

To discard the ideas of culture, social structure, and personality is to ignore their explanatory power. The sociology of knowledge suggests that the gross sociocultural milieu or historical era in which one is found has a powerful influence over what one is able to think about and how one thinks about it. The skillful and informative use of social structural concepts in the explanatory mode has been demonstrated repeatedly, for example, in Weber's work with religion or Marx's with social class. The great analytic power of the concept of culture when carefully applied is similarly undeniable. This is in contrast to the naive and frequently stereotyped use of these constructs by the person on the street who explains and excuses all behavior on the grounds of the actor's race, nationality, sex, age, social class, etc. This distortion of what the person's own methods must indicate occurs, we suppose, as a result of "authoritative" evidence to the contrary provided by social scientists in the mass media.

What is ultimately called for in understanding human behavior is some comprehension of the interaction between action and setting—the ways in which the definition of the immediate situation is mediated by certain preconditioned and predisposing factors. It is this mediation between situations and what goes on beyond the immediate situation to which Maines (1982) refers with his idea of mesostructure (see also Hall 1987, 1991; and Pestello and Voydanoff 1991a, 1991b). In its simplest form, the problem is, Under what conditions will what kinds of people define situations differently from other kinds of people under other conditions? Furthermore, How do certain situations come to be available at certain times?

Good students and thoughtful critics constantly confront the problem of determinism. To eliminate the notion of helpless, irresponsible individuals relentlessly pushed one way or the other by their culture or personality or social structure is a reasonable goal. But when we suggest a situational sociology are we not substituting a new form of determinism for the older ones? Are we not arguing, from evidence, that people helplessly follow the cues provided in their immediate social situation? Like automatons, they step off the curb following a stranger. Like mindless machines they are programmed to sign or not sign a petition. Like an army of Frankenstein monsters they kill or maim others if that seems to be what is called for. This does not seem to us what W. I. Thomas intended when he discussed the definition of the situation. Nor is it what G. H. Mead and later Blumer have described in their analyses of the construction of the social act.

Along with Blumer (1969) we prefer to believe that people are situation-assessing, speculative, role-taking animals who consider various lines of action by asking themselves, What if . . . ? Having tried to imagine themselves in another's shoes, they then act. But, as E. C. Hughes once asked, "What Other?" How is it possible for the role-taking person of G. H. Mead to inflict pain on others? Easy! As pathetic as the plight of the experimental subject or the national minority may be, the scientist and the national leader are people of wisdom and authority. If, in assessing the situation, the person in the street must take the role of one at the expense of the other, we suspect the choice is predictable. Fortunately, the prediction will be wrong in a large minority of instances.

Katz (1988) grapples with the issue of determinism and comes to a conclusion similar to ours in his recent work on crime. He is troubled by criminologists' focus on the background of criminal events, what we here call culture and structure. He points out that many who share the most damaging background characteristics do not resort to crime and many who are privileged do. He advocates that criminologists begin by focusing on the "foreground," the context within which action takes place. One aspect of situations that we have not explicitly addressed is emotion. Katz suggests that humans engage in "genuine experiential creativity" as their actions unfold in the criminal situation (p. 8). He considers how criminal situations are imbued with emotion, and the "moral emotions" that emerge in them:

> The closer one looks at crime, at least at the varieties examined here, the more vividly relevant become the moral emotions. Follow vandals and

amateur shoplifters as they duck into alleys and dressing rooms and you will be moved by their delight in deviance; observe them under arrest and you may be stunned by their shame. (p. 312)

We will take up the issue of emotion in the next section. Let us first consider the persistent minority who resist the pressures of the majority to conform.

In every piece of evidence we have seen, no matter how convincing, there remained that large and stubborn minority of research subjects who resisted group pressures toward conformity. Recall, that many of Milgram's subjects said No! to the teacher's demands and refused to administer an electric shock. We also know that such minorities exist in real life, sometimes under conditions that could have disastrous consequences for them. The people described by the Oliners (1988) as "rescuers" in Nazi Europe provide a poignant example. Their study of non-Jews who helped Jews escape Nazi persecution in Europe found no difference between rescuers and a control group in any of the characteristics they were able to identify, including age, sex, socioeconomic status, *or political affiliation!* The rescuers were as likely to be Nazis as the controls. Furthermore, there is a minority of people in everyday life who are willing to publicly act contrary to the expectations of others. Some people may take the difficult and lonely step of becoming whistleblowers, attempting to expose the wrongs of their group (see Glazer and Glazer 1989). It is possible that under the continuous development of social action that occurs in real life (in contrast to experimental situations), the minority who fail to go along may sometimes succeed in altering norms and thus alter the majority's definition of the situation.

This is one source of social change. But how does it happen that some people come to define a situation differently from others and how does it happen that some of these are able to resist the pressures of the majority? Although Mead provides an escape hatch with his concept of "generalized other" (which we read as an underlying notion of the actor about what people in general think—the ubiquitous "they" in What will they say if . . . ?), it seems clear that at this point some of the traditional perspectives of psychology, sociology, and anthropology must be brought into play.

Current Fad or Telling Signpost?
The Sociology of Emotions

When last we considered the relationship between words and deeds in *What We Say/What We Do*, the study of emotion was dormant. The 1970s produced a surge of interest among social scientists on the emotional aspects of human behavior. We find that some of this work is relevant to the sentiments-acts controversy, particularly research on the constructed nature of emotions and the interrelationship between emotion, talk, and action.

Constructionists maintain that separate sentiments are created as social actors learn, through the socialization process, to differentiate their emotional cues and to combine them with gestures, social relationships, and beliefs. It is through "sentiment socialization" that young social actors also learn how to read others' sentiments and how and when to control their own (Gordon 1981). Hochschild (1983, 1989, 1990) has documented the learning and use of emotion management techniques among adults and finds that people use feeling and expression rules to appropriately adapt their emotion displays to the situations they face. This is particularly evident in service work, where individuals sell their emotional displays to their employer—like flight attendants who are required to be pleasant and sympathetic regardless of the abuse they confront, or bill collectors who must remain indifferent to the hardships of overdue creditors (Hochschild 1983).

Of central concern to any socialization process is talk. In the study of emotions, attention to language is particularly evident in research attending to the flexibility and mutability of emotion expressions and feelings. For Perinbanayagam dialogue is the "defining principle of all actions and interactions" (1991, p. xii). Emotions, acts, and cognitions are intertwined and bound together through talk (pp. 146, 164–65). This relationship between cognition and emotion is empirically explored by Mills and Kleinman (1988), who find that feeling and thought (reflexivity about self) operate independently and thus can be either consistent or inconsistent with each other. Examples of the latter include battered women who can have strong emotions yet feel numb (Mills and Kleinman 1988) and physicians who are socialized to suppress emotions and approach patients in an analytic fashion (Smith and Kleinman 1989).

Scheff (1983, 1990) attempts to theoretically integrate the constructivist approach (feelings are socially learned) with the positivist approach (emotions are biologically based). According to his theory, communication (largely conveyed through linguistic symbols) and emotion (predominantly communicated with nonverbal gestures) are distinct, but interwoven processes, which social actors utilize to create, maintain, and destroy the bonds between them. Like Perinbanayagam (1991), Scheff (1990) views emotion as critical to discourse. Their approaches reveal a point of convergence between our work on the relationship between sentiments and acts and their respective research on emotions. What they add to our discussion of talk and behavior is emotion, a dimension we did not explicitly address in our previous work. Scheff argues that feelings undergird talk. They are implied and hidden. For Perinbanayagam talk and action are surrounded by and infused with emotion.

We too reject the assumption of rationality in human behavior and have emphasized the fact that the rational logic of scientists isn't very helpful when it is evoked to explain the attitudes or behaviors of ordinary people. We have argued that people have their own logic, which we are obliged to discover if we are to understand their statements and their actions. This folk logic may be viewed by "scientists" as irrational or emotional. We chose the word *sentiments,* in part, because it implies an emotional overtone to what people feel and say. It is clear to anyone who does empirical research that people do not behave rationally. This is an inconvenient fact of life that many social scientists—especially economists—prefer to ignore. Somehow they find it more expedient to assume that workers will change jobs if the pay is higher or move to another community if there is better work there, etc. This view assumes that people have no sentiments or emotions, that they are not influenced by loyalty to old employers or love of their hometown, or a desire to live near their extended families and old friends. Most sociologists tend to understand such sentimental motivation despite the fact that they sometimes ignore it. The continued growth of the sociology of emotions holds the promise that we will come to understand it better.

Although emotion researchers are prone to many of the pitfalls that attitude researchers have experienced, there is potential for convergence between these two areas of investigation. Emotion researchers cover some of the same conceptual terrain carved out by attitude researchers decades earlier. Hochschild denies, however, that emotion researchers are simply "using new words for what used to be referred to as 'values' or 'attitudes'" (1990, p. 117). While we do not entirely agree with her, in the field of attitudes and behavior the emotional dimensions of attitudes have been neglected.

We are interested in what people say and do but it is important to know the emotions that accompany talk and action. Emotions are used to convey messages, sometimes louder than spoken words, and emotions are "read" in the interpretation of messages, sometimes given greater weight than the speaker's words. We may, for example, show anger while speaking, which demonstrates the seriousness of our intent, and conversely we might not feel obliged to follow through on something because it was said in a moment of anger.

There seems to be little doubt that our talk and behavior are embedded in emotions and the relationship between the two. Feeling, talk, and action are linked in the situations we encounter in everyday life. Teasing out the role of emotion is essential for a full understanding of the words-deeds relationship. The phenomenological-constructivist approach to emotions offers a strong beginning in that direction.

The sociology of emotions contains elements that are clearly compatible with the kind of situational sociology that evolved in this volume and incorporates ideas that have been central to our thinking. This movement is not novel and may go the way of other fads and fashions in social science. Nevertheless, the critique it provides and the alternatives it emphasizes are useful and necessary. Even though such movements may themselves fade away, they provide a valuable service to social science by reminding us of certain failures in our own procedures.

All The World *Is* a Stage

The backdrop and the stage props provide the setting within which the action occurs. But it is the script with its dialogue and its cues that creates the action itself. Culture, personality, and social structure, like the backdrop and props, provide broad suggestions of what range of action seems appropriate. An audience expects different action in a subway scene from what they expect in a bedroom scene, different action in an automobile from what they expect in a bordello, different action in a dining room from what they expect in a jewelry store. Let us ignore, or treat as "deviant," the fact that people occasionally do sleep in subways, make love in automobiles, and have breakfast at Tiffany's.

The essential point of the analogy is that even within the restrictions of the backdrop and props, an almost infinite number of dramas may be constructed and played out. This is true even in situations that appear to be tightly scripted, like a Naval Reserve training weekend or a maximum security prison (Thomas 1984; Zurcher 1984). Likewise, within one's presumed cultural, personality, and social-structural constraints, there are nearly infinite lines of action that can develop. To the extent that this is true, it follows that the gross concepts throw little light on how or why we choose to act and interact as we do. To pursue the analogy, the difference between the revolutionary and the reformer is that, in their efforts to bring about social change, revolutionaries would demand a new set and new props for the stage; reformers, in contrast, would attempt to edit the script.

The image of the tailor-made person—neatly fitted into culture, hemmed in by personality, and sewed down by the social structure—the "oversocialized conception of man" as a "judgmental dope," is of limited utility. It is also potentially tragic because of its impact on popular conceptions of the nature of people in society. As long as social science posits an image of the tailor-made person, we are not only incorrect in our perception, but, perhaps of greater consequence, our translation of knowledge into social policy will be couched in terms of creating better controls and constraints—to tailor the individual so that behavior becomes predictable and expected.

When we free ourselves of this deterministic image of the culture-bound, personality-bound, or social structure–bound person and temper it with the interacting, situation-assessing, emotion-guided person, the translation into social policy then becomes couched in terms of designing roads to freedom—not to constraint. Everett Hughes reminds us, in the admittedly sexist language of the time, that this is the person W. I. Thomas would have called "creative" and David Riesman calls "autonomous." This person is no automaton,

> not a reed blown about by the wind, but a man of many sensitivities who would attain and maintain, by his intelligent and courageous choice of the messages to which he would respond, by the choice of his "others," freedom of a high but tough and resilient quality. (Hughes and Hughes 1952, p. 126)

11

Stimulus-Response Is for Animals (Symbols Are for People)

It's What's in Between That Counts

In the 1920s, following his remarkable breakthrough in discovering and documenting the conditioned reflex, Pavlov considered the relationship between his findings with animals and possible generalizations to human behavior. Pavlov, whose brilliant researches have been so distorted by sycophantic followers, was impressed by what he called a "second signal system" in human beings. The physical stimuli to which all animals respond, and which are the focal concern of Pavlov's conditioning experiments, are the first signals. The second signals are primarily *words:*

> The word created a second system of signals of reality which is peculiarly ours, being the signal of signals. On the one hand, numerous speech stimuli have removed us from reality. . . . On the other, it is precisely speech which has made us human. (1927, p. 357)

It is this symbolic construction of reality, largely through language, that, according to Pavlov, makes it inappropriate to generalize from the behavior of experimental animals to the behavior of human beings. "Of course," he insists,

> a word is for man as much a real conditioned stimulus as are other stimuli common to men and animals, yet at the same time it is so all-comprehending that it allows of no quantitative or qualitative comparisons with conditioned stimuli in animals. (p. 407)

Pavlov recognizes that one may, with great pains, create an experimental situation where human beings, like other animals will learn to avoid pushing a red lever because they associate an electric shock with it (and to press a black lever because they associate the receipt of jelly-beans with it). This complicated conditioning process is, however, easily bypassed and even thwarted by human subjects. If, as a person is about to press a lever, someone whispers, "Press the black one," instant conditioning takes place—the second signal system. Or the someone might be mischievous and say "Push the red one." In either case the person might or might not listen to the directions, and might or might not act in accord with the instructions. But, regardless of how the comment is interpreted, the fact is that the physical conditioning process that uses first signals has been sabotaged by a different process—one that, if not exclusive to the human race, is employed more extensively and more pervasively by us than any other animal.

The behaviorist's laboratory is an unexpected source for confirmation of the essentially symbolic nature of human behavior. Razran (1939), for example, showed his subjects a list of words while they were eating, conditioning them to salivate at the sight of certain words. One of those words was *style*. Having conditioned subjects, Razran proceeded to introduce a new series of words to them—including both *stile* and *fashion*. Even though *stile* is similar to *style* in both appearance and sound, and *fashion* is most dissimilar in these respects, conditioning was, in fact, generalized from *style* to *fashion* and not to *stile*. The generalization is semantic—related to invested meaning—rather than dependent upon objective visual or auditory clues.

Of equal importance is a follow-up experiment conducted by Riess (1946), this time with children rather than adults as subjects. Among children, the generalization was to the homophone rather than the synonym. It appears that the invisible and inaudible similarity between *style* and *fashion* is one that we must learn to impute and that comes to supersede the less salient sensory similarities: For the child, *style* and *stile* resemble one another and *fashion* is unrelated to either. This is not so for the adult, to whom things have come to stand for something other than themselves.

All of this is not to say that, in many respects, human behavior cannot be understood on the same terms as animal behavior. We are animals and we do share with other animals whatever forces may drive them. But there is something else, perhaps a second signal system, that impinges upon and has great influence in human conduct. It is to this something else, this symbolic quality, that George Herbert Mead (1934) directed his attention and that Herbert Blumer devoted a career to transforming into a different kind of social science.

Blumer (1966) provides a theoretical link between Meadian social psychology and the kind of situational sociology that evolved in the previous chapter. Furthermore, his work is rich in methodological implications. In his 1956 article "Sociological Analysis and the 'Variable,'" Blumer argues not simply that we need to get away from bivariate analysis. Most social scientists would agree with that. Instead, he is convinced that we need to get away from the very idea of variables, and very few social scientists would agree with that. Let us consider his reasoning.

The Legacy of Blumer

Blumer's thesis is a familiar one in other contexts. For example, sociologists have traditionally clung to an antireductionist argument (in part, we suppose, out of disciplinary self-preservation), whether it is the classic Durkheimian position that a social fact is a reality *sui generis,* not of a kind with the psychological facts to which some would reduce it, or a more modern C. Wright Mills (1959) distinction between private troubles and public issues. An image of the social world as consisting of a set of discrete variables that can be isolated from one another is, according to Blumer, a form of reductionism. In "Sociological Analysis and the 'Variable'" (1956) his opening paragraphs are misleading and beside the point he is trying to make. In them he grumbles about using the wrong kind of variables, not clearly enough identifying them, the fact that they are historically bound, that they tend to be unstable in their empirical reference (as a result of arbitrary operational definitions), or that they deal with class terms that are tied in with the local conditions they study. It is not until he finishes what appears to us to be a digression along these lines that he shifts ground and challenges variable analysis per se. He begins his basic argument, and the one relevant to our purposes, when he raises the "important question of how well variable analysis is suited to the study of human group life" (p. 685).

It is the process of interpretation—of defining the situation—that Blumer believes is overlooked in variable analysis. In Chapter 10 we observed how alterations in the actor's definition of the situation appear to influence actions or sentiments. The evidence is supportive of Blumer's basic image of human behavior and social processes:

> Our world consists of innumerable objects . . . each of which has a meaning on the basis of which we act toward it. . . . We can and, I think, must look upon human group life as chiefly a vast interpretative process in which people, singly and collectively, guide themselves by defining the objects, events, and situations which they encounter. (p. 686)

Blumer's image is not restricted to minute interpersonal influences, but is extended to large organizations, institutions, and social change as well. If, procedurally, in our efforts to analyze human group life, we take this interpretive framework into account, then variable analysis becomes questionable. It does so because it is not the variable as objectively defined by the scientist that exerts influence on the action; to the contrary, *it is the actor's interpretation of what that variable means that is related to action*. Clearly, the same variable may be interpreted differently by different categories of people and sometimes by different individuals. Furthermore, it may be interpreted differently by the same people at different times.

Outcomes, as we perceive them, are not the consequence of the play of certain objective variables; they are the consequence of the actor's interpretation of such variables or social objects. This argument underlies our discussion of prediction in Chapter 4: The relationship between an "independent" and a "dependent" variable by design ignores the basic interpretive process. In employing that relationship, we blind ourselves deliberately to the locus of the action. What remains is the sometimes useful, but hardly scientific model of human behavior based on input and output alone. In our quest of understanding, it is indeed what happens in between that counts.

Let us again emphasize that, even though Blumer's examples are all bivariate, this is not an argument against bivariate analysis. Its logic extends to multivariate analysis as well. Witness, for example, Wicker's (1971) study of the relationship between attitudes toward church and church-related activities. He finds that even when a number of other variables are controlled and collectively taken into account, 75 percent of behavioral variance remains unaccounted for by attitudinal responses.

One can see Blumer's perspective clearly reflected, for example, in Aaron Cicourel's (1967) approach to problems of fertility and population control. Cicourel uses gross demographic data to provide preliminary cues for the location of the action. For final cues to problems of population control, Cicourel turns to definitions of the situation by husbands and wives—the actors who are most responsible for making babies. In doing his research, Cicourel treats with respect Blumer's argument that the "intervening interpretation is essential to the outcome" (1956, p. 687). Variable analysis assumes that the independent variable predetermines its own outcome: the dependent variable. The rhetoric implies as much. But if the meaning is conferred on the variable by the actor, then it is to that semantic process that we must turn if we are to understand what is happening.

Blumer considers the possibility of treating this intervening interpretive process as a variable in its own right—an intervening variable. This is possible as long as we do not forget that it is this intervening process that is the key to the action. It is not simply a link between the independent and the dependent variables, it is the central subject of research. In terms of our own problem, it then becomes clear that it is inappropriate to view the initial *sentiments* and the ultimate *acts* as the objects of study. The simple relationship between words and deeds, attitudes and behaviors, verbalizations and actions, is no longer the question to which we address ourselves. It becomes, literally, what's in between that counts!

A Small Step Forward:
The Discovery of "Intervening Variables"

Since the midsixties there has been, among students of the attitude-behavior relationship, a growing awareness of "what's in between." Although it remains couched in terms of variable analysis, it is a significant step forward. Scholars began to concentrate less on the sentiments-acts dichotomy (the input-output model) and more on such intervening processes as "social constraint" (DeFriese and Ford 1969; Warner and DeFleur 1969; Frideres, Warner, and Albrecht 1971), "salience" (DeFriese and Ford 1969), "reference groups" (Fendrich 1967b; Acock and DeFleur, 1972), "social distance" (Warner and DeFleur 1969), "commitment" (Fendrich 1967a), public and private conditions (Albrecht, DeFleur, and Warner 1972), the opportunity to do the action or express the sentiment, and what might generally be termed actor competence, including both knowledge of how to behave and ability to implement that knowledge (Ehrlich 1969). Reflecting the awareness that was developing at the time, and most closely approximating what Blumer intends by the definitional process, is Albrecht's (1973) work in the early seventies. It focused on the relationship between verbalizations and the expectations of significant others. Some thirty years after LaPiere's classic study, researchers were beginning to understand that the independent variable (sentiments) has very little if anything to do with the dependent variable (acts). It is to the complex interpretive process that these studies were turning.

We will consider this new wave of research below. It does not represent the subtle alteration in perspective that Blumer demands. It does, however, begin to focus on what happens in between. According to Blumer, the act of interpretation simply cannot be converted into a variable—intervening or otherwise:

> One cannot, with any sense, characterize the act of interpretation in terms of the interpretation which it constructs; one cannot take the product to stand for the process. Nor can one characterize the act of interpretation in terms of what enters into it—the objects perceived, the evaluation and

assessments made of them, the cues that are suggested, the possible definitions proposed by oneself or by others. These vary from one instance of interpretation to another and, further, shift from point to point in the development of the act. This varying and shifting content offers no basis for making the act of interpretation into a variable. (1956, p. 687)

What variable analysis does is to remove or to neutralize (hold constant) the central defining process—and this is not how things happen. Returning again to our own problem, it can be argued that we needed first to confirm the fact that variable analysis is inappropriate. Blumer does concede that there is a legitimate place for and use of variable analysis in studying those areas where the interpretive process is at a minimum. In fact, variable analysis helps us to locate such areas. In like manner, it seems to us that it helps us locate areas where the interpretive process is critical. These are areas where we find the relationship between variables to be highly unstable and to alter radically under different conditions. This is precisely what we do find when we look at evidence that has now accumulated relating sentiments to acts (e.g., Wicker 1969; F. P. Pestello and F. G. Pestello 1991; F. G. Pestello and F. P. Pestello 1991). This is, in part, what we had in mind when we suggested in Chapter 3 that perhaps Linton Freeman's proposed moratorium on data collection should be taken seriously. At least, there is little need for further empirical demonstration that sometimes sentiments and acts are in accord and sometimes they are not.

The kind of data that are required is of a very different order. They are data that inform us on the nature of the process that occurs in between. Once we can sort out those instances where sentiments and acts are related from those instances where the relationship is nonexistent or unstable, we can assume that variable analysis may be appropriate for the former group and turn our attention to the unrelated or differentially related instances, of which there appear to be very many. It is in these cases that, as Blumer suggests, we need to study how things come about, rather than the relationship of fragments to one another. This is not an easy undertaking with our present modes of analysis. Let us consider the hypothetical instance where a citizen is asked in an interview if he or she would act in some manner to assist a stranger who was being mugged. The citizen responds affirmatively. But we cannot check that response against behavior unless an opportunity arises for the citizen to observe a mugging.

In the late 1960s Ehrlich responded to us (Deutscher 1966) and others who were arguing that behavior could not be predicted from attitudes. Ehrlich maintained that "the evidence for inconsistency can be rejected on both methodological and conceptual grounds" (1969, p. 29). He makes a number of good observations. Much of the insight he provides has to do with intervening variables. One of those to which he directs our attention is opportunity, reminding us that not everyone has the opportunity to follow words with actions. Is it inconsistent that actions do not follow words, since the opportunity does not present itself? That hardly seems reasonable.

Ehrlich also reminds us that even if the citizen does have the opportunity to act, knowledge for action may be lacking. That is, one needs to be able to conjure up something to do or else he or she may end up standing helplessly by as the stranger gets mugged. Is this inconsistent? That doesn't seem a reasonable interpretation either. Ehrlich continues to remind us of other intervening factors. The pathetic person, having committed verbally and having the opportunity to act and knowing what to do, may still turn out to be incompetent. In the haste to be helpful she or he may slip and be knocked unconscious or engage in any other amount of well-intentioned but inconsequential bumbling while the mugging is successfully completed.

Nor is this the end of what can happen in between. Consider Milgram's observation of a direct relationship between the callousness of a subject administering a shock and the physical remoteness from the "learner" who is getting blasted. Although there is little doubt about the influence of proximity on behavior, its influence varies under different conditions. In interpersonal situations, Milgram finds an inverse relationship between proximity and callousness. Ransford's (1968) data on intergroup relations confirm Milgram's association by demonstrating that isolation from whites increased the willingness of blacks to take violent action in the Watts riots.

From Milgram's evidence we might infer that people who say they will help and find themselves in close proximity to the victim are more likely to help than those who are more remotely located from the mugging. A final intervening variable is suggested by Darley and Latané (1968) in observations made under conditions similar to our hypothetical case. Their work suggests that the likelihood of a bystander assisting a stranger in trouble is a function of the number of bystanders. Respondents who indicated they would help may find themselves observing a mugging along with many other witnesses, and honestly think they should help, and probably would, except that there are lots of other people who can do it, so it really seems unnecessary.

When we come to understand why persons do not act as they talk, the discrepancy is no longer an inconsistency. The process of exploring the actor's perception of the situation clarifies the actor's logic. The dimensions used in the hypothetical example above were considered as if they occurred in sequence. But in everyday social processes they might appear in almost any order. Furthermore, they would probably criss-cross each other, as well as other dimensions, before any outcome could be determined. Under such conditions it makes no sense to continue asking what the relationship is between sentiments and acts. It becomes necessary to focus on the intervening process. But how does one go about understanding this messy, complicated, unordered process, which consists largely of unspoken definitions by the actor?

Ehrlich and most other contemporary researchers insist that we simply need to improve upon the standard methodology in order to fully understand the attitude-behavior link. As we elaborate in the following two chapters when discussing the current state of research, these improvements involve the inclusion of relevant social and situational intervening variables, and refining variable measurement. Blumer, however, insists that refinements in variable analysis will never allow for an understanding of the interpretive process:

> The very features which give variable analysis its high merit—qualitative constancy of the variables, their clean-cut simplicity, their ease of manipulation as a sort of free counter, their ability to be brought into decisive relation—are the features that lead variable analysis to gloss over the character of the real operating factors in group life, and the real interaction and relations between such factors. (1956, p. 689)

He provides a hint of the methodology necessary to understand this process when he touches on procedures:

> This procedure is to approach the study of group activity through the eyes and experience of the people who have developed the activity. Hence, it necessarily requires an intimate familiarity with this experience and with the scenes of its operation. It uses broad and interlacing observations and not narrow and disjunctive observations. (p. 689)

It is no accident that participant-observation techniques are closely related to symbolic-interactionist theory. If an observer can gain intimate knowledge of the processes of social life as those who live it see them, then it becomes possible to understand this interpretive area between the independent and the dependent variables. Most other techniques in social science assume a fragmented, variable-laden world, which can be understood by hooking up the fragments in an input-output manner. To the extent that Blumer's perception is correct, social science will have to rethink its methodology and manufacture a new set of methods. For under the conditions described by Blumer, variable analysis, as we presently understand and employ it, is useful only in certain routine, highly stable areas of social life. It is true that some objects have a relatively fixed and standardized meaning—they have common shared interpretations. This permits variable analysis in such instances as long as we recognize their transiency: If common meaning can be agreed upon, it can also be redefined. What this seems to us to imply is that our current methods are more likely to be appropriate (1) in small, simple, homogeneous, stable societies and (2) in the study of stable institutionalized forms of social life. In large complex, heterogeneous, changing societies it is unlikely that variable analysis is useful in any but a preliminary manner or in residual areas of social life where consensus survives and change is minimal. Traditional methods may be retained in a future social science as detecting or problem-locating devices, largely exploratory and parameter setting, or for the analysis of the remaining fragments of a once larger consensus.

It is difficult to disagree with Blumer when he insists that "the process of interpretation is not inconsequential or pedantic. It operates too centrally in group and individual experience to be put aside as being of incidental interest" (1956, p. 688). It was the interpretive process that Pavlov identified with language and that he saw as messing things up when, in our research, we treat human beings like other animals. Whether we accept Pavlov's concern for "the word" intervening between stimulus and response, or whether we prefer Blumer's notion of an "interpretive process," makes little difference. What is important is that something happens between the input and the output and, in attempting to understand human behavior and social processes, it is that something that must become the object of our studies. What are the chances that future research may recognize this? That is the question that launches Chapter 12.

12

Rising Expectations and Later Disappointments: Research into the 1980s

The Hopeful Signs of Research in the Late Sixties and the Early Seventies

At the time that *What We Say/What We Do* was being completed, some encouraging lines of research were beginning to pay attention to the "in-between" process. Among the encouraging signs of the late sixties were James Fendrich's 1967 publications. To the extent that Fendrich's work was typical of what was happening during those closing years of the sixties, things were looking up. Taking his cue from Linn (1965), Fendrich (1967a, p. 348) is primarily concerned with intervening definitions of the situation, rather than a primitive straight-line notion of cause-and-effect prediction. Fendrich finds that attitudes explain only a small proportion of the variance in overt behavior (12 percent) while the intervening process of "commitment" accounts for 69 percent of that variance. Further he finds that the two different definitions of the situation he imposed experimentally have markedly different consequences, "producing one set of responses that were consistent with overt behavior and one set of inconsistent responses" (Fendrich 1967a, p. 354). Fendrich recognizes that "it is dangerous to assume that participants are willing, but docile subjects in social research, rather, they are active agents who define a social situation and play what they perceive to be the appropriate role" (p. 354). He turns this observation to constructive use in designing his experiment.

His other 1967 paper represents a further effort to escape what he calls "theoretical monism"—the idea that "one independent variable can account for all the variance in the dependent variable" (Fendrich 1967b, p. 960). In that paper he presents four possible theoretical models relating reference group behavior to racial attitudes and overt behavior. The one that his data appear to support suggests that reference group behavior determines both racial attitudes and overt behavior, while racial attitudes simultaneously act as an independent determinant of overt behavior. That paper represents an important movement from description of relationships to explanation of relationships.

It is interesting that DeFriese and Ford (1969) report a field study two years later that confirms the theoretical model proposed by Fendrich, although they are apparently unaware of his paper. They interpret their data as suggesting that attitudes are indeed directly related to behaviors, but so too are reference group perspectives and it is more expedient to use indices of the latter. Although Fendrich's experimental evidence was weak, this field confirmation provides a degree of convergence that enhances its credibility.

Warner and DeFleur, writing in 1969, point out that some students assume a necessary relationship between attitude and behavior while others assume independence between them. But the accumulating data seem not to allow either of these positions; instead, "the results strongly suggest that such interactional concepts as norms, roles, group memberships, subcultures, etc., pose *contingent* conditions which can modify the relationship between attitudes and action" (p. 154, emphasis in original). They are convinced that an adequate theory of attitude must "take into account the intervening situational variables which modify the relationship between attitudes and action" (p. 154).

Although this position is a long way from Blumer's insistence that the intervening process is the legitimate and appropriate object of study in itself, it is, nevertheless, an improvement over the older stance, which searched for a simple relationship between an independent and a dependent variable. The two intervening variables that Warner and DeFleur seek to control are "social constraint" and "social distance." The latter is of particular interest since it would become the theme of a number of studies during the ensuing years. But the idea of social constraints is also interesting because it illustrates some of the problems that result from attempts to treat the intervening processes as an intervening variable. In a sense the whole intervening process can be described as one of social constraint, and almost anything that influences the expression of a sentiment or an act can be subsumed under social constraint: reference groups, significant others, its public or private nature (disclosure), or perceptions of social distance.

Warner and DeFleur borrow their definition of social constraint directly from Durkheim's conception of a collective conscience. This more deterministic Durkheimian perspective brings them into sharp contrast with the more voluntaristic, pragmatic perspective of the symbolic interactionists: For example, "Sociologists hold it to be axiomatic that a person acting in relation to others is directly and indirectly compelled to *behave as others expect*" (p. 155, emphasis in original). This has been the dominant sociological perspective, but the symbolic interactionists, reflecting the pragmatic philosophy of the Chicago school, would never choose such a word as *compelled*. Blumer, we suspect, would have stated the "axiom" in a fundamentally different way—something like: In attempting to construct a line of action, a person must *take into account* the expectations of others. Whether or not the actor properly assesses those expectations, chooses to conform or deviate from them, is capable of carrying through intentions, and other such contingencies are the stuff out of which inconsistencies between sentiments and acts are made.

We want only to highlight the fundamental differences between "to be compelled to behave as others expect" and "to take into account what others expect." Central to their research is Warner and DeFleur's notion of the relation between a social-psychological self and "others" in the definition of the social situation. Although they miss it completely, they do skirt very close to Blumer's formulation: "[T]he presence of others, either in the immediate sense or in the actor's psychological definition of the situation, exerts pressure to act in accordance with what those others are perceived to feel as appropriate and desirable conduct" (p. 155). It is the element of a compelling drive to conform that is absent in Thomas's notion of the definition of the situation and Mead's notion of the significant other.

Throughout this volume the dimension of private and public opinions and actions has intruded as a central theme of our discussion. It is also the central theme of Warner and DeFleur's 1969 article. What they suggest is that social constraint is a more powerful influence on the expression of an attitude or the performance of an act under public than it is under private conditions. Like Ehrlich, they use the term *disclosure* to refer to what happens when the actors are aware that others will know of their attitude or act. As they put it, how do actors behave when they know their behavior is under "surveillance" in contrast to the situation in which they believe anonymity is preserved? This matter of surveillance is seen by Mayhew (1968) in a field study as the major controlling factor in constraining women to abide by the birth control proscriptions of their churches. His logic is that peer surveillance is provided when people marry coreligionists. The church, in the person of the spouse, is exercising surveillance over sex behavior. On the other hand, women who marry outsiders can practice birth control because of the absence of surveillance by coreligionists. In this sense, Mayhew argues that people comply with their church proscriptions of birth control in accordance with how public (observable) their sex behavior is. He finds that verbal acceptance of the belief—the religious proscription—does not predict high fertility. What does predict fertility differentials is the intervening variable of surveillance of sex behavior by one's own co-religionists. Mayhew's analysis suggests that there are reasonable empirical grounds for considering, as Warner and DeFleur do, this matter of surveillance.

In their piece of the late 1960s, Warner and DeFleur were beginning to focus on the complex intervening process as the molder of eventual outcomes. There is not only a suggestion that the process is a total entity in and of itself, but of equal importance, a recognition that it must be viewed from the perspective of the actor. We have here an awareness of the need for a phenomenological view:

> [S]social distance, social constraint, and attitude form a single system of interactional considerations, a *gestalt*, confronting the actor. That is, they are experienced by a subject as a single system of variables impinging upon his decisions concerning acceptance or rejection of the attitude object. (p. 156)

What is suggested here is that people may not think of an act in terms of "variables" at all. Rather, they think and act and take into account the totality of the situation as they size it up!

Variables may be useful functions for facilitating the scientist's work, but they do not exist in the everyday world of authentic human behavior. Without reviewing the design details of the Warner-DeFleur study, which deals with racial attitudes and behaviors, we can see that its most significant feature is that its factorial design allows the analyst to identify sources of variance that derive from the interaction between and among variables. With this design it is no longer necessary to restrict our conception of human behavior as resulting from the action of isolated variables. They are still variables, but at least they are now working in conjunction with each other. The design also encourages the analyst to keep separate the two kinds of consistency and the two kinds of inconsistency identified in Chapter 9.

Warner and DeFleur (1969) do find that the factor of social constraint (the threat of public disclosure) has a powerful effect on both highly and mildly prejudiced subjects. Furthermore, that effect is different for these two groups of subjects. The complex interactions they discover seem more closely to approximate what happens in everyday life than the earlier simplistic variable studies: "Since the requested act was one generally disapproved within relevant norms, the exposure to potential surveillance provided by the condition of high social constraint produced inconsistency between attitudes and action for the least prejudiced subjects" (p. 164). This inconsistency is sharply contrasted with the situation for the most prejudiced subjects, where "a condition of high social constraint tended to produce substantial consistency between attitudes and action" (p. 164).

Shortly after the publication of the 1969 article, Warner and DeFleur and their associates for the first time undertook to extend their research comparatively. In a series of papers they have reported experiments dealing not with attitudes and behaviors of whites toward blacks, but with attitudes and behaviors of students toward marijuana smoking (Albrecht, DeFleur, and Warner 1972). Their work uniformly reflects an abandonment of the view that a direct relationship necessarily exists between attitudes and behaviors and adopts a concomitant emphasis on the intervening process. It is of considerable interest that, having abandoned their earlier perspective, they find that there sometimes is a direct relationship—that people do under some conditions act in accord with their sentiments. The conditions under which such concordance might be expected have been illustrated as well as theoretically articulated by Blumer (1948).

By 1972, Albrecht, DeFleur, and Warner were beginning to take a phenomenological perspective in their experiments on marijuana use. They speculate that a primary source of error in predicting the effect of disclosure on the sentiments-acts relationship may result from a lack of information about how subjects define the situation. Citing W. I. Thomas, they observe that the crucial factor affecting the individual's response is not the group's position, but the individual's perception of the group's position (Albrecht, DeFleur, and Warner 1972). As the researchers begin to treat this position with respect, they must inevitably also begin to move away from concern with variables and concern with the attitude-behavior relationship, toward an interest in the intervening process as the object of study. This new slant leads them to the observation that it is what's in between that counts. And, in fact, the kinds of information these investigators see as essential data become phenomenological: Data are obtained from the vantage point of the subject! [For an extensive discussion and critique of their conclusions see *What We Say/What We Do* (pp. 276–80).]

Whether the problem be one of race, drugs, or anything else, it would be unwise to ignore Milton Rokeach's persistent plea that it isn't only intervening variables that must be considered. There is also the whole complex paraphernalia of attitudes, beliefs, and orientations we all carry around with us. It may be that, other things being equal, prejudiced whites will reject blacks as associates, but the facts of life are that other things never are equal.

Some psychologists focus more directly on the intervening process and on situational factors and even on the crucial distinction between public and private expressions. In a summary article Allen (1965) reached the conclusion that to establish a relationship between an input variable and an output variable is not a very informative accomplishment. Thus, two people appear to be conforming, let us say, publicly. One has private beliefs that lead to this public conformity. The other is conforming publicly under some form of social pressure not because of private beliefs, but in spite of them. These two persons who express the same public opinion certainly cannot be expected to act the same in private and may vary in public depending upon the nature of the perceived social constraints. The reverse is also possible: Apparent differences may cloak basic similarities just as apparent similarities can cloak basic differences.

The issue of public and private conformity becomes even clearer when we consider Allen's analysis of Asch-type experiments. Asch had his subjects provide judgments on the comparative length of lines in the presence of confederates who, by plan, judge aloud that longer lines are shorter and shorter lines are longer. Unlike the Sherif autokinetic experiments, the Asch model deliberately leads the subjects to accept factually erroneous conclusions by the group. Allen suggests that conformity under these conditions is purely public, with private views not being altered at all. He uses Asch's own interview data as suggesting that "actual change" rarely occurs. Although subjects publicly agree with the group, they remain privately certain that the group is wrong (Asch, 1956). Luchins and Luchins (1955, 1961) further pursued this by readministering the entire set of stimuli (lines) to subjects after they had taken the basic experiment and conformed to the majority. This time the subjects made no objectively incorrect choices. Their second study produced less clear results. Taking the stimuli in private immediately after the experiment, the subjects tended to provide the same erroneous results as they had under social pressure, but one day later these same subjects made no errors.

However we prefer to see them, as intervening variables or an intervening process, it is becoming increasingly apparent that the things that occur in between require attention if we are to understand more fully the sometimes lack of relationship between sentiments and acts. For example, Ehrlich (1969) correctly suggests that discrepancies may result from ignorance, lack of logical discipline, or educational deficiency. But he fails to note that, on the other hand, the best educated, logically trained scientists can behave contrary to their beliefs and knowledge. In smoking, for example, there appears to be no relation between knowledge and behavior. There is evidence that certain cancer research scientists who link smoking with lung cancer still maintain their smoking behavior (Lawton and Goldman 1958). Baer concludes in his comparison of several types of smokers and nonsmokers that "present smokers who smoked cigarettes only, would like to have stopped smoking, believed they smoked too much, believed in a relationship between smoking and lung cancer, believed in a reduction in life expectancy from smoking" (1966, pp. 69–70).

What is true of cigarette smokers may be equally true of the inconsistency between knowledge and activity common to many areas of habitual or pleasurable behavior. Such behavior may have known consequences ranging from a high risk of contracting a sexually transmitted disease to a high risk of accidental death. Psychoanalytic theory might permit us to avoid confronting such knotty problems with notions about self-destructive behavior, a death wish, or other inferential explanations. We suspect, however, that Jeremy Bentham's quaint idea of a hedonistic calculus makes more sense. The smoker continues to smoke against the odds like the reckless driver continues to speed against the odds because both types of behavior are fun. The actors' assumption is that the long shot will pay off. Far from wanting to die, many people want to eat their cake and have it too (see Katz 1988).

Certainly there are social constraints that intervene between a sentiment and a related act. But to name the process in that manner brings us closer to understanding human behavior and social processes only to the extent that it directs our attention to the proper locus of exploration. It is important that we recognize that it is not input and output or independent and dependent variables or stimulus and response that is our proper concern. It is more likely what's in between that counts. Of all of the reasonable alternatives Ehrlich provides for us in seeking intervening variables, we think that *opportunity* deserves to be singled out for special attention. Perhaps we are influenced by the large impact that little idea has had on our understanding some kinds of juvenile delinquency [Cloward and Ohlin 1960; see also Coleman (1989) on white-collar crime]. The fact is that regardless of all other social, psychological, and physiological forces, an opportunity must be present before we can behave in a given manner and the absence of such an opportunity severely limits the likelihood of such behavior. Opportunity is, then, a condition that is always salient to human behavior.

The absence of opportunity to behave in an approved manner can be illustrated with the results of an educational program for soldiers who are in prison. Imprisoned soldiers who have gone over the hill (i.e., who are absent without leave) may well become convinced as a consequence of an educational program that going over the hill is not a reasonable thing to do. They may even honestly intend to refrain from doing so in the future. But when there is trouble at home and they cannot get a leave, they apparently continue to go over the hill—regardless of their good intentions (Allen, Simonsen, and Vetter 1971). Generally this series of reports on the results of educational programs for imprisoned soldiers shows a remarkable change in attitudes as well as remarkable changes in a wide variety of observable military behaviors. However, 40 percent of these men fail to report back to duty after release. Comparisons between these failures and the successes, on both attitudinal and behavioral items, show no difference. It can be said that they did not have the opportunity to act according to their intentions. Under such conditions, it is the intervening situation with its lack of opportunity that requires attention.

Once these intervening processes are understood, the discrepancies between sentiments and acts need no longer be viewed as inconsistent. Our understanding has removed the designation *inconsistent*; it has not, however, removed the discrepancy. The fact is that people sometimes do not do as they say and it is important to be attentive to such discrepancies. Although they may sometimes be more apparent than real, they are sometimes very real. Rather than attempting to explain such discrepancies away as "spurious," it is gratifying to recognize them for what they are and to begin to understand the processes that account for them. That is the function of science.

The Disappointment of Research in the Eighties

In the preface we noted that in 1986 we undertook a review of the attitude-behavior literature in order to see what advances had taken place in the field since the publication of *What We Say/What We Do*. We did a comprehensive search, trying to locate all articles published on the topic in the four preceding years. One of the things that we had hoped to determine was the extent to which the hopeful signs of the late 1960s and early 1970s had borne fruit. Many of the conclusions we were able to draw were published in two articles, one of which focused on attitude conceptualization and measurement. Our methodology is more fully described there (F. P. Pestello and F. G. Pestello 1991). The other article focused on behavioral dimensions (F. G. Pestello and F. P. Pestello 1991). In this section and throughout the next chapter we will elaborate upon what we found.

It was immediately clear to us that interest in the area burgeoned in the middle 1960s and voluminous research has been published on the topic since then (Dawes and Smith 1985, p. 555). We discovered that Schuman and Johnson (1976), and other social scientists who are convinced that attitudes and behavior are related, argue that studies that fail to show a relationship are technically flawed. Fishbein and Ajzen state this position clearly: "[A]ppropriate measures of attitude *are* related to appropriate measures of behavior" (1975, p. 352, emphasis in original). Common flaws they identify are failure to measure variables at the same level of specificity and failure to use multiple-act criteria. Hill reaches similar conclusions: "Moderate relations between attitudes and behaviors have been found consistently when attitudinal measures and behavioral criteria correspond on the dimensions of target [at which action is directed] and action" (1981, p. 356).

Although we were optimistic about the trends observed in the early 1970s, our optimism soon turned to dismay. Several models specifying the attitude-behavior relationship began to emerge in the mid-1970s. The most widely cited and applied is the theory of reasoned action (Fishbein and Ajzen 1975; Fishbein 1980). Fifty-two of the sixty-two articles we were able to find on the attitude-behavior relationship cite the work of Fishbein or Ajzen and Fishbein. All of this work was reported after their model was developed. Most of these fifty-two articles are either a test of, response to, comparison with, or elaboration of the reasoned action model.

The model is a psychological one, which relegates social and situational influences to an antecedent position. Two assumptions undergird the theory. The first is human rationality. Actors are assumed to rationally process and use information in choosing their actions. The second assumption pertains to volition. According to the model, one can only expect behavior that is under the voluntary control of the actor to be influenced by the actor's attitudes.

The theory of reasoned action posits a four-stage, recursive model. The immediate determinant of behavior is one's intention to engage in that behavior. Fishbein and Ajzen (1975) argue that the correlation between intention and behavior should approach unity, if nothing intervenes to alter intention.

Intentions are hypothesized to be contingent upon two variables, attitudes and subjective norms. Attitudes are positive or negative evaluations toward performing the "target" act (Fishbein 1980, p. 67). Subjective norms are the actor's perception of how relevant others would view the performance of the behavior in question by the actor. Fishbein (1980) argues that the relative importance of the two variables depends on the intention under investigation.

Beliefs provide the foundation for attitudes and subjective norms. One's personal beliefs about the behavior predict attitudes about performing the behavior. One's beliefs about how others would view one performing the behavior shape subjective norms. It is in this single variable, subjective norms, that all pertinent social and contextual factors are captured.

The model is parsimonious: Beliefs determine attitudes and subjective norms, which in turn determine behavioral intentions, which finally determine behavior. Because the model focuses upon cognitive precursors to behavior, self-administered questionnaires and interviews have remained the dominant means of data collection. We dwell on this "model" in such detail not because of its merits, but because it has clearly dominated recent publications in the area of our concern.

Some contemporary research does display a greater theoretical concern with the influence of context, or situation, on the attitude-behavior relationship. As we would expect, findings consistently support the influence of intrapersonal and situational variables on the relationship between attitudes and behaviors (Sherman and Fazio 1983; Liska 1984). Sherman and Fazio (1983), in a review of research on attitudes and traits as predictors of behavior, discuss situational factors, and person by situation interactions, which moderate the attitude-behavior relationship. Snyder and Kendzierski (1982b) attribute some of the observed consistency between attitudes and behaviors to the fact that individuals choose situations that will allow them to perform behaviors consistent with their attitudes. Fazio and his collaborators (1982, 1983, 1984) conclude that it is a subject's definition of the immediate situation that links attitudes to behavior. Budd and Spencer (1984) provide evidence that high latitude of rejection, centrality, and certainty of attitudes produce more attitude-consistent behavior. Self-interest, self-focused attention, and self-analysis have also been found to be important mediating variables (Sivacek and Crano 1982; Gibbons and Wicklund 1982; Wilson, Dunn, Bybee, Hyman, and Rotondo 1984; Ajzen et al. 1982), as has a perception of moral obligation (Gorsuch and Ortberg 1983; Pagel and Davidson 1984; and Kantola, Syme, and Nesdale 1983). Other researchers have found that direct experience stabilizes the formation of attitudes (Fazio et al. 1982, 1983, 1984; Borgida and Campbell 1982; Raden 1985) and that attitudes formed as a result of direct experience increase their accessibility (Raden 1985).

Liska (1984) applauds such research on "other" variables. He argues, however, that it has not adequately been incorporated into attitude-behavior models, because the dominant Fishbein-Ajzen model "treats these conditions more like methodological nuisances to be controlled or randomized, rather than as conceptual issues, the model neither guides nor organizes the extensive research aimed at identifying them" (p. 69). Researchers have tried to address the inadequacy of the Fishbein-Ajzen model (e.g., Liska 1984; Bagozzi and Burnkrant 1985; Budd and Spencer 1984), but the large number of moderating variables potentially yields cumbersome models that are difficult to calculate (Liska 1984, p. 70).

As we noted earlier in this chapter, a more fundamental problem with the "other variables" approach is that no study can include all possible modifying variables. Thus, researchers search for a manageable set of variables that will make clear the nature and extent of the attitude-behavior relationship (Liska 1984). The quest for the appropriate set of modifying variables is an effort to adequately define the interactional context. Lalljee, Brown, and Ginsberg explain that this effort is futile:

> Specifying context seems impossible since the features of a context relevant to its evaluation are indefinite. Further, if we are concerned with a particular person's attitude, the specification of context would be incomplete unless it took into account the motives of the actor. (1984, p. 238)

These researchers, like some of those of the late sixties and early seventies, are moving toward Blumer's position that the inherent problem with variable analysis is its inability to incorporate the interpretive quality of human interaction. People define and interpret situations to give them meaning, and then act on that basis. Contexts and situations are not "neutral mediums" through which independent variables pass.

The moderating-variable approach allows researchers to incorporate measures of context without having to change their conceptualization of the problem, or adopt more time-consuming methodologies. One need only ask more questions of subjects. The modified models retain the same assumption evident in simpler precursors that a discrete set of variables allows for adequate understanding of behavioral outcomes. Models and statistical analysis become more complex, but understanding of process does not advance.

Zuckier cuts to the heart of the methodological problem in his critique of the personological orientation that dominates most social-psychological research. Behavior is reduced to an individual phenomenon, because it is easier to understand and study, but this conceptualization ignores our social nature:

> Psychologists, like laymen, have conceptualized the person as autonomous and self-contained. They have recognized, of course, that human behavior is intricately embedded in its environment and moderated by its sociocultural context. However, these powerful sociocultural influences . . . have been treated more as extraneous contingencies whose adulterating effects only obscured the picture of man's psychological processes. The discrete individual alone was the proper unit for scientific psychological

investigation, and his entanglement with the world could and should be unraveled. (1982, p. 1075)

Social psychologists are trying to filter out the contaminating world so that subjects' "true" attitudes and behaviors will be revealed. This approach disregards the fact that our thoughts and actions are based on meanings derived from and modified through interaction with others.

We believe that it is because of this approach that the attitude-behavior relationship remains a perennial problem (Liska, Felson, Chamlin, and Baccaglini 1984). We know no more about the relationship between what people say and do from the literature in attitude-behavior investigations today than we did a quarter-century ago—and we knew little then (Deutscher 1966). The concept of attitude still has not been adequately defined. The fundamental issues involved in the relationship are yet to be resolved.

Some studies do conclude that there is a close, direct attitude-behavior relationship (e.g., Jaccard and Becker 1985; Manstead, Profitt, and Smart 1983; Manstead, Plevin, and Smart 1984). There is, however, much evidence to the contrary. A number of researchers are finding that attitudes are highly unstable and add little to predicting behavior beyond knowing past behavior (Acock and Fuller 1984; see also Davidson et al. 1985; Fredericks and Dossett 1983). Many studies note that little variance in behavior is explained by their models (e.g., Baumann and Chenowith 1984; Hill et al. 1985; Kantola et al. 1982). Every study that tests the reigning model finds it in need of some sort of modification (e.g., Davis 1985; Kantola et al. 1983; Pagel and Davidson 1984; Wittenbraker, Gibbs, and Kahle 1983). While most research presumes a unidirectional causal path from attitude to behavior (frequently measured as intention), several studies suggest that under at least some conditions the relationship is reciprocal, or reversed—behavior causes attitudes (e.g., Acock and Fuller 1984; Liska et al. 1984; Stults, Messé, and Kerr 1984; Thornton, Alwin, and Camburn 1983). And no one studying attitudes and behavior is actually looking at the relationship between what people say and what they do.

There is another source of observed discrepancies, which is very different from those discussed up to this point. Recall the difficulty we had in finding appropriate names for the dimensions we have been considering in this volume. By and large it has been implied, for purposes of discussion, that we are exploring the relation between two phenomena (attitudes and behavior, words and deeds, sentiments and acts, etc.). The difficulty in naming these two phenomena reflects much more than an inconvenience; behind that difficulty lies the variety of *different phenomena* that are subsumed under the two gross categories. The confusion that results from this conceptual muddiness has consequences for understanding the relationship between what people say or think or feel and what they do. Although our earlier discussion of language broached this problem, the next chapter will consider in some detail the manner in which conceptual confusion can sometimes lead to attempts to add apples and oranges—can lead to comparing phenomena that are in fact not comparable. We now turn to the concrete issue of the building blocks of theory—to the matter of concepts and how they can be a source of confusion as well as a source of clarification.

13

Concepts and How Their Confusion Can Mess You Up

Making Distinctions and Connections

The problem of conceptual confusion stems from the fact that an individual may simultaneously or sequentially harbor a number of different orientations toward the same social object. It becomes difficult to accumulate comparative knowledge unless it is clear what kinds of orientations are being elicited and observed. This is the problem of conceptual confusion. It implies the need to make more meaningful distinctions in the connotations of words employed in interviews and research instruments. Although, like some of the methodological arguments, it suggests that some observed discrepancies are more apparent than real, it also suggests that there is a large and undifferentiated set of possible relationships between orientations toward the same phenomenon. In this chapter we will concentrate on the confusions that result when we fail to make clear conceptual distinctions.

In our earliest efforts to understand the relationship between what people do and what they say, we complained that we knew so little that we couldn't even find an adequate vocabulary to make the distinction (Deutscher 1966). At that time we were more irritated by the profusion of terms than we were aware of the confusion of concepts. At some point, however, it occurred to us that some of the studies we were attempting to analyze comparatively were dealing with different phenomena (frequently under the same name). It became increasingly clear that behavioral intentions, observed behaviors, and self-reported behaviors were not necessarily the same. It became equally clear that beliefs, aspirations, norms, values, and knowledge might possibly be unrelated or, at least, differentially related.

The distinction between attitude and behavior is vulgar! So too is the distinction between sentiments and acts, or any other that implies a dichotomy. There are many kinds of sentimental orientations, possibly as different from each other as each is from the many kinds of action orientations.

Some reputable scholars avoid this issue by classifying, as B. F. Skinner (1957) does, all orientations toward social objects as behavior. The operant-conditioning psychologists and their sociological counterparts argue that the concept of attitude is a useless fiction that can be eliminated from our conceptual repertoire. This is precisely the position Tarter eloquently advocates. From this perspective "attitudes are just another of the many hypothetical and largely unproductive mental states that behavioral scientists have tried to measure and use in prediction of overt behavior" (1970, p. 276).

Tarter would prefer to discard the "mentalistic" term *attitude*, but he recognizes that this is unrealistic in view of the vested interests and prejudices of social scientists. If some scholars would prefer that everything be seen as behavior, there are others who suggest that all orientations toward social objects be embraced by the concept of attitudes (DeFleur and Westie 1963). Although both arguments have merit, neither is ultimately very helpful. The sole achievement of this line of reasoning is to rename the study of human interaction as the study either of human behavior or of human attitudes. This is a version of the naming game that the Hugheses (1952) have described as sociological exorcism.

The creation of euphemisms, epithets, or otherwise relabeling a phenomenon has little scientific import, although it may have social value as in the case of the self-fulfilling prophecy. There is another sense in which it is not very helpful to call everything either behavior or attitudes. Concepts, if they are to be useful and informative, must distinguish among relatively homogeneous categories of phenomena. Otherwise, they cannot facilitate understanding of the relationships among such phenomena. A category makes no sense unless there are at least two of them; it cannot help us make connections when there is nothing left with which to connect. To subsume all orientations toward an object under a single conceptual umbrella is a nominalistic nullification of the problem. It is magic and not science.

It should be clear by now that the concept of a concept being purveyed here is quite different from the operational formulation originally suggested by Bridgman (1927). Bridgman's notion has been widely adopted in the social sciences because it permitted us to avoid embarrassing attempts to understand what was going on in the real world. Instead, Bridgman argues for the creation and study of artificial worlds because they are simpler, clearer, more controllable, and conform to our abilities to measure them: "In general, we mean by any concept nothing more than a set of operations: the concept is synonymous with the corresponding set of operations" (p. 5). It is assumed in this chapter that a concept is synonymous not with a corresponding set of operations, but with the recurring, empirically observable phenomena of everyday life to which it refers, which it identifies, and which it distinguishes from unlike phenomena and relates to like phenomena.

A phenomenological perspective suggests that the scientific definition of concepts is unimportant relative to the definitions employed by the people we are interested in learning about. No effort is made here toward attempting to order a scientific concept of attitude or of behavior. Instead, what is suggested is that a great amount of confusion and misinformation results when we assume that people are providing us with a single datum because we have a name for it. The important variations in definition are those employed by our respondents. This is true not only because people shift perspectives as a result of subtle verbal clues (e.g., believe, think, expect, like, approve), but also because the range, intensity, and intervals respondents customarily employ may differ from the ranges, intensities, and intervals imposed by social scientists in their scaling devices (Jordan 1965).

Occasionally a thoughtful sociologist recognizes this problem. Shalom Schwartz, for example, in his efforts to relate attitudes and behaviors of people regarding the donation of organs for transplanting, writes: "I am now working on a scale to measure sense of moral obligation to serve as a transplant donor. . . . This normative scale runs from −1 'obligation *not* to,' to 0 'no obligation,' through 5 'strong obligation.' This seems closer to the reality of people's natural conceptual scales" (1969, personal communication).

On Adding Apples and Oranges

The distinction between covert sentiments and overt acts, although a necessary starting point, remains a first-order distinction of the grossest kind. There is a large number of possible cognitive, verbal, and overt action orientations toward the same object, whether that object be a black person, a spouse, or a political candidate. The extent and direction of covariance among these multiple orientations remains as problematic as the relationship between the components of the basic dichotomy—sentiments and acts. If for no other reason, the fact that the relationships among these various orientations are unknown makes it imperative that we clearly distinguish which of them we are dealing with in our investigations. Although it would be helpful if there were a standard usage of such terms as *values, norms, beliefs, aspirations,* and *opinions,* this is not the central problem. The problem is to make the necessary distinctions between orientations and to understand what kind of orientation we intend to tap and what kind of orientation our respondents are providing us with.

Studies reported by Westie (1965) and Rodman (1966) illustrate our argument by documenting what happens when conceptual discrepancies are recognized. What happens is the elimination of a considerable amount of confusion in the comparisons of sets of presumably similar data. The social object in which Hyman Rodman is interested is nonlegal marital unions in Caribbean societies—especially the orientations of members of the lower classes toward such unions.

There appears to be consensus regarding the overt behavioral orientation: Such unions occur frequently among the Caribbean lower classes. The problem arises when various investigators attempt to assess "attitudes" toward this same object. A rash of contradictory and inconsistent findings is reported. Scanning reports by Rodman (1963), Blake (1955, 1958, 1961), Simey (1946), Goode (1960), Braithwaite (1957), and Hatt (1952), we find it difficult to believe that these social scientists are all talking about the same thing. And, as it turns out, they are, in fact, not talking about the same thing, although they sometimes employ the same name to refer to it. There are many possible sources of explanations for the variance found among these studies, but Rodman (1966) has isolated the one that seems to account for a great deal. *He is able to reconcile what appear at first blush to be inconsistent findings by making a simple conceptual distinction.*

The inconsistent findings discussed by Rodman result from the reports by some investigators "that within the lower class the nonlegal marital union and the resulting illegitimate children are deviant patterns, and that marriage and legitimate childbirth are normative" (1966, p. 673). Rodman points out that no distinction has been made by these analysts between preferential orientations and normative orientations. Asking people which of two alternatives is better is not the same thing as asking them if a pattern is acceptable. In order to document this observation, Rodman isolates responses from the same people to three preferential questions and to three normative questions, all referring to the same social object. "Looking at the percentages for the total sample, marriage tends to be 'favored' on the preferential questions. On the normative questions *living*—the alternative arrangement—tends to be 'favored'" (p. 676). Misunderstandings occur when inferences about norms are made from responses to preferential questions.

In Rodman's terms, an example of a preferential question is, Is it better for . . . ? An example of a normative question is, Is it all right for . . . ? To add responses to such questions is indeed to add apples and oranges. They tap different attitudinal dimensions. Furthermore, to expect comparable findings from different studies that employ one or the other type of question is to expect apples and oranges to add up to something. Perhaps they do add up to something, but the synthetic fruit has about as much basis in reality as a synthesis of different orientations toward the same social object.

A second illustration of the way in which meaningful conceptual distinctions can lead to clarification derives from Gunnar Myrdal (1944) and is reported by Frank Westie (1965). In his classic book on race of the midforties, Myrdal wondered how American whites lived with a fundamental dilemma. Westie summarizes Myrdal's concern: "Americans suffer from a basic ambivalence because they embrace, on the one hand, the Christian-democratic tenets of the 'American Creed' and, on the other, any number of unChristian and undemocratic valuations defining relations between Negroes and whites" (1965, p. 528).

Contrary to popular distortions, Myrdal did not pose a dilemma between democratic ideology and American discriminatory acts. The distinction he *discovered* and employed as the basic guideline in his analysis of American race relations was between two independent cognitive orientations: valuations and beliefs. We emphasize the word *discovered* advisedly. Myrdal did not invent concepts in the manner advocated by Bridgman. He suggested, rather, that in peoples' minds there is no necessary relationship between conceptions of what ought to be (valuations) and conceptions of what is (beliefs).

This discovery not only guides Westie's empirical research, but also provides him with a useful device for content analysis of interview probes: "[R]esponses were classified as *valuations* where they contained any 'ought to be' elements whatever, and *beliefs* where they included any statements of 'what is,' 'what was,' or conceptions of reality" (p. 530, emphasis in original). Although Westie leaves open the question of the extent to which individual Americans experience a dilemma as a result of inconsistent valuations and beliefs, his data leave little doubt that such inconsistencies occur.

Since preference (in Rodman's terms) is frequently directed toward a prejudice orientation in our society, individuals who find themselves agreeing with specific nonprejudiced orientations find themselves in an awkward position. The more general faith in the platitudes of the democratic ideology is also "preferred." Thus, from one perspective, consistency means agreeing with both preferred positions—specific prejudice and general egalitarianism. This, of course, is not what the social scientist and the logician define as consistency. *Their* definition of consistency is perceived by respondents as somehow deviant and requiring explanation. In effect, what is consistent from one perspective is inconsistent from another.

Just as Westie demonstrates that sometimes there is a critical difference between actors' beliefs about what is and their beliefs about what ought to be, sometimes there is a clear difference between beliefs and facts. Lipset provides one example of how people's cherished beliefs about prejudice are not affected by indisputable evidence to the contrary:

> Polls taken among contributors to the San Francisco Jewish Community Federation have found that one third agree that a Jew can not be elected to Congress from San Francisco. A poll reported such results in 1985 when all three members of Congress from contiguous districts in or adjacent to the city were Jewish, as were the two State Senators, the mayor, and a considerable part of the city council. (1990, p. 22)

We have referred above to the simple dichotomous distinctions clarified by Rodman and Westie, as first-order ones. As we said, the complex interrelationship among various orientations remains a mystery. We do not know what the matrix of such a set of orientations might look like (much less how that matrix shifts under varying conditions). We have been inclined to treat such orientations as interchangeable parts in social science research—and sometimes they may be (Wicker 1971; Cagle and Deutscher 1970). But, as Rodman and Westie testify, there is evidence that sometimes they are not. Rarely does a research report provide us with an indication of what the matrix of relationships among several of these dimensions might look like.

In their analysis of white Brazilian students' responses to queries about blacks, Bastide and van den Berghe (1957) supply one such matrix. In *What We Say/What We Do* we adapted the titles of classification of their data and then compared the matrix we developed from their data to a similar matrix reflecting the relationship among orientations toward a more mundane situation: observations of pedestrians who either conform to or violate a Don't Walk signal at an intersection (Deutscher 1973, pp. 317-19). We found that there are three orientations common to both the study employing Brazilian student respondents and the one employing American pedestrian respondents.

For both the Brazilian students and the American pedestrians beliefs and values were more highly correlated (.60 for the students and .16 for the pedestrians) than values and self-reported behavior (.51 for the students and .14 for the pedestrians), which were more highly correlated than beliefs and self-reported behavior (.25 and .06, respectively). The correlations between racial orientations in Brazil are uniformly higher than the correlations between pedestrian orientations in the United States. The fact that there are no discrepancies in the ordering of these two sets of coefficients is less important than the fact that there is no apparent contradiction between them other than their absolute size. Our purpose in noting this is only to indicate the complexity of the relationships found among various orientations toward the same social object.

We have not yet expressed our concerns with polemics on the proper definition of attitude. Thus far we have been concerned with evidence of the existence of many dimensions of human behavior, the relationships among which are unknown, but which are frequently lumped under a single rubric. Sometimes that rubric is attitude; sometimes it is something else. Nor have we expressed our concerns with the annoying lack of uniformity in the symbols assigned to the various orientations subsumed under attitudes. So what exactly is an attitude? And, for that matter, what exactly is a behavior?

In the following sections we will consider how attitudes and behavior are conceptualized by contemporary researchers. Our discussion comes largely from two recently published articles, one on the conceptualization and measurement of attitudes (F. P. Pestello and F. G. Pestello 1991), the other on the conceptualization and measurement of behavior (F. G. Pestello and F. P. Pestello 1991). Let us consider attitude first. Its conceptualization has received considerably more attention.

Attitude: Something That Cannot Be Defined

The concept of attitude has a long history in the social sciences. It was used in works of one of the founders of the field of sociology, Herbert Spencer (1862). By 1918 Thomas and Znaniecki (1918, pp. 20–86) had defined social psychology as the scientific study of attitudes (subjective dispositions). Nearly seventy-five years later, attitude remains a central variable in social-psychological theory and research. The quantity and diversity of the literature on attitudes is enormous (Fishbein 1967, p. v).

In contrast to its seeming importance, back in the mid-1950s Blumer concluded that attitude "fails miserably to meet the requirements of a scientific concept" (1955, p. 59). He drew this conclusion on the basis of three critical criteria. First, the concept is empirically ambiguous and thus pieced together through inference. What gets included in a study is decided arbitrarily on the basis of personal impressions and preconceptions of the researcher. Second, attitude is an omnibus term, and thus fails to distinguish a class of objects to which it refers. Finally, there has been no cumulative building of knowledge on what an attitude is. Based on our reading of current literature, nothing that would contradict Blumer's conclusions has happened since his observations were published.

Despite the extraordinary attention devoted to the concept, there is still no consensus on what constitutes an attitude (Fishbein and Ajzen 1972, p. 488; Hill 1981, p. 348). Social psychologists are preoccupied with determining causation "rather than with the logically prior problem of identifying, measuring, and validating the theoretical constructs that participate in causal relations" (Breckler 1984, p. 1204). Dawes and Smith's chapter on "Attitude and Opinion Measurement" (1985, pp. 509–66) in the most recent edition of *The Handbook of Social Psychology* demonstrates that attitude conceptualization and operationalization is done by fiat.

While they defend the situation, Dawes and Smith observe that social scientists often research phenomena "at great length without knowing what they're talking about. So it is with *attitude*. . . . There is little agreement about the definition of *attitude* and hence what aspects of attitudes are worth measuring" (p. 509). They go on to observe that most papers on attitude discuss the classical definitions and then conclude "with a statement of what the researcher himself or herself will mean by the term. How cumulative science can survive this Humpty Dumpty operationalism is not entirely clear" (p. 509).

Dawes and Smith were not the first to quantify the lack of consensus on the operationalization of attitudes. Based on an exhaustive review of articles published from June 1968 through December 1970, Fishbein and Ajzen "found almost 500 different operations designed to measure 'attitude'" (1972, p. 492). "Over 200 of the studies reviewed employed more than one dependent measure of an 'attitudinal' variable, and about 70 percent obtained different results when different measures were used" (p. 493).

The many definitions of attitude can be roughly categorized into either affective conceptualizations or tripartite models of affect, cognitive, and conative components (Dawes and Smith 1985, p. 510; see also Bagozzi and Burnkrant 1985; and Dillon and Kumar 1985). The most widely cited definition is Allport's, and it is an affective one. In his classic article on the topic, Allport states: *"[A]n attitude is a mental and neural state of readiness, organized through experience, exerting a directive or dynamic influence upon the individual's response to all objects and situations with which it is related"* (1935, p. 810, emphasis in original). This definition of attitudes establishes both the sentiments-acts relationship and the direction of causality.

While advocates of the tripartite conceptualization persist (e.g., Breckler 1984), there is consensus among most attitude-behavior researchers upon the essence of the affective conceptualization (Liska et al. 1984, p. 18). Fishbein and Ajzen note:

> [A]lthough definitions of attitudes vary considerably, there is general agreement that a person's attitude towards some object constitutes a predisposition on his part to respond to the object in a consistently favorable

or unfavorable manner (cf. Allport 1935). This view has led to the widespread assumption that attitudes and overt behavior are closely related to each other. (1974, p. 59)

Most studies use "general measures" of attitude (p. 59) typically obtained with traditional attitude scales. Those who develop these scales usually share conceptualizations of attitudes similar to Allport's. Thurstone, who gave birth to modern scaling, defines attitude as "the sum total of a man's inclinations and feelings, prejudices or bias, preconceived notions, ideas, fears, threats, and convictions about any specific topic" (1928, .p. 77). Conceived as an internal phenomenon, Thurstone observes that attitudes can only be measured indirectly. He states that the best way of assessing them is through the opinions one expresses (p. 78). To measure these opinions he developed an elaborate technique for constructing a scale, which was then administered to subjects by questionnaire.

Osgood and his colleagues define attitudes as "inferred states," which are "predispositions to respond, but are distinguished from other states of readiness in that they predispose toward an *evaluative* response" (Osgood, Suci, and Tannenbaum 1957, p. 189, emphasis in original). They maintain that social scientists share the view that "attitudes can be ascribed to some basic bipolar continuum with a neutral or zero point, implying that they have both direction and intensity and providing a basis for the quantitative indexing of attitudes" (pp. 189–90). Given these conditions, attitudes can be measured through the use of a questionnaire with a series of bipolar evaluations, each containing the same number of identically scored choices, which are summed to get a scale score (p. 191).

Like a handful of others, including Likert (1932) and Guttman (1944), Thurstone and Osgood developed relatively easily employed questionnaire strategies that yield precise numerical measures of a nebulous concept that cannot be directly observed. Attitude researchers have ratified their reasoning by embracing their techniques. In the mid-1970s Schuman and Johnson noted that no research in this area investigates spontaneous opinions expressed in ordinary life (1976, p. 163).

On the basis of their observation, Schuman and Johnson state that they, like the research they review, will "limit attitude to explicit questionnaire responses" (p. 164). *Attitude is thus defined in terms of its operationalization. This logic allows social psychologists to evade clarifying the concept.* Dawes and Smith (1985, p. 510) imply that the present state of research is no different from what it was in the mid-1930s when Allport observed that "attitudes are measured more successfully than they are defined" (1935, p. 9).

Practically all of the current research being done on the attitude-behavior relationship uses either self-administered questionnaires, a slightly modified form of questionnaire, or interviews to measure subjects' attitudes. The questions asked of the respondents in these studies are usually in the form of Likert scales, semantic differentials, or other similar, closed-choice, bipolar, evaluative ratings. Guttman and Thurstone scales are also used, but considerably less frequently than the others.

Allport cautions others that

> in forcing attitudes into a scale form violence is necessarily done to the unique structure of man's mind. Attitude scales should be regarded only as the roughest approximations of the way in which attitudes actually exist in the mental life of individuals. (1935, p. 832)

Osgood notes that the widely used semantic differential "is an indirect method in the same sense that an intelligence test, while providing objective and useful information, does not directly measure this capacity" (1952, p. 26). Dawes and Smith admit that even for a technique with strong internal (consistency of responses to similar items) or external (ability to predict behavior) validity, a subject's responses cannot be interpreted literally because they *"may be determined by many factors other than his or her attitude"* (1985, p. 539, emphasis in original). What is created in the practice of research, according to these researchers, are approximate, indirect, difficult to interpret, measures of a concept that, as noted above, cannot be satisfactorily defined.

Only one of the sixty-two articles we found in the mid-1980s literature acknowledges the confusion and takes issue with the base assumptions of attitude conceptualization and measurement. The authors of this theoretical paper, Lalljee, Brown, and Ginsberg (1984), maintain that the standard intrapersonal, nonsocial conceptualization of attitudes is untenable, and the methodology employed to measure attitudes is thoroughly inappropriate. Their critical argument is largely based on two facts. First, "sufficient evidence has been amassed to indicate that neither the idea of a neutral situation, nor that of true attitude which is more accessible in neutral situations, is defensible" (p. 236). All situations are active influences on the attitudes one expresses; "there is no non-influential, 'neutral' context" (p. 236). Second, "self-report approaches to the study of attitude entail communicative acts which involve context, multiplicity of actual and often imagined perspectives and self-presentation (Schlenker 1982); those approaches do not and cannot simply measure 'predispositions to respond'" (Lalljee et al. 1984, p. 237).

Lalljee, Brown, and Ginsberg conclude that attitudes should be construed as expressive communicative acts occurring "as features of situated social encounters" (p. 239):

> Rather than debating the nature of the actor's true attitude, the psychologist's task should be to consider how these expressive acts are displayed, what inferences are drawn from them, and how people maintain claim and counter claim about the evaluation it implies.

Attitudes should be studied for what they are, one means for controlling and coordinating interaction (p. 242). By following this course, researchers would eliminate the attitude-behavior problem because they would no longer seek "to reify one expressive act as 'the true measure of attitude' and look for 'situational constraints' which prevented its expression" (p. 242).

These arguments are grounded in contemporary theories of impression management, self-presentation, and speech act theory. From these perspectives, individuals are viewed as self-monitoring agents who act differently in different situations to achieve certain interactional goals (p. 233). The result of this combination of theoretical positions is that attitudes are reconceptualized as a self-referent speech act implying evaluation, the clearest case of which would be of the form "I approve/disapprove of entities type X" (p. 233).

In summarizing the implications of their work Lalljee, Brown, and Ginsberg state:

> Expressing a particular attitude may serve to assert one's social identity and one's orientation to the interaction as well as imply a commitment to other acts, expressive of a similar evaluation, in the future. Attitude expressions also enable other interactors to classify the individual and to form certain expectations regarding the actor's future behaviour. (1984, p. 242)

Through their conceptualization of attitudes in terms of its social functions Lalljee, Brown, and Ginsberg (1984) provide a promising proposal for extricating research from the quagmire Blumer observed in 1955, we first found in the late sixties and early seventies (Deutscher 1966, 1969, 1973), and we rediscovered in our review of research in the 1980s (F. P. Pestello and F. G. Pestello 1991). The definition of attitude they advance is unambiguous. Also, unlike traditional conceptualization, this new view of attitudes requires that the concept be grounded in direct study of individuals expressing evaluations in their everyday social worlds.

Because of the way in which the concept of attitude was traditionally conceptualized we were not surprised to find that in practice attitudes are operationalized through paper and pencil measures. It was exhilarating to discover the work of Lalljee and his colleagues. After all of our reading, it seemed an island of reason in a sea of mystification.

Behavior: Something That Should Not Be Observed

Behavior, in contrast to attitudes, has received little theoretical or methodological scrutiny by attitude-behavior researchers. Although every edition of *The Handbook of Social Psychology* and most social psychology textbooks include at least one chapter on the conceptualization and measurement of attitudes, similar chapters on behavior are absent. Behavior's visibility and accessibility may make its definition and measurement seem more obvious than the relatively obscure attitude (Ajzen and Fishbein 1980). In this vacuum the measurement of behavior has followed the path of attitude research. Researchers rely primarily upon survey techniques using standard attitude scaling procedures to create indices of behavior based on intentions, or self-reports (see F. G. Pestello and F. P. Pestello 1991). Visible and accessible behavior disappears from the equation through the alchemy of operationalization.

In such research, conceptual distinctions between attitudes and behavior frequently become muddled. When explicitly considered, behavior is usually thought of as "overt acts that are studied in their own right" (Fishbein and Ajzen 1975, p. 13), while attitudes are treated as internal predispositions to respond in a favorable or unfavorable manner toward some object. In conducting research, however, both attitudes and behavior are typically measured on a single questionnaire and some authors include a behavioral component in their definition and measurement of attitude.

Fishbein and Ajzen maintain that answering questions about attitudes (i.e., checking boxes) is a behavior, which serves as an indicator of an attitude. Answering questions about behaviors also may serve as an indicator of an attitude (p. 357). The same measure, however, is also used as a measure of behavior. By their criteria, subjects engage in behaviors (checking boxes on a questionnaire) to provide data about their behavior (their answers), which serve as indirect but accurate measures of either behavior or attitudes, depending on how the researcher wishes to take them.

Context and process are dismissed, since contemporary researchers "usually have little interest in a specific context or a specific point in time" (Ajzen and Fishbein 1980, p. 34). Scholars seek to examine generic behaviors that transcend place and time, just as attitude researchers have sought to measure attitudes devoid of time and context. The result is that researchers have become further removed from observing people acting in their everyday social worlds. This is obvious in studies that rely on measures of intention for the operationalized behavior of interest.

The most common strategy of measuring behavioral intentions is to ask respondents a single bipolar question. For our collection of studies in the mid-1980s, fourteen (27 percent) of the fifty-two articles that were based on original data use behavioral intentions as the dependent variable.[1] In many of these studies the behavior under study is so hypothetical that it is difficult to believe that responses are anything but conjecture, plausibly tainted by the context in which intentions are elicited. In one study, for example, adult Baptist Sunday School students are asked if they would return an erroneously sent five-hundred-dollar refund check to the government (Gorsuch and Ortberg 1983).

A few researchers do acknowledge that intentions may not translate into action. Two studies we found compare intentions to other measures of behavior. Results lead the authors to question the assumption that intentions are accurate indicators of actions (Breckler 1984; Stutzman and Green 1982). Despite such concerns Fishbein (1980) has been adamant in his advocacy of measuring intention as a preferred substitute for actually observing behavior.

Fishbein believes that when nothing intervenes to alter intentions between the time they are measured and the time a *volitional* behavior occurs, the relationship between the two will always be perfect. There is, therefore, no need to observe behavior itself:

> Since direct behavioral observation is often impossible and always time-consuming and costly, our options are rather limited. . . . The insistence of many investigators on direct behavioral observation, . . . has not only been inappropriate, but it has actually impeded rather than advanced scientific knowledge. (p. 78)

Even if we were to assume that intentions and volitional behavior were perfectly correlated, how much behavior in the real world is truly volitional? Very little, and what could be considered volitional is not usually of much interest to *social* scientists. Most of the behaviors that attitude-behavior researches have concerned themselves with could not reasonably be considered volitional.

Some sentiment-act consistency may be attributed to the fact that questionnaire measures of intention eliminate the complexity and inconsistency of intentions as they are found in everyday life. People hold seemingly inconsistent intentions, but intentions that researchers deem contradictory denote "error in measurement." *Studies are designed in a manner that does not allow for inconsistency.* Chassin and his colleagues (1984) provide an example in their study of smoking among high school students: "Subjects were eliminated for giving inconsistent answers to the behavioral intention items at time 1, that is, for reporting that they both intended to smoke and not to smoke in the future" (p. 227). This led to the elimination of 197 students (6.5 percent of their sample), because the researchers could not envision how students could both intend to smoke and not intend to smoke. We can and do know of at least one such case. The existence of 197 instances in their own sample did nothing to weaken their insistence on its implausibility. We have repeatedly observed, however, that people do hold inconsistent beliefs and attitudes.

Let us consider an empirical instance. A former colleague of ours, who was about forty years old at the time, quit smoking cigarettes because she was concerned about its adverse health effects. Quitting was difficult for her. The sacrifice was made easier, she claimed, by promising herself that upon reaching age sixty-five she would reward her success and start smoking again. She figured that at that age any ill effects will have taken so many years to develop that she will have reached a ripe old age if and when stricken with a smoking-related disease. So our colleague intended to both not smoke and smoke! And when this anecdote is told to former smokers, they frequently respond in the same manner.

By operationalizing behavior as intentions, researchers eliminate another key research problem. Intentions and actions are made one by methodological design. Yet among the conclusions we have been able to draw with certainty is that people sometimes do *not* do what they say they will. Researchers must come to accept that and strive to understand when and why inconsistency occurs. This inconsistency comprises a critical piece of the attitude-behavior puzzle.

Some of the concerns over the disjuncture between intentions and actions are eliminated by measuring behavior through self-reports of past acts. Twenty-two (42 percent) of the fifty-two original data articles we located rely upon retrospective accounts of behavior, making this the most common measure of behavior in contemporary research.[2] Typical of their haste, laziness, and penuriousness, Ajzen and Fishbein (1980, p. 38) advocate self-report measures *because they require less time, effort, and money*, than actually observing behavior (p. 38).

Like measures of intention, however, there are serious validity problems with operationalizing behavior through self-reporting of past acts. Significant discrepancies between self-reports and actual behavior have been found for the most simple and discrete acts like voting (Hill 1981; Phillips 1971). Seemingly straightforward questionnaire data can be extremely unreliable (Sacks, Krushat, and Newman 1980). Some are particularly suspicious of the ability of self-reports to measure "mundane, regularly occurring behaviors" (Blalock 1989), which is what attitude-behavior researchers generally explore.

Several of these studies use a complementary measure to verify respondents' reports. Introducing the second measure substantially increases confidence in the accuracy of outcome measures. The processes involved in the construction of behavior, however, remain either neglected or distorted.

Most research presupposes a unidirectional causal path between attitudes and acts. Cross-sectional designs correlating current attitudes with reports of past behavior are ill suited to test that premise. When data are collected at more than one point in time, attitudes are usually measured at one time and a measure of behavior is administered at a later time, thus elevating the directional nature of the attitude-behavior relationship from an hypothesis to an untestable assumption. Furthermore, survey studies that do include measures of attitudes and behaviors at two different times produce findings that undermine the assumption of a unidirectional attitude-to-behavior link, as do longitudinal studies with direct measures of behavior (Acock and Fuller 1984; Fredericks and Dossett 1983; Thornton et al. 1983).

Sixteen of the articles based on original data (31 percent) include a direct measure of behavior.[3] Most of these studies employ experimental designs, usually conducted in university laboratories, few of which incorporate a temporal dimension. Although laboratory experiments permit the direct study of behavior under rigorously controlled conditions, they suffer from a number of long-standing concerns, as we outlined in Chapter 8.

The few studies that directly examined behavior outside a laboratory conceptualize it narrowly. Such measures are usually circumscribed and isolated from other actions in which the research subject normally engages. People engaging in everyday, ongoing activity are rarely examined. Only two of the articles we located in our literature search examine behavior in a natural setting, and the behavior examined is quite transitory (Katzev and Averill 1984; Wurtele, Roberts, and Leeper 1982). This is unfortunate.

Beyond Concepts: A Hatful of Explanations

Our work would be a bit easier if conceptualization of the basic variables were not in the perpetual state of shambles we just described. Standardization of terminology, however, has little to do with the deeper conceptual problems that plague contemporary social science. Those problems revolve in large part around our inability to identify the distinctions people make in their everyday discourse. Without the conceptual tools that facilitate the making of such distinctions in our research instruments, we find ourselves unable to make the kinds of abstract connections that are the building blocks of theory. Furthermore, we simply throw away annoying observations such as the fact that people appear to intend to smoke and to not smoke simultaneously.

Until we are able to sort out the kinds of orientations toward social objects reflected by our instruments, the possibility of cumulative knowledge is dim. Spurious cumulations, little houses of cards, are of course as possible as they are misleading and dangerous insofar as they have any influence on policy or programs. Such spurious cumulations are possible because they are generated by a philosophy that holds costs, time, and facility to be the primary criterion of appropriate methodology. Furthermore, they are built on operational definitions—fictions created in the minds of social scientists in order to assure comparability. But it isn't very helpful in understanding human behavior to have at our disposal a mass of comparable irrelevancies.

Without a clear understanding of what kinds of orientations our instruments are and are not tapping, it is difficult to know what can be compared with what—what is an apple and what is an orange. Without the ability to make such distinctions we are confronted with the unhappy choice between knowledge limited to the time and place of specific studies or the irrelevant generalizations of operationalists. We would prefer, to either of these alternatives, that researchers continue to identify the various perspectives or orientations people may have toward social objects and proceed to learn how these orientations covary under different conditions.

Why do people sometimes not act in accord with their sentiments? It should be clear by now that there are no grounds for assuming such consistency to be a natural or expected state of affairs. The evidence suggests that sometimes they do act as they say and sometimes they do not and sometimes there is no relationship at all. It can be legitimately argued that much of this evidence must be heavily discounted if not discarded on methodological grounds. The observed discrepancy between sentiments and acts (as well as the observed concordance) is sometimes more apparent than real. Our measurement techniques as well as our research designs can produce such findings artifactually. Furthermore, our methodology—the way we think about our procedures—can also result in findings that require reinterpretation: Sentiments and acts may represent a continuum—a scale ranging from easiest to hardest expressions—rather than a categorical dichotomy.

Technical and methodological analysis may indeed screen out much of the supposed "evidence." It is also true, as our discussion in this chapter suggests, that there are many kinds of sentiments and many kinds of acts and many kinds of indicators of both, and their relationship is obscure. Discrepancies between sentiments and acts sometimes disappear when conceptual clarification is achieved. These explanations all lead to the conclusion that inconsistency may be more apparent than real. So too does the issue of the definitions of an inconsistency. We have seen instances where one person's inconsistency is another's congruence.

The conceptual problem is not only confounding because sometimes people try to compare apples and oranges, but because, as Rokeach (1970) has argued, an individual's acts are influenced by a number of attitudes rather than any single one. He points out that we not only have attitudes toward objects that may be different from our attitudes toward situations, but we are likely to entertain several attitudes toward any given object or toward any given situation. The full ramifications of Rokeach's argument can be seen in a concise and comprehensive analysis of the attitudinal dimension by Robert Lauer (1971). Lauer reminds us that attitudes are interdependent and they are multidimensional. He also points to the need to distinguish between attitudes that are central and those which are peripheral, attitudes that are primary and those which are secondary, and, finally, between what he refers to as "extrapolated attitudes" and "existential attitudes." This last dimension is related to subjects' definitions of what constitutes "reality."

The double screen does not sort out everything. When methodological credibility is ascertained and conceptual clarity achieved, it still appears that sometimes people do otherwise than what they say or what they think or what they believe. There is one explanation that appears to be shared by social scientists regardless of their theoretical persuasion. Tarter (1970, p. 277), an avowed behaviorist, explains the improved predictability of behavior in his own research in terms of the similar stimulus properties present in both the attitudinal measurement and the actual behavioral situation. Jordan (1963, Chapter 4; see also Jordan 1968), using a Lewinian rhetoric, argues that when the attitudinal field and the behavioral field are similar, there will be concordance, and when they are different, there will be a discrepancy. Blumer, the symbolic interactionist, insists that when people define the interview situation in the same manner in which they define the situation in which they are called upon to act, then the words and the deeds will coincide. Otherwise they may not. In his relatively detached summary of literature in this field, Wicker concludes that "the more similar the situations in which verbal and overt behavioral responses are obtained, the stronger will be the attitude-behavior relationship" (1969, p. 69). This broad agreement cannot be ignored. It would seem clear that there is a relationship between actors' definition of the situation in which they speak and their definition of the situation in which they act, and the extent to which talk and action are concordant.

Great emphasis has been placed on subjective definitions by actors during the course of this volume. That is not because we set out to demonstrate the importance of this factor, but because it emerged from our review and analysis of the literature. Evidence from every conceivable source can be brought to bear on the conclusion that individuals size up a situation in terms of its external features and their internal assessment and *then they act*. They do not simply respond to stimuli; they interpret the scene.

Behaviorists would repudiate any internal interpretive process as "mentalistic" and unnecessary and they would hold to an older input-output model of behavior. But it is our impression that they are lonely these days. Most social scientists, regardless of theoretical or methodological differences, are coming to recognize a need to concentrate on the intervening process rather than on the sentiment and the act. In these terms the question What is the relationship between sentiments and acts? becomes irrelevant. We begin to ask how a variety of events (or factors or characteristics or variables) interact with each other, exerting different kinds of influences under different conditions and eventually culminating in one or another outcome. The focus on what's in between seems to be most promising; it is also most difficult to implement.

Underlying any explanatory mode is the inescapable need to assume that the social act is in a constant state of development and that one cannot expect it to be the same at one time as at another or in one situation as in another. People are flexible—even the most rigid of them! Without such flexibility social survival would be difficult, if not impossible. The lack of consistency in human behavior has been an inherent part of the paraphernalia of traditional sociological concepts. The Linton-Parsons structural concept of social roles (like Mead's active verbs, "to take a role" and "to play a role") is a device that permits us to view inconsistent behavior and attitudes as "normal."

The problem of understanding the relationship between sentiments and acts need not be seen as a social-psychological or a microsociological one. Blumer spells out potential extensions of his interactionist theory to larger groups and societies. But there are other theoretical clues. W. F. Ogburn's notion of "cultural lag" (Ogburn 1957), for example, can be extended to encompass the sentimental as well as the behavioral and technological elements of a society. If we do this, it becomes possible to see certain peculiar inconsistencies in rapidly changing societies as resulting from a "lag," say, between traditional values and industrial behaviors.

Our hatful of explanations would be incomplete without drawing attention to the fact that people are political animals. The subtlest of psychological and sociological explanations sometimes fail to compare in explanatory power to this superficial quality. People may and do act counter to their sentiments for no better reason than expediency. In ruminating over the fate of idealism among medical students, Becker and Geer put it this way: "[W]hen a man's ideals are challenged by outsiders and then further strained by reality, he may salvage them by postponing their application to a future time when conditions are expected to be more propitious" (Becker and Geer 1958, p. 56).

People frequently act in ways that they feel are in their own interest or that will facilitate achievement of ultimate ends regardless of their beliefs or values. This reflects a degree of rationality, but irrationality is also a characteristic of human beings. We may act in ways that we know to be counter to our best interests *and* to our sentiments, for reasons we ourselves are unable to understand. Continued cigarette smoking among those who believe in the connection with morbidity is one example. Finally, as our earlier discussion of compartmentalization suggests, we may refuse to make any association between orientations that appear to others to be inconsistent. To help us understand this we need to consider the phenomenological tradition in sociology.

Notes

1.   The fourteen articles that measure behavioral intentions are Bagozzi and Schnedlitz (1985), Breckler (1984), Budd and Spencer (1984), Crawford and Boyer (1985), Gorsuch and Ortberg (1983), Jaccard and Sheng (1984), Kantola, Syme, and Campbell (1982), Kantola, Syme, and Nesdale (1983), Katz (1982), Klandermans (1985), Lord, Lepper, and Mackie (1984), Pagel and Davidson (1984), Shepherd and O'Keefe (1984), and Stutzman and Green (1982).

2.   The twenty-two studies that employ retrospective accounts of behavior are Acock and Fuller (1984), Ajzen, Timko, and White (1982), Baumann and Chenowith (1984), Begley and Alker (1982), Brinberg and Durand (1983), Chassin, Presson, Sherman, Corty, and Olshavsky (1984), Dalton and Todor (1985), Davidson and Morrison (1983), Davidson, Yantis, Norwood, and Montano (1985), Fisher (1984), Gardner, Tiemann, Gould, DeLuca, Doob, and Stolwijk (1982), Hill, Gardner, and Rassaby (1985), Jaccard and Becker (1985), Katz (1985), Manstead, Profitt, and Smart (1983), Manstead, Plevin, and Smart (1984), Prothero and Beach (1984), Sjoberg (1982), Thornton, Alwin, and Camburn (1983), Vaughn (1983), Warshaw and Davis (1985), and Wittenbraker, Gibbs, and Kahle (1983).

3.   Sixteen studies that use a direct measure of behavior are Borgida and Campbell (1982), Fazio, Chen, McDonel, and Sherman (1982), Fazio, Herr, and Olney (1984), Fazio, Powell, and Herr (1983), Fredericks and Dossett (1983), Gibbons and Wicklund (1982), Katzev and Averill (1984), Lobel (1982), Schlenker and Goldman (1982), Sivacek and Crano (1982), Snyder and Kendzierski (1982a, 1982b), Stults and Messé (1985), Stults, Messé, and Kerr (1984), Wilson, Dunn, Bybee, Hyman, and Rotondo (1984), Wurtele, Roberts, and Leeper (1982).

14

A Phenomenological Approach: Toward a Situational Sociology

Social Reality as a Social Creature

In the late nineteenth century, German idealism began to exert an influence over intellectuals in Northern Europe. It was short-lived—doomed by the massive payoffs of twentieth-century science, whose positivism the idealists challenged. This antiquated idealism is the source of many of the notions we have been discussing in relation to contemporary social science. The idea of "reactivity" derives directly from Kant and is reflected in Heinrich Rickert's insistence that the very act of knowing transforms the object of knowledge (Coser 1971, pp. 453–55). The Austrian psychologist Franz Brentano built his psychology around the notion of "intention": "Psychical activity 'intends' or is primarily directed upon *objects*. . . . The objects thus intended may exist or not exist, but the fact that they are intended lends them their objective character" (Becker and Barnes 1952, p. 906, emphasis in original).

It is to Brentano that one pair of social historians attributes the origin of phenomenology in social science. They do, however, allow that it was a student of Brentano's, Edmund Husserl, who established phenomenology under that name as "the descriptive study of consciousness of objects" (Becker and Barnes 1952, p. 906). Since Husserl first applied the name to that activity, we will let it be his, just as we will let "symbolic interactionism" be Herbert Blumer's and "ethnomethodology" be Harold Garfinkel's for the same reason. It does seem to us that these men gave a very specific name (of their own coinage in the cases of Blumer and Garfinkel) to a set of ideas they were proposing. We may disagree with those ideas, or modify them, or enlarge them, but in so doing we should recognize that what we are talking about is no longer what they were talking about and we ought not to retain the inappropriate label.

This cursory review of the origins of many of the ideas in this volume is based largely on secondary sources. It is intended simply to remind the reader that these notions were not invented yesterday and to give credit where credit seems due. With some merit, Johan Goudsblom has suggested, however, that we are not talking about phenomenology in the original sense of that term, but about what Weber called *verstehen*.

Although Weber's term may be more appropriate and might be acceptable to both symbolic interactionists and ethnomethodologists, Garfinkel has explicitly described his antecedents as phenomenological. Ethnomethodologists think of themselves, and are thought of by other sociologists, as phenomenologists. For this reason, we think it would cause more confusion than clarification to change names in midstream. We have urged that we treat labels with due respect. Nevertheless, it is less important what we call the matters we are dealing with than it is to attempt to understand the distinctions, assumptions, and procedures at issue.

Alfred Schutz, writing from the early thirties into the forties, took "seriously the phenomenological method in the original sense of Husserl" (Salomon 1945, p. 612). It is to Schutz that Garfinkel acknowledges his greatest debt (see Garfinkel 1964). The direct line of descent for ethnomethodology is, then, from Kant to Brentano to Husserl to Schutz to Garfinkel.

Ethnomethodology also owes a debt to the structural-functional tradition of Parsons. Garfinkel's comments on his teacher are laudatory: "Parsons's work, in particular, remains awesome for the penetrating depth and unfailing precision of its practical sociological reasoning on the constituent tasks of the problem of social order and its solutions" (Garfinkel 1967, p. ix). While the roots of ethnomethodology predate Garfinkel's confrontation with functionalism (Doubt 1989), Garfinkel's writings are seen as a reaction and response to Parsons. Heritage notes that the differences between them "crystallize[d] around the question of whether the actor's point of view, and its role in the organization of action, should be analyzed and treated by means which were intrinsic to, or external to, the structure of the actor's experience" (1984, pp. 9–10). In the phenomenological tradition, Garfinkel treats the actor's point of view as intrinsic. For Parsons, "action was to be analyzed as the product of a causal process which, although operating 'in the mind' of actors, were [*sic*] all but inaccessible to them and, hence, uncontrollable by them" (Heritage 1984, p. 22).

Since Descartes, philosophers have been concerned with the problem of knowledge—epistemology, as they call it. It is out of that concern that (through Hegel to Marx and Scheler and Mannheim) the sociology of knowledge, as we know it today, emerged. The rationalistic school was laying the groundwork for a superscientific method that could deal with any kind of knowledge, while the counterattack was coming from the more humanistic "idealists" such as Locke and Hume (see Delaney and Widdison 1990).

Comte, the original hard-nosed sociologist, rejected idealism out of hand. For him there is only one way of understanding the rational order of the universe and that is the scientific method. There is only one reality and there is only one way to grasp it, but Kant was not that clear. His distinction between the phenomenal world and the noumenal world is at the heart of the issue. For Kant both were real and each was different in its knowability.

It is an oversimplification to class Kant as an idealist because he reacted against rationalism. Although he does not hold with the positivist position that human understanding passively reflects the inherent nature of things in themselves, as they really are, or whatever, he also rejects the notion that mind itself is the only reality or that mind creates its world. Kant accepted both noumena and phenomena. The basic Kantian idea is that people create their own history, culture, and selves, and these creations have to be understood by methods other than those by which nature can be understood.

We have traced above the intellectual passage of one brand of contemporary phenomenology from Kant to Garfinkel. There is, however, a rather different and considerably older phenomenological tradition in American sociology. It culminates in what Herbert Blumer calls "symbolic interactionism." Like ethnomethodology, symbolic interactionism is clearly a Kantian derivative. Blumer is explicit about his debt to George Herbert Mead and Mead is equally explicit about his debt to Kant. This makes the tracking problem simple. The strong influence of Kant on Mead's ideas of the relationship between subject and object (the "I" and the "me"), and on the development of the self, can be found throughout his lectures on nineteenth-century philosophy. Mead (1936) never lets the reader forget that the issue is realism vs. idealism and, ultimately, that there is little worth bothering with that is "real." The world we must come to understand is a phenomenal world constructed by its actors.

Mead preached the social construction of the act and a mentalistic psychology in which the important things all happened inside people's heads—in conversations with themselves. We suppose this is why the Chicago school of sociology has always been such a puzzle. In its heyday that school produced innumerable descriptive monographs—pure empiricism: the *real* world as only the sociologist could discover it (see Bulmer 1984, Chapter 6)! The focus was on "empirical research at the expense of social theory" (Kurtz 1984, p. 15). On the other hand, Mead's symbolism was ever present, manifesting itself, for example, in Thomas's classic "Definition of the Situation," which was to become a widely accepted sociological postulate. Most pervasive was the translation of Mead's "taking the role of the other" into a methodology that demanded that the social world be described from the perspective of the actors in it. What made Chicago sociology distinct is that Chicago sociologists "were more concerned about developing their own theories of society, based upon their research, and were more closely related to the American philosophical traditions than to the European theorists" (Kurtz 1984, p. 18). While we recognize that there is also a long overlooked quantitative tradition at Chicago (see Bulmer 1984, Chapter 10), participant observation or ethnography remains the trademark of what is called Chicago-style sociological research.

There is some controversy about Blumer's interpretation of Mead, Mead's importance for the development of symbolic interaction, and Mead's contribution to the Chicago school of sociology. Much of this critique comes from the department of sociology at Illinois [see, for example, the exchange in the *American Sociological Review* begun by McPhail and Rexroat (1979) responded to by Blumer (1980) to whom McPhail and Rexroat (1979) reply]. Perhaps the most controversial of recent criticisms is that by Lewis and Smith (see the review symposium in *Symbolic Interaction* volume 6, number 1). Building upon dissertations they wrote at Illinois, Lewis and Smith use much of their book on American sociology and pragmatism to build a case that calls "into question the assumption . . . that Mead was a progenitor of symbolic interaction" (1980, p. xix). They argue "that the basic principles of Mead's social behaviorism and philosophy of perspectives are entirely contrary to the voluntaristic, nominalist assumptions of the psychical interactionism of Cooley, Thomas, Ellwood, Blumer, and others" (p. 250). In their view the pragmatist roots of symbolic interactionism are to be found in the James and Dewey brand of pragmatism, social nominalism, which is critically different than that of Mead and Peirce, social realism [the significance of this distinction is questioned by Rochberg-Halton (1982)]. Many have disagreed with this analysis (see Kurtz 1984, pp. 34–36, 44–45).

Rather than arguing about who "misunderstood" Mead, as if there were an objective reality to Mead's writing, Lewis and Smith might better have adopted a more subjective perspective. In his lectures, Blumer attributed to Mead literally every idea he presented. When students suggested to Blumer that, although stimulated by Mead, much of his theoretical and methodological reasoning was his own, he smiled modestly and changed the subject. Ultimately the argument rests on our assumption that symbolic interaction is a term invented by Blumer and consists of what Blumer did. Mead becomes important then, if for no better reason than that Blumer thought he was important.

Our sketch of nineteenth-century antecedents of contemporary phenomenology in sociology—both symbolic interaction and ethnomethodology—has failed to mention some of the more important and better known of the German idealists. Wilhelm Dilthey, for example, expressed his antipositivism in his emphasis on "meaning" as the crucial element in understanding history. Salomon (1945, p. 591) describes him as the German William James. It was Dilthey who developed the method of "verstehen," which was later to become associated with the name of Max Weber. Dilthey was clearly in the phenomenological tradition, insisting that one had to become immersed in a phenomenon in order to grasp its meaning.

It is equally clear that Weber failed to embrace this tradition, possibly for political reasons. Weber's sociology seems to us one in which people are driven by overwhelming external forces over which they have little or no control. The idea of verstehen provided, for Weber, some sort of preliminary familiarization with the phenomenon under study. Weber seems to be conceding that one ought to take a look at and try to make sense out of the object of study before really getting down to the sociological business of studying it. But the real business of sociology is a rational, positivistic one.

Weber does recognize the subjective, irrational qualities of humanity, as his essays on values and objectivity indicate (Weber 1949). But those same essays reflect his failure to understand that sociologists are people. He recognizes a world populated by irrational, emotional, value-laden human beings. He even suggests that it is these very properties of human nature that may be the most important focus of the sociologist's concern. But he never for a moment concedes that the sociologist is also human. He is oblivious to the idea of reactivity and to the constraints suggested by the sociology of knowledge. Both of these ideas were endemic in the intellectual milieu in which Weber matured. Weber argued that the sociologist, as scientist, is a superperson who transcends the value-laden qualities of human nature, and views them objectively from a superior position as detached observer.

If German idealism survives at all in American sociology, it is thanks largely to Georg Simmel, who has played a more prominent role than Alfred Schutz. Schutz's link with the American pragmatists, especially Mead and James, is clearly reflected in his footnotes, but Simmel eschewed footnotes. There can be no doubt about the Kantian influence, and Coser suggests that Husserl left traces on Simmel's work as well. His distinction between the forms of social interaction and their specific content is reminiscent of Kant, and "historical knowledge to Simmel, like the knowledge of nature to Kant, is a product of . . . thinking. It is never given; it has to be created" (Coser 1971, p. 202).

The impact of Simmel on the Chicago school is reflected from its origins with Robert Park through the works of Louis Wirth and Everett Hughes. Park, who studied under Dewey at Michigan and James at Harvard, was already steeped in the pragmatic philosophy when he spent a semester attending Simmel's lectures. Coser (1971, p. 374) believes this was probably the most important academic semester in Park's life (see also Lengermann 1988). Simmel's influence is clearly evidenced in Park and Burgess's *Introduction to the Science of Sociology* (1921), in which selections from and citations to Simmel are more prevalent than any other author.

In suggesting that phenomenology in American sociology ultimately took only the forms found in Blumer's symbolic interaction and Garfinkel's ethnomethodology, we have oversimplified. Midwestern sociologists, steeped in the Chicago tradition, have used Mead as a basis for a more positivistic sociology. The Iowa school of Kuhn and his students is the most striking example (see Meltzer and Petras 1970), but there are others, like Stryker (1980). In like manner there are sociologists who came under the influence of Schutz during his tenure at the New School for Social Research and whose phenomenology has nothing to do with Garfinkel's ethnomethodology (e.g., Berger and Luckmann 1966; Blum and McHugh 1971).

The Subject as Methodologist

The unifying element, the core that permits the diverse sociologists discussed above to be called phenomenological, is that they generally share a perspective on human behavior and social processes. What they have in common is that each of them insists that the proper study of people must attempt to understand the world as those people do—to view it from their perspective. The phenomenological orientation always sees reality as constructed by people in the process of thinking about it. It is the social version of Descartes's *Cogito, ergo sum*. For the phenomenologist it becomes *Cogitamus, ergo est*—we think, therefore it is! We have done our best to introduce that perspective into this book, because we believe it can resolve some of the problems plaguing contemporary social science, particularly in the study of sentiments and acts.

Taking a leaf from Kant, we submit that there are two worlds out there: One that is objectively perceived by the senses as real. The other is a world that we create in the process of thinking about it. We refuse to opt for either as the proper perspective for the study of social actors. It seems to us that there may be some things we can know better one way; some can be better understood the other way; and some can only be understood when we figure out how these two worlds are fit together by people doing the things they do.

The fact that we cannot always define reality into existence is evidenced, for example, by the large numbers of people who get killed with "empty" guns. No matter how sincere the definition of the situation, the fact remains that, if there is a bullet in the chamber, there will be empirically observable consequences. However, the way in which this death is explained by others—accident, suicide, or homicide—is not so clear. And anyone who has ever run out of gas while driving on an isolated stretch of highway is well aware that the failure to define the gas tank as empty was utterly ineffective in altering objective reality. The interpretation a passenger will give to this event again is not clear from the objective reality.

It is our impression that Blumer and Garfinkel each get around the problem of objective reality in different ways. Both concede that to the extent that subjective definitions become widely shared, they become objectified. For them it is a matter of degree. Garfinkel's is based in Schutz's notion of "typifications" while Blumer's is in Mead's distinction between the symbolic and the nonsymbolic social world. The phenomenological perspective sensitizes us to the centrality of "meaning" and "intention" in human behavior, but the positivistic perspective alerts us to the existence of objectively real consequences as well as socially constructed consequences of human action.

The need for both perspectives can be illustrated in efforts to understand suicidal behavior. There is adequate documentation of the fact that suicide attempters and completers tend to have very different social and demographic characteristics. The objective fact of killing oneself is, however, not sufficient for making the distinction. In trying to understand the discrepancy between suicidal sentiments and suicidal acts, it becomes necessary to take intentionality into account. Persons intent on completing a suicidal act may nevertheless fail if, for example, they believe that four aspirins are a lethal dose or a leap from a third-story window will inevitably kill. Objective reality interferes with their definitions of the situation. To put it more bluntly, incompetence becomes an intervening variable. Tragically, the reverse is also possible. The individual, symbolically engaging in a "cry for help," may end up objectively dead regardless of intentions otherwise.

We find the phenomenological perspective useful in beginning to unravel the relationship between what people say and what they otherwise do if—rather than playing objective scientist, rather than trying to develop a theoretical framework within which we can organize their words and their deeds—we take a cue from Garfinkel and treat them as if they were methodologists. What calculus does the person in the street employ in constructing lines of action? If we can come to see the world as the social actor does, then we can begin to understand the relationship between talk and action as the social actor does. This seems more effective, as Garfinkel suggests, than assuming that ordinary people are cultural and psychological dopes.

Although Blumer's perspective has always seemed persuasive to us, we had trouble finding a technology for research that seemed faithful to that perspective. Garfinkel (1964) began to open such technological doors with reports of "little studies" designed to stimulate research of commonsense activities. He notes the need for such studies by observing that the social sciences are preoccupied with "the familiar commonsense world of everyday life" (p. 225). Despite the centrality of this topic it had been ignored as a ground for sociological inquiry. "An immense literature contains little data and few methods with which the essential features of socially recognized 'familiar scenes' may be detected and related to dimensions of social organization" (p. 225).

Garfinkel argues that most of the work in the social sciences merely assumes, or settles by theoretical representation, the commonsense world (p. 225). Results are misleading because subjects are cast as "judgmental dopes":

> By "cultural dope" I refer to the man-in-the-sociologist's-society who produces the stable features of the society by acting in compliance with preestablished and legitimate alternatives of action that the common culture provides. The "psychological dope" is the man-in-the-psychologist's-society who produces the stable features of society by choices among alternative courses of action that are compelled on the grounds of psychiatric biography, conditioning history, and the variables of mental functioning. The common feature in the use of these "models of man" is the fact that courses of common sense rationalities of judgment which involve the person's use of common sense knowledge of social structures over the temporal "succession" of here and now situations are treated as epiphenomenal. (p. 244)

Through studies that breach expectations Garfinkel (1964) demonstrates his point. By acting deviant in various situations, the researcher reveals subjects' judgmental work and the commonsense knowledge upon which it is based. Through the responses of subjects to upset expectations, subjects' background expectancies and the environments they comprise are made available for study. Researchers can then begin to see how everyday affairs are produced by social actors, rather than determined by social structures or mental states.

Ethnomethodology has grown dramatically since its inception over thirty years ago. It is no longer a homogeneous endeavor. Although the phenomenological roots are still evident in some ethnomethodological work, other strands have taken on a more structuralist and behaviorist bent (Atkinson 1988, p. 447). Atkinson finds that "some versions of ethnomethodology have returned to the judgmental dope as their model actor" (p. 449).

For many of these ethnomethodologists, the importance of meaning and interpretation is subordinated to a concern with how actors sequence their activities. This trend is most apparent in conversation analysis (p. 447), which explores minute intricacies of talk and action (Heritage 1984; Hilbert 1990). For this now dominant version of ethnomethodology, talk assumes a privileged place in understanding human activity because talk is deemed the most "pure" and "authentic" form of data available. These scholars argue that transcribed natural conversations come the closest to being "an unmediated, literally represented social reality" (Atkinson 1988, p. 454; see also Frank 1985).

When doing conversation analysis, the ethnomethodologist transcribes tape-recorded talk:

> Little or no reference is made to the situation in which the conversation took place, and little may in fact be known about it, the ethnomethodologist is exterior to his or her materials for analysis. But in the method of analysis, the ethnomethodologist grants him or herself a significant interiority: he invokes his competence as a member of the same speech community as the speakers in order to claim to know enough of what they are doing in the speech to enable him to get on with the analytic problem of how these doings are accomplished, i.e., what conventional resources are required. (Frank 1985, pp. 108–9).

Such analysis is crassly empirical. What actors are talking about or why they are engaged in conversation is irrelevant. Talk is recorded, transcribed, and continually reinspected in an attempt to assess objective dimensions of sequencing patterns. Gregory (1983) provides an example with his computer reconstruction of temporal symmetry in dyadic conversations through the analysis of voice frequency levels (see also Gregory, Webster, and Huang 1990).

Although conversation analysis is the most extreme in its neglect of context, meaning, and interpretation, Gallant and Kleinman (1983) suggest that the difficulty may be endemic to all of ethnomethodology. Ethnomethodologists examine meaning and reality construction quite differently than symbolic interactionists. Ethnomethodologists concentrate on "the individual act—a member's procedure for creating a sense of order when others are co-present" (pp. 10–11). They want to identify

rules and typifications used by social actors that transcend the immediate context and interaction. Interactionists, by contrast, are fundamentally concerned with *joint* action. They do not separate meaning from
context and interaction, because they find meaning to be created and
accomplished through joint action in a particular situation. For the interactionist, meaning emerges from interaction; for the ethnomethodologist, meaning construction occurs within the individual.

We noted earlier that Garfinkel and his followers have worked to
reveal the hidden rules that precede and undergird all situations and
interaction. Other sociologists, largely in the interactionist tradition,
have explicitly explored the negotiation process by which definitions of
reality are socially constructed (e.g., Emerson 1970; Scheff 1968). Strauss
is one of the first and strongest proponents of a negotiated-order perspective (see Strauss 1978, particularly pp. 4–5). This approach attempts
to show how social order is both achieved through the extensive negotiations of social actors while also giving form to the negotiations and
social interactions that take place within it (Maines 1982, p. 275).

Maines uses the term *mesostructure* to refer to this perspective:

> It is through interaction that structures are enacted, but in that process,
> interaction becomes *conditional* interaction. In terms of classical theory,
> mesostructure portrays freedom as possible through constraint and con-
> straint as a consequence of freedom. The center of that domain thus con-
> sists of mediating processes and the webs of significance and group affilia-
> tion that form the interstitial arenas of social life. (1982, p. 276, emphasis in
> original; see also Maines 1977)

People are influenced by seemingly invariant external forces, setting a
stage with established scripts for social action. Individual performances,
however, are flexible and mutable within those established scripts (Hall
1987; Pestello and Voydanoff 1991a).

While ethnomethodologists demonstrate the rules underlying talk,
interactionism and other interpretive sociologies view talk as a "socially
shared resource in the construction of meaning and the constitution of
everyday reality" (Atkinson 1988, p. 449). The former provides too narrow a view of the way in which social actors use talk to coordinate and
give meaning to their activities. One example of the latter that is central
to the words-deeds relationship is motive talk.

From the phenomenological perspective it becomes essential to learn
how members of society provide satisfactory accounts for what is happening. This is the root of the sociological analysis of actors' ascription of
motives. Rather than viewing motives as internal characteristics that
cause individuals to act, a sociological approach treats motives as a

means of using language to render behavior relevant so that it can be seen as normative (Blum and McHugh 1971, pp. 99–100).

In his seminal article, Mills treats motives as "accepted justifications for present, future, or past programs or acts" (1940b, p. 327). They serve to undo snarls and integrate actions (1940b, pp. 327–28). When successful, motive talk neutralizes untoward behavior and allows interaction to get back on, or remain on, track. Sykes and Matza (1957) were among the first to apply this approach. They discovered that juveniles use "techniques of neutralization" to justify their delinquent behavior. By employing these neutralization techniques, juveniles can violate norms while denying that they are being violated.

Expanding Sykes and Matza's techniques, Scott and Lyman (1968) developed the concept of "accounts": statements that explain unanticipated or untoward behavior. Accounts prevent conflict by verbally bridging action and expectation (p. 344). Noting that the concept of accounts is limited to the retrospective reconstruction of meaning, Hewitt and Stokes (1975) created the concept of "disclaimers": "A disclaimer is a verbal device employed to ward off and defeat in advance doubts and negative typifications which may result from intended conduct" (p. 3). By successfully providing such talk before acting, individuals may behave in untoward ways with impunity.

In an attempt to tie together these concepts, and several other related notions, Stokes and Hewitt (1976) present a broad view of the use of language to render problematic situations nonproblematic (see also Hunter 1984). They group all of these concepts under the umbrella of "aligning actions": "largely verbal efforts to restore or assure meaningful interaction in the face of problematic situations" (Stokes and Hewitt 1976, p. 838). The focus of aligning actions has largely been on how individuals provide talk to repair, or keep from damage, identities that are threatened by their acts.

Through our research we discovered that *groups* are also able to act contrary to their principles and still preserve their ideals. We called this collective aligning action "discounting" (Pestello 1991). Through discounting, group members negotiate conceptualizations that allow the discrediting features of problematic acts to be disregarded. Just as we "scientists" discount evidence, so too do ordinary people going about their ordinary actions.

Work on aligning actions provides insight into one important means by which talk and action—in this case untoward action—are related, and situationally constructed in concert with others. Unfortunately, as we noted in the previous chapter, the standard attitude-behavior literature is based largely on intrapersonal, asituational models. Most scholars look for consistency within individuals instead of examining how consistency is established and maintained in interaction. Lest the reader think this is a trivial matter, let us consider how our understanding of human behavior depends upon whether or not social scientists can grasp and accept this logic.

It Makes a Difference

What difference does a phenomenological perspective make in the work of the social scientist? The differences discussed below tend to be stated in either-or terms for expository purposes. In fact, many of these differences can be viewed as matters of degree or emphasis rather than as absolute dichotomies. For purposes of contrast we will compare a phenomenological approach—situational sociology—with the more traditional positivistic approach—variable analysis—in social science. Again, this is a device for present purposes only. We have already seen the variety of peoples and activities that can be subsumed under the phenomenological rubric where situational sociology is found. This variety is even greater within a "traditional positivistic" rubric.

In this chapter we began contrasting the two views of the study of social actors by noting their major differences in perspective: The phenomenologist seeks to understand the social world from the point of view of the actors in it. Positivistic scientists, rather than attempting to discover the actors' categories, create their own scientific categories and employ them for making sense out of the behavior of others. The phenomenologist sees actors as active creators of their own social world—fitting together their lines of action as they assess and define situations. The self-styled scientist, in contrast, tends to explain behavior in terms of passive reaction to external forces—actors respond to stimuli. Scientists are "objective," outside and separate from the behavior they study, detached and value free. In contrast, the phenomenologist takes the position that in order to understand human behavior one must be or must have been a part of the situation under study. It is necessary to take the role of the other—to walk in others' shoes—in contrast to maintaining a scientific distance from one's subjects.

It follows that phenomenologists would employ an inductive method in building knowledge. They begin with minute observations of particular events and build up from there, perhaps creating theories about more general events from their little observations. Positivistic scientists, on the other hand, need broad scientific theories as a starting point for testing little empirical observations. They move out deductively from general theories, verifying them with specific observations. The scientist works in an atomistic world where parts can be dissected and understood in themselves, with knowledge accumulating as more and more parts are catalogued. Situational sociologists cannot work with such "variables" because they make sense only in context—only in relation to their setting—only as a *gestalt*.

For the scientist one discovers the whole by summing up the individual parts; not so for the phenomenologist, who sees the whole as something different from the sum of its parts. The scientist, who experiments with variables, trying to understand their relationship with one another, views with some contempt the phenomenologist, who has regressed into ancient mysticism with questions about "meaning" and "intentions." The phenomenologist is essentially a social semanticist while the positivist is concerned with syntax.

Consistent with these two sets of views is the further distinction between process, as emphasized by the phenomenologist, and structure, as emphasized by the positivist. The Hegelian idea of "becoming" is central to the phenomenological perspective. Human behavior is a social process—constantly reforming, reshaping, and redirecting itself. The positivistic scientist's emphasis on input and output or on independent and dependent variables makes no sense to phenomenologists since they see all of the important things as happening "in between."

From the phenomenological perspective, to slice up time makes as little sense as slicing a social situation into component variables. The phenomenological focus on process assumes that change is the normal state of affairs in human social life. The positivistic focus on being (in contrast to becoming) assumes that stability or balance is the normal state of affairs.

This idealized set of distinctions carries with it methodological paraphernalia. The phenomenologist must study social life as it is found in its natural milieu, while the behaviorist may isolate bits and pieces or simulate them for study in isolation. The phenomenologist must in one way or another and to some degree use subjective knowledge as a member of society, while positivists attempt to isolate themselves personally in order to preserve objectivity. The phenomenologist is inclined to make observations through time, while the positivist can observe a slice of time as easily as a slice of behavior. The phenomenologist must attempt to discover the categories used by ordinary citizens—the scales they carry around with them are the only legitimate scales for the phenomenologist. The positivist creates scientific categories—built on logic, scales that are then tested and applied to subjects. For the phenomenologist the empirical world provides the raw materials out of which theory may be constructed bit by bit. The positivist applies reason and logic, developing an overarching scheme that seems to make sense and then testing, modifying, and altering this scheme in the empirical world.

The phenomenologist must preserve the essential subjectivity of hu-

man behavior by subtly entering into it, while the positivist must objec-
tify human behavior and make it measurable. Definitions must be operational not only because that makes them scientific (i.e., consistent with
the social construction of the scientist), but because such definitions
have objective measurement explicitly built into them. By now it should
be clear that the only measurement that makes sense to the phenomenologist is the measurement employed by the people studied.

The scientist may be satisfied to measure color along a light spectrum
or heat with a thermometer. But the phenomenologist must be attentive
to the color categories people themselves utilize or the manner in which
they define hot and cold. The warm beer and cold soup about which a
truck driver may complain in a roadside diner make no sense at all to the
positivist. The thermometer indicates that the warm beer is many
degrees colder than the cold soup. To the scientist the truck driver is
being unreasonable in complaining. To the phenomenologist the categories of warm and cold are defined by that member of society in that
particular context (and it is a shared definition, not an idiosyncratic one).
It is definitions that determine actions. Finally, Blumer's critique of variable analysis is a purely phenomenological argument, implying that the
proper object of research is the intervening process and not the irrelevant independent and dependent variables.

The phenomenologist might take the skeptical view that the scientist
is ethnocentric in attempts to impose a scientific perception of reality on
everyone else. Scientists can in turn argue that their perception of reality
is as good as anyone else's. It is shared by a large scientific community
and permits the accumulation of knowledge in a manner that is hardly
possible if we allow to every person or group its own definitions of the
situation. Both views are well endowed with their own cultish adherents, but the essential pragmatic question is, What use is it all?

The kinds of evidence and arguments that have appeared throughout
this volume should bear witness to our own catholicism on this matter.
Whatever contributes to understanding, in whatever small way, to the
relationship between sentiments and acts, is admissible as evidence.
Such an eclectic stance sometimes creates problems of inconsistency in
basic assumptions, but we believe these can be compartmentalized in
the same manner as we compartmentalize the variety of perspectives
that impinge upon us in our everyday life. For our part we will draw
from whatever compartment we may find useful.

There are matters that ought not to be confused with the issue we
have been discussing. The ancient functionalist debate in sociology is
not central here. A self-styled functionalist may as well be a phenomenologist as a positivist and may have strong objections to either position. For example, a functionalist may take a static rather than a process
view of social life (positivistic), but may also insist that a society is a

gestalt with all of its parts intimately interrelated with each other (phe-nomenological) so that any interference with a part automatically upsets the whole system.

It is, in fact, possible to undertake a positivistic form of phenomenolo-gy—in spite of the use we made of these two for purposes of contrast. We have referred to the work of such symbolic interactionists as Man-ford Kuhn and Sheldon Stryker. These men have attempted to apply posi-tivistic science to phenomenological theory. One of the great strengths in the variety of contributions made by Arnold Rose was eclecticism. He could be passionately loyal to the Chicago school and to symbolic inter-action on the one hand, but he could also put to work whatever methods based on whatever assumptions were required to meet his necessary research goals.

It would also be an error to assume that such versions of phenomenol-ogy as ethnomethodology and symbolic interaction are the same. Their strongest adherents become almost violent in their contempt for each other. Much of this reflects the cultish quality of both schools, but there are also very real differences. Ethnomethodologists see themselves as belonging to a new discipline—a radical perspective on human behavior and its study. Symbolic interactionists see themselves as part of an old and respectable tradition in sociology and see their mission as the revi-talization of a discipline gone stale. Out of this difference emerges a different view of the history of social science. The ethnomethodologist is likely to argue that there is no literature worth reading—that the jour-nals are loaded with irrelevancies, that history begins with ethno-methodology. The anti-intellectual overtones of this argument seem hor-rendous to the more traditional scholars of the symbolic interactionist school.

When *What We Say/What We Do* was published in 1973, ethnometh-odology was just coming into its own. It is now out of its infancy and into middle age (Frank 1985). It is no longer the new kid on the block. It has been supplanted by more "radical" approaches, like postmodern-ism. In its maturity, ethnomethodology seems more conventional, se-date, and respectable than it once did. Pollner (1991) maintains that in becoming accepted, ethnomethodology has, unfortunately, abandoned its "radical reflexivity." The differences between it and symbolic interac-tion, however, are still quite apparent. Ethnomethodologists disavow structure, focusing only on what is "empirically real" (see Hilbert 1990). Interactionists want to understand how people process structure in the course of their interactions (see Maines 1982).

For the purist of either school there is also a basic methodological difference. The symbolic interactionist is immersed in the world she or he studies—wallows in it. Ethnomethodologists, however, if they are to take note of the taken-for-granted rules that guide the behavior of members of their world of study, must maintain sufficient distance so that they do not come to take those rules for granted like everyone else. They must maintain the detachment necessary to make explicit the rules that participants implicitly accept. The emphasis on rules results in a somewhat more deterministic, somewhat less volitional view of the social actor than found among the symbolic interactionists. The latter tend to see free actors constructing their lines of action in terms of their own definitions of the situation. The rule-guided person of the ethnomethodologist is not quite that free.

A rapprochement may be possible between the conversation-analytic methods of ethnomethodology and the participant-observation methods of symbolic interactionism (see Atkinson 1988; Boden 1990). Atkinson suggests that many ethnographers have failed "to develop a systematic approach to language use in natural settings" (1988, p. 119), while conversation analysts have often severed conversations from context. He identifies what he finds to be their complementary strengths and potential pitfalls:

> The ethnographer ignores at his peril the interactional foundations and interpretive procedures he draws on. But the conversational analyst treads on equally thin ice if he becomes seduced by the ideal-type of the decontextualized, "mundane" talk of the two party encounter in which rights and resources are equally available. (p. 130)

In effect, ethnomethodology may be viewed as the study of microsocial organization, in contrast with symbolic interaction, which is a social psychology. Traditionally in sociology we have been inclined to view the study of little interactions as "social psychology" and the study of big systems as "social organization" or "social structure." But as Garfinkel is prone to remind us, little interactions may be highly structured and, as Blumer is prone to remind us, big systems can operate as symbolically as little ones.

Since the 1920s the debate between positivists and phenomenologists has changed little and slackened not at all. In 1992, a writer for *Newsweek* magazine interviewed the president of the American Sociological Association, James Coleman, along with such other distinguished members of the club as Kai Erikson, Paul Starr, Lewis Coser, Charles Tilly, and Jeanne Ballantine. The major division in the discipline that Kantrowitz identified from those interviews is:

> The thinkers say the quantifiers suffer from "physics envy," an unrequited desire to paint a portrait of reality with numbers rather than insightful observation. The quantifiers say the thinkers are old-fashioned, afraid to subject their ideas to the scrutiny of real science. (1992, p. 55)

15

Toward the Twenty-First Century

How Much Improvement?

This volume is an effort to understand the relationship between what people say and what they do. In the first chapter we identified four major flaws that were largely responsible for the confusing findings in the pre-1970 literature. Those flaws are found in (1) research techniques, involving largely a failure to be attentive to the validity of data; (2) concepts, especially the lack of clarity regarding the different kinds of sentiments and acts being analyzed; (3) assumptions, in particular the assumption of a psychological need for consistency among ordinary people as well as a reliance upon the scientists' rather than the people's definitions of consistency and inconsistency; and (4) flawed theory, which viewed human behavior as a static phenomenon that could be dissected into slices and then understood by discovering which variables accounted for how much of the variance. Such theoretical orientation was convenient for research purposes but failed to acknowledge the empirically observable fact that human behavior is an ongoing process and that it is to that flow of action, as it shapes and reshapes both sentiments and actions, that the observer must be attentive.

Validity

Research through the 1960s was attentive to issues of reliability. There was much less concern with the equally important issue of validity. We had hoped to find that researchers in the 1980s were relying less upon operational definitions, a convenient means of sidestepping the issue of validity, and paying more attention to convergent validity (consistency of findings using different methods of data gathering), searching for unobtrusive measures, or direct observation of the phenomena in question.

Unlike the period of investigation through the 1960s, most contemporary researchers find some degree of relationship between sentiments and acts. They do so only at the expense of credibility. Our review of recent research shows that the methodological decline from the 1930s to the 1960s continued into the 1980s. Most researchers rely on a narrow set of reactive methodologies to indirectly study circumscribed behaviors among small samples of unrepresentative subjects.

The most prolific attitude-behavior researchers strongly discourage the actual measurement of behavior because it is too time-consuming. As a result, researchers make unwarranted leaps of faith in assuming a correspondence between what they measure and what takes place in the complex, everyday world in which people talk and act. We are disheartened to find that convenience continues to take precedence over validity.

Concepts

Prior to 1970, there was no consensus on definitions of even the most basic variables that were studied. The same terms were used to refer to different mental or behavioral orientations. This made it difficult to compare studies and build knowledge. In our examination of the post-1970s research, we looked for increased precision in conceptual distinctions. We paid particular attention to the conceptualization of attitude and what orientations were being referred to as behavior. We found little change in a long tradition of definitional sloppiness and neglect.

Researchers still fail to define their terms and persist in applying the same terms to different orientations. There is ample evidence of a lack of consensus on what constitutes an attitude. Scholars who acknowledge this lack of definitional precision are complacent about it. And while authors continue to draw conclusions about behavior, their findings are often based instead on behavioral intentions or self-reports of past acts. It is on the point of conceptual precision that we regret the positivists' failure to take a cue from the natural scientists they seek to emulate.

Consistency

There were two problems in the pre-1970s literature having to do with consistency. The first problem stems from the assumption that people feel compelled to be consistent. The second involves who determines what is consistent and what is inconsistent. Is it the scientist or the actor? We found in the pre-1970s literature that scientists were not attentive to actors' definitions. Instead, they assumed that everyone was compelled by logic to face what the scientists considered to be an inconsistency. These flaws remain in contemporary studies. Virtually all the work we examined was based on the researchers' definition of consistency and on the assumption that subjects feel they should act consistently. There is no attempt to determine what subjects consider consistent or inconsistent. Nor does anyone explore the conditions under which subjects do and do not feel compelled to act in a manner that they define as consistent.

Starting in the mid-1970s, leading researchers declared that the battle was won. Attitudes and behaviors, they claimed, are directly related. With that self-declared victory, questions of consistency were also settled. Research based on reigning models presumes a drive toward consistency as the researchers conceive it. Unfortunately, this precludes from investigation many fundamental questions related to variations in consistency and inconsistency that we know to exist in the sentiments-acts relationship.

Process

It is not appropriate to make initial sentiments and ultimate acts the principal objects of investigation. People act on their definitions of the situation in which they find themselves. What comes in between initial attitudes and ultimate behavior needs to be the central focus of research. We were very encouraged in the early 1970s by our observation that researchers were beginning to pay greater attention to what's "in between." Initial attempts to incorporate process and definition of the situation into research came through the inclusion of intervening variables. It was a promising start in the right direction.

Nearly all contemporary research is premised on the belief that attitudes alone do not determine behavior. However, little else is usually measured beyond "norms," typically conceptualized as how relevant others (predetermined by the researcher) would feel about the subject, if the subject were to engage in the particular act in question. Certainly the feelings of others are an important factor bearing on what people do, particularly if those others are present when the act is committed. But norms are usually measured out of context on the same questionnaire with attitudes and intentions or self-report of past acts. Process itself is never studied nor are most of the other factors that people take into account when defining situations. This is perhaps the most fatal of the four flaws. It is truly a shame that the fledgling start to overcome it became institutionalized as a single intervening variable in the few narrow path models to which most researchers slavishly adhere.

Conclusions

To overcome the flaws we have identified, a radically different approach is needed: a situational sociology. We have demonstrated that the history of investigation in this area has been infused with a positivistic bent. In Chapter 2 we explain why we think this has happened: "Science" proved to be very seductive. As it manifests itself throughout this book, the phenomenological perspective undermines the positivist stance of most sentiments-acts researchers. This perspective is apparent in Chapter 1 where we considered the need, as Mills suggested, to discount research reports as the products of researchers. In Chapter 2 our discussion of epistemology and the sociology of knowledge was essentially phenomenological in its argument that ways of knowing are intimately related to the temper of the times. We considered arguments in Chapter 5 that social data are a social product. Our quarrel with extreme operationalism in that chapter was based on the phenomenological grounds that definitions on which people act are their own definitions and not those imposed by scientists. In Chapter 7 our discussion of language and social research is also grounded in phenomenology. Research needs to examine the situated talk of social actors.

Much of the methodological critique in Part II hangs on the problem of reactivity—of the active role played by the researcher in producing research results. Those chapters were also concerned about the inability of much of our current research techniques to reflect the world as perceived by its members. To this extent those methodological chapters were phenomenological in their orientation. When we conclude in Chapter 10 that the actors' definition of the situation becomes central in understanding their actions, we make a phenomenological conclusion. And our use of Blumer's arguments in Chapter 11, along with the analysis of evidence related to the intervening process between sentiments and acts, is explicitly phenomenological.

It is discouraging to analyze the research of that small group of positivists that is responsible for producing most of the research in this field while contributing little or nothing to our understanding of the relationship between sentiments and acts. Our hope is that researchers in the growing phenomenological traditions will be attentive to the manner in which words and deeds are and are not related. This matter lies at the heart of all social science. Furthermore this issue has serious consequences for the future of applied social science and its practice.

Fiddling with People's Lives

Although, on the surface, this book may appear to be a harmless quest for knowledge about the relationship between people's sentiments and their actions, that quest clearly implies knowledge about *changing those sentiments and those actions*. It is an easy jump to apply such knowledge to consumer polling, public opinion surveys, clinical sociology, social consulting, or applied and policy work of a variety of types, including the design and evaluation of programs that plan to intervene in and alter ongoing social processes. It is at this point that we begin fiddling with people's lives and need to consider the consequences of such knowledge: Who will use it for what purposes?

We concur with the sentiment that it is "difficult to imagine a truth that . . . as a whole . . . [we are] better off not knowing" (R. A. Gordon 1969, pp. 249–50). But knowledge can hardly be divorced from the uses to which it may be put. We will resist the temptation to document this opinion with reviews of Nazi medical research on concentration camp inmates or United States Public Health Service research on syphilitic African American patients (Jones 1981), among other possible examples.

We have no more answer to this question of values and morality in research than to caution the researcher to take account of it—to consider the consequences of other peoples' use of research findings. But there is an equally urgent issue for which we do have answers. That issue has to do with efforts to apply social science research that is of questionable validity. This volume, like its predecessor, has leaned heavily on that issue and this final section will attempt to spell out some of the ways in which our findings bear upon the application of social research.

We make no Columbus-like claim to discovery of this problem. Some of the most distinguished sociologists of the past half-century have alerted us to the central issues. Robert S. Lynd's (1948) *Knowledge for What?* is subtitled *The Place of Social Science in American Culture*. The punishing attack on his contemporaries by Pitirim Sorokin (1956), one of the most prominent sociologists of the century, has been virtually ignored by the discipline's establishment. Sorokin's title is fair warning of his message: *Fads and Foibles in Modern Sociology and Related Sciences*. More recent additions to this tradition include the disillusioned Derek Phillips's (1971) *Knowledge from What?*, the "disappointed" applied sociologists Scott and Shore (1979), who agonize over the question of *Why Sociology Does Not Apply*, and the persistent Alfred McClung Lee (1978), who asks, *Knowledge for Whom?*

Perhaps the last gasp of this tradition before the malaise of the Reagan years settled over American society (including its social science) was found in Sam Sieber's (1981) documentation of the manner in which a failure to consider unintended consequences of social actions may create the very problems such actions were designed to cure. His *Fatal Remedies* transcends social science, including others who attempt to induce social change for a variety of reasons. The best evidence of the failure of social science to make a difference might be found in Bernard Barber's (1987) somewhat immodest compendium of the eight best cases he was aware of in *Effective Social Science*. If this is all (or at least the best) we have, then the radicals of the 1960s need not have feared us serving as "tools of the establishment." We were not very good tools.

This volume provides some clues as to how we might become sharper tools. If nothing else, the reader of this book ought to be persuaded that people do not always do as they say. When we couple this conclusion with the observation that the bulk of social science research is based upon what people say (in the form of polls, interviews, questionnaires, and the like), it follows that we know a great deal more about sentiments than about acts. We would not argue that sentiments are any less important than actions. They are not! We would argue that *if it is to actions that sociological practice is addressing itself, then knowledge of sentiments may be irrelevant and even misleading.*

As we have documented, the attitudes people hold are not always the same as the behaviors they engage in and a change in one does not necessarily lead to a change in the other. Does it make sense to use a verbal instrument to measure the effectiveness of a social program designed to change people's behaviors? Would not the direct observation of such behaviors (or at least indirect records or "traces" of them) be a more accurate means of evaluating such a program? The repeated evaluations of Project Head Start are a case in point.

In 1981 we analyzed twenty-eight evaluations of that program conducted between 1965 and 1980 (Deutscher and Bass 1986). The analysis of those studies suggests that Head Start has generally no effect on poor preschool children and may even occasionally be harmful. We will not dwell on the absurdity of such a conclusion, but only point out that most of the studies were rigorously designed experiments, that employed highly reliable "cognitive" measures and the most elegant analytic techniques that the state of the art made available.

There were a few exceptions in which primitive behavioral measures were employed. The most dramatic of these was conducted by a local Head Start teacher who kept her own records from Head Start through the end of high school (McDonald and Monroe 1981). She reports that of those children who began Head Start in 1967, 50 percent graduated from high school in 1980. This was in contrast with the 33 percent of graduates among her eligible children who did not attend Head Start. This simple behavioral indicator is a valid reflection of the intent of the program (in contrast to the "cognitive" measures of unknown validity employed in all twenty-eight studies). For a lot less money and effort we have a persuasive and easily understandable finding.

The elegant, expensive analyses had the potential for doing great damage to a lot of children. Fortunately, the politicians exercised better judgment than the social scientists in this instance. How long this political wisdom can survive remains unclear. Consider the response of the White House to the violence in Los Angeles, and elsewhere, that followed the acquittal of the police officers who had assaulted Rodney King in May 1992. The administration blamed the violence on the "failed" programs initiated under the Johnson administration—including Project Head Start. Following the riots, George Will, a conservative columnist, enjoyed citing "evidence" that Head Start failed to keep children in school. He repeated this announcement frequently on television news and talk shows. It follows from our analysis that this is probably untrue. However, it adds useful political ammunition to the conservative effort to eliminate all social programs. Although it may be Washington wisdom that all such programs have failed, we are not aware of any scientific evidence demonstrating the failure of any of the Great Society programs. It is in this sense that the elegant, expensive, and largely irrelevant studies have the potential for doing great damage to a lot of poor children.

As the Head Start evaluation case illustrates, validity is of the utmost importance in applied and policy research. In basic research one can afford the luxury of playing with novel techniques or methods or theories. In applied work one is playing with the lives of people and organizations. Brinkerhoff and Dressler (1990, p. 113) write of "double validity," the first being the kind of validity on which we have dwelled (the need to measure what you are supposed to be measuring). The second type of validity is peculiar to applied and policy research. It is the requirement that your measure provide useful information to the people who need to make changes. They call this "implemental validity." The present discussion is, in fact, a consideration of Brinkerhoff and Dressler's notion of double validity.

In social science work, which has direct consequences for the everyday lives of ordinary people, one must be extremely cautious when dealing with verbal statements of intentions to act. We have seen from Milgram's experiments using his electrical shocking machine as a "teaching" device (Chapter 8) that ordinary people are likely to succumb to authority and inflict pain on others *in spite of their contrary sentiments*. One of the criticisms of Milgram's work is that his subjects were aware of the experimental ploy and played along with it. Yet this same anomalous response to authority is found in a controlled study of nurses in both public and private hospitals (Hoffling, Brotzman, Dalrymple, Graves, and Pierce 1966). Twenty-one out of twenty-two nurses responded to a telephone request from an unknown physician to administer twice the maximum dosage of a drug to a patient with whom they were unfamiliar. This clearly violates nursing dictums related to telephone orders, unknown physicians, excessive dosages, and unfamiliar cases. A group of student nurses to whom this scenario was described uniformly agreed that they would not respond to such a request.

Although the investigators, being psychiatrically oriented, explain the anomalous behavior of their nurse subjects with such concepts as "repression" and "self deception" (p. 177), we have seen in Chapter 10 how easy it is for people to compartmentalize all kinds of sentiments and acts. Again, there is evidence that in their everyday life people may not do as they say, may not do as they believe, may not do as they intend, and are easy prey to persons in authority positions. Policy must not be based on utterances of intentions or other sentiments in such instances. As in the design of this study, valid conclusions must be based upon behavioral observations.

Even when using measures of behavioral intentions, rather than observing behavior, inconsistencies with attitudes can be found in applied research. The work of Kegeles and associates (1988) on the use of condoms by sexually active adolescents provides one such example. They find it "disquieting" that such adolescents, although they believe that condoms protect them from disease and attach great importance to such protection, have no intention of using condoms themselves or having their partners do so. Nickerson reminds these investigators that there are problems involved with their "attitude-behavior" research, including "the failure to consider the nature of adolescent sexual behavior and the social context in which it occurs, both of which impose situational constraints on behavioral intentions" (1990, p. 1174). The response of the investigators is that they really had no intention of dealing with the attitude-behavior discrepancy (Adler, Kegeles, and Irwin 1990).

We have seen the violence people are capable of wreaking on each other whether as a result of knuckling under to authority or for any number of other reasons. Recall that the research that initially created the itch to explore the relationship between sentiments and acts had to do with prejudice toward Orientals in the American West in the thirties (LaPiere 1934). That same author had previously studied race prejudice in France and England (1928) and would later look at Californians' views of Armenians (1936). His work was truly comparative and he found universally that people do not act toward minorities in the same way they talk about them. Almost all of the early research we found on attitude and behavior had to do with American race relations. We attributed the concentration of research in that substantive field to its clear distinction between prejudice (reflected in talk) and discrimination (reflected in overt behavior). In recent decades that useful conceptual distinction appears to have dissolved into the single word *racism*. Before becoming so vague and diffuse as to lose their value, the terms *racism* and *sexism* in our vocabulary of intergroup relations referred to the subtle, often institutional, and frequently unrecognized ways in which prejudice and discrimination manifested themselves in largely unintentional but conventionalized patterns.

The conceptual distinction between prejudice and discrimination needs to be retained, if actions to reduce these phenomena are to be properly directed. They are central to one journalist's in-depth series of interviews on race relations with soldiers in a paratroop platoon that had recently returned from the Gulf War: Duke concludes, "But while the military can change behavior, it cannot necessarily change minds" (1991, p. A12). Apparently these combat soldiers behave toward each other with the respect and camaraderie that the military situation demands of them, while continuing to harbor whatever racial stereotypes they may have brought to the situation.

In spite of the civil rights movement of the fifties and sixties and the resultant reduction of overt discrimination, racial prejudice persists in the United States. It may be a constitutional irony that we will have to live with mean and vicious thoughts and speech while carefully policing actions with considerable care. The American Civil Liberties Union, a defender to the extreme of the equal rights of all citizens, has argued vehemently against the right of university officials to expel or otherwise punish students who make racist, anti-Semitic, or homophobic remarks in public. It is the conduct of these students, they claim, and not their words that is at issue (Brown 1991). The Supreme Court took a similar position with its unanimous decision to strike down a St. Paul, Minnesota, ordinance banning hateful speech (see Jaschik, 1992). We applaud the clarity of the distinction, although we have reservations about its consequences. Words (verbal *behavior*) can hurt as much as sticks and stones, as Vissing and Straus (1989) demonstrate in their research on parents' "verbal aggression" toward children.

In recent years, elections that have involved both African American and Caucasian candidates have been instructive. They suggest that Blumer's critique of public opinion and our analysis of private and public sentiments may have been too limited. The election in 1989 of Virginia's black governor by a narrow margin, contrary to the easy victory projected by the polls, suggests that those polls were disguising private opinions behind public ones. This observation is confirmed by the defeat of black North Carolina senatorial candidate Harvey Gant in his challenge to the white Jesse Helm in 1990. It would appear that white voters do not consider it *de rigueur* to admit to pollsters what they admit in more intimate circles.

Blumer (1947) argued that election polls were one of the few exceptions to the more general irrelevance and inaccuracy of polls. Since the polling situation so closely resembled the voting situation, he thought it likely that the intention expressed to the election pollster would be the same as the behavior expressed in the voting booth. These two recent cases suggest otherwise—at least where the expression of deeply held racial prejudices is constrained by notions of propriety in public situations. The pollster is a stranger and we do not speak openly to strangers as we would to intimates on such matters.

The study of racial and ethnic animosities in America goes back at least to the work and thinking of Park and the Chicago sociologists in the 1920s, yet the rippling problems that fan out through American society as a consequence of these animosities continue into the last decade of that century. It would be serious enough if such problems were merely parochial American ones, but they are not. Wherever in the world one may look, there are people living within the bounds of a nation who are despised by the dominant group in that nation. This has been true throughout human history and it remains true today—in Europe, in Asia, in Africa as well as in North and South America. Sociology, with its long history of concern and research, can contribute to the peaceful resolution of this worldwide condition of ethnic conflict. The proposals and caveats found in this volume can be helpful in that pursuit (cf. Deutscher 1993 [forthcoming]).

It is unlikely that the self-styled "scientists" in the social sciences will pay any more attention to the evidence or arguments posed in this volume than they did to its predecessor. Whether such ignorance is explained by the sociology of knowledge, the great need some have for "scientific respectability," or a vested interest in the research ideology they harbor is essentially irrelevant. We had hoped that research would have moved in the directions we anticipated in the seventies. One of the major purposes of this volume was to determine the extent to which such movement has taken place. It has not. On the other hand, the social science practitioners, with a clearer view of the immediate consequences of their practice, may find useful clues here for the improvement of that practice.

As social scientists we have responsibility for encouraging and working for social change. There is no question about that. The question is, Change for what and for whom and why? The typical social-science-fiction future, projected by novelists, is one where, having learned how to alter people's sentiments and actions, that knowledge is ruthlessly imposed in order to achieve an accommodating uniformity in society. People are manipulated and adjusted so that they behave themselves. If Orwell's 1984 is behind schedule, it remains a possibility. It is, in fact, a not unreasonable future to project. But it is not the only one. Marx's dream became Stalin's reality; it did not have to.

One of our themes has been that people construct their lines of action and that they can do so intelligently or stupidly, with knowledge or with ignorance, benignly or maliciously. They are not, as Dennis Wrong (1961) has reminded us, helplessly socialized robots responding automatically to whatever stimuli are thrust at them. They are, rather, more like the people described by Everett C. and H. M. Hughes (1952)—people who are creative and who are autonomous. These are people who achieve their freedom through their ability to make intelligent choices among their many "others" and to interpret the situations in which they find themselves, in ways that create a reality, the social meaning of which we could all share: a good life in a good world.

References

Acock, A. and M. L. DeFleur. 1972. "A Configurational Approach to Contingent Consistency in the Attitude-Behavior Relationship." *American Sociological Review* 37:714–26.

Acock, A. and T. Fuller. 1984. "The Attitude-Behavior Relationship and Parental Influence: Circular Mobility in Thailand." *Social Forces* 62:73–84.

Adler, N. E., S. M. Kegeles, and C. E. Irwin. 1990. "The Utility of Multiple Strategies for Understanding Complex Behaviors." *American Journal of Public Health* 80:1180–82.

Adler, P. 1985. *Wheeling and Dealing: An Ethnography of an Upper-Level Drug Dealing and Smuggling Community.* New York: Columbia University Press.

Ajzen, I., R. K. Darroch, M. Fishbein, and J. A. Hornick. 1970. "Looking Backward Revisited: A Reply to Deutscher." *American Sociologist* 5:267–72.

Ajzen, I. and M. Fishbein. 1980. *Understanding Attitudes and Predicting Social Behavior.* Englewood Cliffs, NJ: Prentice-Hall.

Ajzen, I., C. Timko, and J. B. White. 1982. "Self-Monitoring and the Attitude-Behavior Relation." *Journal of Personality and Social Psychology* 42:426–35.

Albrecht, S. L. 1973. "Verbal Attitudes and Significant Other's Expectations as Predictors of Marijuana Use." *Sociology and Social Research* 57:196–207.

Albrecht, S. L., M. L. DeFleur, and L. G. Warner. 1972. "Attitude-Behavior Relationships: A Re-examination of the Postulate of Contingent Consistency." *Pacific Sociological Review* 15:149–68.

Alexander, C. N., Jr., L. G. Zucker, and C. L. Brody. 1970. "Experimental Expectations and Autokinetic Experiences: Consistency Theories and Judgmental Convergence." *Sociometry* 33:108–22.

Allen, H. E., C. E. Simonsen, and H. J. Vetter. 1971. "Attitudes and Behavior: A Test." Paper presented at the annual meeting of the Ohio Valley Sociological Society.

Allen, V. L. 1965. "Situational Factors in Conformity." Pp. 133–75 in *Advances in Social Psychology,* Vol. 2, edited by L. Berkowitz. New York: Academic Press.

Allport, G. W. 1935. "Attitudes." Pp. 798–844 in *Handbook of Social Psychology,* edited by C. Murchison. Worcester, MA: Clark University.

Almond, G. and S. Verba. 1963. *The Civic Culture.* Princeton, NJ: Princeton University Press.

Anderson, B., B. D. Silver, and P. R. Abramson. 1988. "The Effects of Race of the Interviewer on Measures of Electoral Participation by Blacks in SRC National Election Studies." *Public Opinion Quarterly* 52:53–83.

Anderson, R. B. W. 1967. "On the Comparability of Meaningful Stimuli in Cross-Cultural Research." *Sociometry* 30:124–36.

———. 1969–1970. "Hidden Translation Problems in Mono-Cultural Research." *Sociological Focus* 3:33–42.

Asch, S. E. 1951. "Effects of Group Pressure upon the Modification and Distortion of Judgment." Pp. 177–90 in *Groups, Leadership and Men*, edited by H. Guetzkow. Pittsburgh: Carnegie-Mellon University Press.

———. 1956. "Studies of Independence and Submission to Group Pressure: A Minority of One Against a Unanimous Majority." *Psychological Monographs* 70:416.

Atkinson, P. 1988. "Ethnomethodology: A Critical Review." *Annual Review of Sociology* 14:441–65.

Baer, D. J. 1966. "Smoking Attitude, Behavior, and Beliefs of College Males." *Journal of Social Psychology* 68:69–70.

Bagozzi, R. P. and R. E. Burnkrant. 1985. "Attitude Organization and the Attitude-Behavior Relation: A Reply to Dillon and Kumar." *Journal of Personality and Social Psychology* 49:47–57.

Bagozzi, R. P. and P. Schnedlitz. 1985. "Social Contingencies in the Attitude Model: A Test of Certain Interaction Hypotheses." *Social Psychology Quarterly* 48:366–73.

Bakan, D. 1968. *On Method: Toward a Reconstruction of Psychological Investigation.* San Francisco: Jossey-Bass.

Bannister, R. C. 1987. *Sociology and Scientism: The American Quest for Objectivity 1880–1940.* Chapel Hill: University of North Carolina Press.

Barber, B. (ed.). 1987. *Effective Social Science: Eight Cases in Economics, Political Science, and Sociology.* New York: Russell Sage Foundation.

Bastide, R. and P. van den Berghe. 1957. "Stereotypes, Norms, and Interracial Behavior in São Paulo, Brazil." *American Sociological Review* 22:689–94.

Baumann, K. E. and R. L. Chenowith. 1984. "The Relationship between the Consequences Adolescents Expect from Smoking and Their Behavior: A Factor Analysis with Panel Data." *Journal of Applied Social Psychology* 14:28–41.

Beck, B. 1970. "Cooking Welfare Stew." Pp. 7–30 in *Pathways to Data: Field Methods for Studying Ongoing Social Organizations*, edited by R. W. Habenstein. Chicago: Aldine.

Becker, H. S. 1989. "Comment on Smith and Carter." *Social Problems* 36:315.

———. 1990. "The Most Critical Issue Facing the American Sociological Association." *American Sociologist* 21:321–23.

Becker, H. S. and H. E. Barnes. 1952. *Social Thought from Lore to Science*, Vol. 12, 2nd ed. Washington, DC: Harren Press.

Becker, H. S. and B. Geer. 1957. "Participant Observation and Interviewing: A Comparison." *Human Organization* 16:28–32.

———. 1958. "The Fate of Idealism in Medical School." *American Sociological Review* 23:50–56.

Becker, H. S., B. Geer, E. C. Hughes, and A. L. Strauss. 1961. *Boys in White: Student Culture in Medical School.* Chicago: University of Chicago Press.

Begley, T. M. and H. Alker. 1982. "Anti-Busing Protest: Attitudes and Actions." *Social Psychology Quarterly* 45:187–97.

Benney, M. and E. C. Hughes. 1956. "Of Sociology and the Interview: Editorial Preface." *American Journal of Sociology* 62:137–42.

Berelson, B. and G. Steiner. 1964. *Human Behavior: An Inventory of Scientific Findings.* New York: Harcourt Brace Jovanovich.

Berger, P. L. and T. Luckmann. 1966. *The Social Construction of Reality: A Treatise in the Sociology of Knowledge.* Garden City, NY: Doubleday.

Bergman, G. 1951. "The Logic of Psychological Concepts." *Philosophy of Science* 18:93–110.

Bernstein, B. 1964. "Elaborated and Restricted Codes: Their Social Origins and Some Consequences." Pp. 55–69 in *The Ethnography of Communication, American Anthropologist,* special publication 66(6), part 2, edited by J. J. Gumperz and D. Hymes.

Bindman, A. M. 1965. "Interviewing in the Search for 'Truth.'" *Sociological Quarterly* 6:281–88.

Blake, J. 1955. "Family Instability and Reproductive Behavior in Jamaica." Pp. 24–41 in *Current Research in Human Fertility.* New York: Milbank Memorial Fund.

———. 1958. "A Reply to Mr. Braithwaite." *Social and Economic Studies* 7:234–37.

———. 1961. *Family Structure in Jamaica.* New York: Free Press.

Blalock, H. M., Jr. 1979. *Social Statistics.* New York: McGraw-Hill.

———. 1989. "The Real and Unrealized Contributions of Quantitative Sociology." *American Sociological Review* 54:447–61.

Blum, A. F. and P. McHugh. 1971. "The Social Ascription of Motives." *American Sociological Review* 36:98–109.

Blumer, H. 1931. "Science Without Concepts." *American Journal of Sociology* 36:515–33.

———. 1946. "Collective Behavior." Pp. 167–222 in *New Outline of the Principles of Sociology,* edited by A. M. Lee. New York: Barnes and Noble.

———. 1947. "Sociological Theory in Industrial Relations." *American Sociological Review* 12:271–77.

———. 1948. "Public Opinion and Public Opinion Polling." *American Sociological Review* 13:542–49.

———. 1955. "Attitudes and the Social Act." *Social Problems* 3:59–65.

———. 1956. "Sociological Analysis and the 'Variable.'" *American Sociological Review* 21:683–90.

———. 1966. "Sociological Implications of the Thought of George Herbert Mead." *American Journal of Sociology* 71:535–44.

———. 1969. *Symbolic Interactionism: Perspective and Method.* Englewood Cliffs, NJ: Prentice-Hall.

———. 1980. "Mead and Blumer: The Convergent Methodological Perspective of Social Behaviorism and Symbolic Interactionism." *American Sociological Review* 405:409–19.

Boden, D. 1990. "People Are Talking: Conversation Analysis and Symbolic

Interaction." Pp. 244–74 in *Symbolic Interaction and Cultural Studies*, edited by M. M. McCall and H. S. Becker. Chicago: University of Chicago Press.

Bonacich, E. 1990. "Reflections of an Outgoing American Sociological Association Office Holder." *American Sociologist* 21:327–30.

Borgida, E. and B. Campbell. 1982. "Belief Relevance and Attitude-Behavior Consistency: The Moderating Role of Personal Experience." *Journal of Personality and Social Psychology* 42:239–47.

Bortner, M. A. 1988. *Delinquency and Justice: An Age of Crisis*. New York: McGraw-Hill.

Bossard, J. H. S. 1945. "Family Modes of Expression." *American Sociological Review* 10:226–37.

Boudon, R. and F. Bourricaud. 1989. *Critical Dictionary of Sociology*, selected and translated by P. Hamilton. Chicago: University of Chicago Press.

Braithwaite, L. 1957. "Sociology and Demographic Research in the British Caribbean." *Social and Economic Studies* 6:541–50.

Brayfield, A. and D. M. Crockett. 1955. "Employee Attitudes and Employee Performance." *Psychological Bulletin* 52:396–428.

Breckler, S. J. 1984. "Empirical Validation of Affect, Behavior, and Cognition as Distinct Components of Attitude." *Journal of Personality and Social Psychology* 47:1191–1205.

Bridgman, P. W. 1927. *The Logic of Modern Physics*. New York: Macmillan.

Brinberg, D. and J. Durand. 1983. "Eating at Fastfood Restaurants: An Analysis Using Two Behavioral Intentions." *Journal of Applied Social Psychology* 13:459–72.

Brinkerhoff, R. O. and D. E. Dressler. 1990. *Productivity Measurement*. Beverly Hills, CA: Sage.

Broad, W. and N. Wade. 1982. *Betrayers of the Truth: Fraud and Deceit in the Halls of Science*. New York: Simon and Schuster.

Brody, J. 1976. "Incompetent Surgery Is Found Not Isolated." *The New York Times* (January 27).

Brown, R. W. 1958. *Words and Things*. Glencoe, IL: Free Press.

Brown, S. 1991. "Free Speech Undermined, Racism Left Untouched: The Brown University Expulsion." *Civil Liberties* 393(Spring/Summer):1–4.

Budd, R. and C. Spencer. 1984. "Latitude of Rejection, Centrality, and Certainty: Variables Affecting the Relationship between Attitudes, Norms, and Behavioral Intentions." *British Journal of Social Psychology* 23:1–8.

Bulmer, M. 1984. *The Chicago School of Sociology: Institutionalization, Diversity, and the Rise of Sociological Research*. Chicago: University of Chicago Press.

Burke, K. 1954. *Permanence and Change: An Anatomy of Purpose*. Los Altos, CA: Hermes.

Cagle, L. T. and I. Deutscher. 1970. "Housing Aspirations and Housing Achievement: The Relocation of Poor Families." *Social Problems* 18:244–56.

Campbell, A. 1965. "Review of *Public Opinion* by R.E. Lane and D.O. Sears." *American Sociological Review* 30:633.

Campbell, D. T. 1955. "The Informant in Quantitative Research." *American Journal of Sociology* 60:339–42.

————. 1957. "Factors Relevant to the Validity of Experiments in Social Settings." *Psychological Bulletin* 54:298–99.

————. 1964. "Social Attitudes and Other Acquired Dispositions." Pp. 159–62 in *Psychology: A Study of Science*, Vol. 6, edited by S. Koch. New York: McGraw-Hill.

Campbell, D. T. and D. W. Fiske. 1959. "Convergent and Discriminant Validation by the Multitrait-Multimethod Matrix." *Psychological Bulletin* 56:81–105.

Campbell, D. T. and J. C. Stanley. 1963. *Experimental and Quasi-Experimental Designs for Research*. Chicago: Rand McNally.

Chassin, L., C. C. Presson, S. J. Sherman, E. Corty, and R. W. Olshavsky. 1984. "Predicting the Onset of Cigarette Smoking in Adolescents: A Longitudinal Study." *Journal of Applied Social Psychology* 14:224–43.

Chein, I. 1949. "The Problems of Inconsistency: A Restatement." *Journal of Social Issues* 5:53–54.

Cicourel, A. V. 1967. "Kinship, Marriage, and Divorce in Comparative Family Law." *Law and Society Review* 1:103–29.

————. 1969–1970. "Language as a Variable in Social Research." *Sociological Focus* 3:43–52.

Cloward, R. A. and L. E. Ohlin. 1960. *Delinquency and Opportunity*. New York: Free Press.

Cohen, A. K. and H. M. Hodges. 1963. "Characteristics of the Lower Blue-Collar Class." *Social Problems* 10:303–33.

Cohn, S. F., S. E. Barkan, and W. A. Halteman. 1991. "Punitive Attitudes Toward Criminals: Racial Consensus or Racial Conflict?" *Social Problems* 38:287–96.

Coleman, J. W. 1989. *The Criminal Elite: The Sociology of White Collar Crime*, 2nd ed. New York: St. Martin's Press.

Coles, R. 1971. "The 'Average Man' Might Fool You." *Life* (May 7):4.

Collins, R. 1975. *Conflict Sociology*. New York: Academic Press.

Congressional Record. 1964. 88th Congress, Second Session, 110, No. 45 (March 12). Washington, D. C.

Converse, P. E. 1964. "New Dimensions of Meaning for Cross-Section Sample Surveys in Politics." *International Social Science Journal* 16:19–34.

Coser, L. A. 1971. *Masters of Sociological Thought: Ideas in Historical and Social Context*. New York: Harcourt Brace Jovanovich.

Couch, C. J., M. A. Katovich, and D. E. Miller. 1988. "The Sorrowful Tale of Small Groups Research in Social Psychology." Pp. 159–80 in *Studies in Symbolic Interaction*, edited by N.K. Denzin. Greenwich, CT: JAI Press.

Crawford, T. J. and R. Boyer. 1985. "Salient Consequences, Cultural Values, and Childbearing Intentions." *Journal of Applied Social Psychology* 15:16–30.

Crew, K. 1983. "How Much Is 'Very.'" P. 225 in *The Practice of Social Research*, 4th ed., edited by E. Babbie. Belmont, CA: Wadsworth.

Dalton, D. R. and W. D. Todor. 1985. "Attitude-Behavior Truncation in Union Stewards." *Journal of Social Psychology* 125:709–14.

Dalton, M. 1964. "Preconceptions and Methods in Men Who Manage." Pp. 50–95 in *Sociologists at Work: Essays on the Craft of Social Research*, edited by P. E. Hammond. New York: Basic Books.

Dannick, L. 1969. "The Relationship between Overt Behavior and Verbal Expressions as Influenced by Immediate Situational Determinants." Unpublished doctoral dissertation, Syracuse University, Ithaca, NY.

————. 1973. "Influence of an Anonymous Stranger on a Routine Decision to Act or Not to Act: An Experiment in Conformity." *Sociological Quarterly* 14:127–34.

Darley, J. M. and B. Latané. 1968. "Bystander Intervention in Emergencies: Diffusion of Responsibility." *Journal of Personality and Social Psychology* 8:36–42.

Davidson, A. R. and D. M. Morrison. 1983. "Predicting Contraceptive Behavior from Attitudes: A Comparison of Within- Versus Across-Subjects Procedures." *Journal of Personality and Social Psychology* 45:997–1009.

Davidson, A. R., S. Yantis, M. Norwood, and D. E. Montano. 1985. "Amount of Information about the Attitude Object and Attitude-Behavior Consistency." *Journal of Personality and Social Psychology* 49:1184–98.

Davis, R. A. 1985. "Social Structure, Beliefs, Attitude, Intention, and Behavior: A Partial Test of Liska's Revisions." *Social Psychology Quarterly* 48:89–93.

Dawes, R. M. and T. L. Smith. 1985. "Attitude and Opinion Measurement." Chapter 10 in *The Handbook of Social Psychology*, Vol. 1, 3rd ed., edited by G. Lindzey and E. Aronson. New York: Random House.

Dayton Daily News. 1991. "Census Asks About Race, Gets Some Strange Replies" (May 12):19-A.

DeFleur, M. L. and F. R. Westie. 1958. "Verbal Attitudes and Overt Acts: An Experiment in the Salience of Attitudes." *American Sociological Review* 23:667–73.

————. 1963. "Attitude as a Scientific Concept." *Social Forces* 42:17–31.

DeFriese, G. H. and W. S. Ford. 1969. "Verbal Attitudes, Overt Acts, and the Influence of Social Constraint in Interracial Behavior." *Social Problems* 16:493–505.

Delaney, H. R. and H. A. Widdison. 1990. "Contributions of American Pragmatism to the Sociology of Knowledge." *Sociological Inquiry* 60:20–34.

Denzin, N. K. 1987. "Under the Influence of Time: Reading the Interactional Text." *Sociological Quarterly* 28:327–42.

————. 1990a. "Presidential Address on the Sociological Imagination Revisited." *Sociological Quarterly* 31:1–23.

————. 1990b. "The Spaces of Postmodernism: Reading Plummer on Blumer." *Symbolic Interaction* 13:145–55.

Desroches, F. J. 1990. "Tearoom Trade: A Research Update." *Qualitative Sociology* 13:39–61.

Deutscher, I. 1958. "The Stereotype as a Research Tool." *Social Forces* 37:56–60.

————. 1966. "Words and Deeds: Social Science and Social Policy." *Social Problems* 13:235–54.

————. 1968. "Asking Questions Cross-Culturally: Some Problems of Linguistic Comparability." Pp. 318–40 in *Institutions and the Person: Essays Presented to Everett C. Hughes*, edited by H. S. Becker, B. Geer, D. Riesman, and R. S. Weiss. Chicago: Aldine.

———. 1969. "Looking Backward: Case Studies on the Progress of Methodology in Sociological Research." *American Sociologist* 4:35–41.

———. 1973. *What We Say/What We Do: Sentiments and Acts.* Glenview, IL: Scott, Foresman.

———. 1993 (forthcoming). "National Policies and Cultural Minorities: The Social Consequences of Pluralism, Assimilation,, and Repression." In *The Changing World Order,* edited by Robert L. Carroll and Musa Alshtawi. Lexington: University Press of Kentucky.

Deutscher, I. and D. Bass. 1986. "The Long-Term Effects of Head Start: An Examination of Twenty Years of Evaluation Research." Paper presented at the annual meeting of the American Sociological Association, New York.

Deutscher, I. and A. Montague. 1956. "Professional Education and Conflicting Value Systems: The Role of Religious Schools in the Educational Aspirations of Nursing Students." *Social Forces* 35:126–31.

Dillon, W. R. and A. Kumar. 1985. "Attitude Organization and the Attitude-Behavior Relation: A Critique of Bagozzi and Burnkrant's Reanalysis of Fishbein and Ajzen." *Journal of Personality and Social Psychology* 49:33–46.

Doubt, K. 1989. "Garfinkel Before Ethnomethodology." *American Sociologist* 20:252–63.

Douglas, J. D. 1967. *The Social Meaning of Suicide.* Princeton, NJ: Princeton University Press.

———. 1970. "Deviance and Order in a Pluralistic Society." Pp. 367–402 in *Theoretical Sociology: Perspectives and Developments,* edited by J. C. McInney and E. Tiryakian. New York: Appleton-Century-Crofts.

———. 1976. *Investigative Social Research: Individual and Team Field Research.* Beverly Hills, CA: Sage.

Drabek, T. E. and J. E. Haas. 1967. "Realism in Laboratory Simulation: Myth or Method." *Social Forces* 45:337–46.

Duke, L. 1991. *The Washington Post* (May 19):A1, A12.

Durkheim, E. [1897] 1951. *Suicide: A Study in Sociology.* Glencoe, IL: Free Press.

Ehrlich, H. J. 1969. "Attitudes, Behavior, and the Intervening Variables." *American Sociologist* 4:29–34.

Ehrlich, H. J. and J. W. Rinehart. 1965. "A Brief Report on the Methodology of Stereotype Research." *Social Forces* 43:564–75.

Elliott, D. S. and S. S. Ageton. 1980. "Reconciling Differences in Estimates of Self-Reported and Official Estimates of Delinquency." *American Sociological Review* 45:95–110.

Emerson, J. P. 1970. "Nothing Unusual Is Happening." Pp. 208–22 in *Human Nature and Collective Behavior: Papers in Honor of Herbert Blumer,* edited by T. Shibutani. Englewood Cliffs, NJ: Prentice-Hall.

Emerson, R. M. 1987. "Four Ways to Improve the Craft of Fieldwork." *Journal of Contemporary Ethnography* 18:123–33.

Erickson, M. 1968. "The Inhumanity of Ordinary People." *International Journal of Psychiatry* 6:277–79.

Etzioni, A. 1968a. *The Active Society: A Theory of Societal and Political Processes.* New York: Free Press.

————. 1968b. "A Model of Significant Research." *International Journal of Psychiatry* 6:279–81.

Ewans, W. L. 1969. "Letter: Looking Backward Through a Glass Darkly." *American Sociologist* 4:251.

Fazio, R. H., J. M. Chen, E. C. McDonel, and S. J. Sherman. 1982. "Attitude Accessibility, Attitude-Behavior Consistency, and the Strength of the Object-Evaluation Association." *Journal of Experimental Social Psychology* 18:339–57.

Fazio, R. H., P. M. Herr, and T. J. Olney. 1984. "Attitude Accessibility Following a Self-Perception Process." *Journal of Personality and Social Psychology* 47: 277–86.

Fazio, R. H., M. C. Powell, and P. M. Herr. 1983. "Toward a Process Model of the Attitude-Behavior Relation: Assessing One's Attitude Upon Mere Observation of the Attitude Object." *Journal of Personality and Social Psychology* 44:723–35.

Fendrich, J. M. 1967a. "A Study of the Association Among Verbal Attitudes, Commitment and Overt Behavior in Different Experimental Situations." *Social Forces* 45:347–55.

————. 1967b. "Perceived Reference Group Support: Racial Attitudes and Overt Behavior." *American Sociological Review* 32:960–70.

Filstead, W. J. 1970. *Qualitative Methodology: Firsthand Involvement with the Social World.* Chicago: Markham.

Fishbein, M. (ed.). 1967. *Readings in Attitude Theory and Measurement.* New York: Wiley.

————. 1980. "A Theory of Reasoned Action: Some Applications and Implications." Pp. 65–116 in *Nebraska Symposium on Motivation 1979*, edited by M. Page. Lincoln: University of Nebraska Press.

Fishbein, M. and I. Ajzen. 1972. "Attitudes and Opinions." Pp. 487–544 in *Annual Review of Psychology*, edited by P. H. Mussen and M. R. Rosenzweig. Palo Alto, CA: Annual Reviews.

————. 1974. "Attitudes Towards Objects as Predictory of Single and Multiple Behavioral Criteria." *Psychological Review* 81:59–74.

————. 1975. *Belief, Attitude, Intention and Behavior: An Introduction to Theory and Research.* Reading, MA: Addison-Wesley.

Fisher, W. A. 1984. "Predicting Contraceptive Behavior Among University Men: The Role of Emotions and Behavioral Intentions." *Journal of Applied Social Psychology* 14:104–23.

Frank, A. W. 1985. "Out of Ethnomethodology." Pp. 101–16 in *Micro-Sociological Theory: Perspectives on Sociological Theory*, Vol. 2, edited by H. J. Helle and S. N. Eisenstadt. Beverly Hills, CA: Sage.

Fredericks, A. J. and D. L. Dossett. 1983. "Attitude-Behavior Relations: A Comparison of the Fishbein-Ajzen and the Bentler-Speckart Models." *Journal of Personality and Social Psychology* 45:501–12.

Freeman, D. 1983. *Margaret Mead and Samoa: The Making and Unmaking of an Anthropological Myth.* Cambridge, MA: Harvard University Press.

Freeman, L. C. and T. Ataöv. 1960. "Invalidity of Indirect and Direct Measures of Attitude Toward Cheating." *Journal of Personality* 28:444–47.

Frideres, J. S., L. G. Warner, and S. L. Albrecht. 1971. "The Impact of Social Constraints on the Relationship Between Attitudes and Behavior." *Social Forces* 50:102–12.

Friedman, N. 1967. *The Social Nature of Psychological Research: The Psychological Experiment as a Social Interaction.* New York: Basic Books.

Frost, R. T. 1961. "Stability and Change in Local Party Politics." *Public Opinion Quarterly* 25:221–35.

Gallant, M. J. and S. Kleinman. 1983. "Symbolic Interactionism vs. Ethnomethodology." *Symbolic Interaction* 6:1–19.

Galliher, J. F. and R. A. Hagan. 1989. "L. L. Bernard and the Original American Sociologist." *American Sociologist* 20:134–43.

Gardner, G. T., A. P. Tiemann, L. C. Gould, D. R. DeLuca, L. W. Doob, and J. A. J. Stolwijk. 1982. "Risk and Benefit Perceptions, Acceptability Judgements, and Self-Reported Actions Toward Nuclear Power." *Journal of Social Psychology* 116:179–97.

Garfinkel, H. 1964. "Studies of the Routine Grounds of Everyday Activities." *Social Problems* 11:225–50.

———. 1967. *Studies in Ethnomethodology.* Englewood Cliffs, NJ: Prentice-Hall.

Gibbons, F. X. and R. A. Wicklund. 1982. "Self-Focused Attention and Helping Behavior." *Journal of Personality and Social Psychology* 43:462–74.

Glaser, B. and A. Strauss. 1967. *The Discovery of Grounded Theory: Strategies for Qualitative Research.* Chicago: Aldine.

Glass, G. R., B. McGaw, and M. L. Smith. 1981. *Meta-Analysis in Social Research.* Beverly Hills, CA: Sage.

Glazer, M. P. and P. M. Glazer. 1989. *Whistleblowers: Exposing Corruption in Government and Industry.* New York: Basic Books.

Glenn, E. S. 1954. "Semantic Differences in International Communication." *Review of General Semantics* 11:163–80.

Goffman, E. 1959. *The Presentation of Self in Everyday Life.* Garden City, NY: Doubleday Anchor.

———. 1964. "The Neglected Situation." Pp. 133–36 in *The Ethnography of Communication, American Anthropologist,* special publication 66(6), part 2, edited by J. J. Gumperz and D. Hymes.

———. 1981. *Forms of Talk.* Philadelphia: University of Pennsylvania Press.

———. 1989. "On Fieldwork." *Journal of Contemporary Ethnography* 18:123–33.

Gold, D. 1969. "Statistical Tests and Substantive Significance." *American Sociologist* 4:42–46.

Goldstein, I. and E. McGinnies. 1964. "Compliance and Attitude Change Under Conditions of Differential Social Reinforcement." *Journal of Abnormal and Social Psychology* 68:567–70.

Goode, W. J. 1960. "Illegitimacy in the Caribbean Social Structure." *American Sociological Review* 25:21–30.

Gorden, R. L. 1952. "Interaction between Attitude and Definition of the Situation in the Expression of Opinion." *American Sociological Review* 17:50–58.

Gordon, L. 1969. "Letter: On Attitude-Behavior Correlations." *American Sociologist* 4:250–51.

Gordon, R. A. 1969. "Letter: Amongst Competent Sociologists." *American Sociologist* 4:249–50.

Gordon, S. L. 1981. "The Sociology of Sentiments and Emotion." Pp. 562–92 in *Social Psychology: Sociological Perspectives*, edited by N. Rosenberg and R. H. Turner. New York: Basic Books.

Gorsuch, R. L. and J. Ortberg. 1983. "Moral Obligation and Attitudes: Their Relation to Behavioral Intentions." *Journal of Personality and Social Psychology* 44:1025–28.

Gould, S. J. 1977. *Ever Since Darwin: Reflections in Natural History.* New York: Norton.

———. 1981. *The Mismeasure of Man.* New York: Norton.

Gouldner, A. W. 1970. *The Coming Crisis in Western Sociology.* New York: Basic Books.

Gregory, S. W. 1983. "Temporal Symmetry in Microsocial Relation." *American Sociological Review* 48:129–36.

Gregory, S. W., S. Webster, and G. Huang. 1990. "Measuring Acoustic Components of Nonverbal Communication in Dyadic Interviews Using Fast Fourier Transform Analysis." Paper presented at the annual meeting of the American Sociological Association, Washington, DC.

Grimshaw, A. D. 1969–1970. "Some Problematic Aspects of Communication in Cross-Racial Research in the United States." *Sociological Focus* 3:67–85.

———. 1981. "Talk and Social Control." Pp. 200–32 in *Social Psychology: Sociological Perspectives*, edited by M. Rosenberg and R. H. Turner. New York: Basic Books.

Gusfield, J. 1967. "Moral Passage: The Symbolic Process in Public Deviance." *Social Problems* 15:175–88.

———. 1981. *The Culture of Public Problems: Drinking-Driving and the Symbolic Order.* Chicago: University of Chicago Press.

Guttman, L. 1944. "A Basis for Scaling Qualitative Data." *American Sociological Review* 9:139–50. Reprinted on pp. 96–107 in *Readings in Attitude Theory and Measurement*, edited by M. Fishbein. New York: Wiley, 1967.

———. 1947. "The Cornell Technique for Scale and Intensity Analysis." *Educational and Psychological Measurement* 7:247–79.

———. 1950. "The Problem of Attitude and Opinion Measurement." Pp. 60–212 in *Measurement and Prediction, Studies in Social Psychology of War*, Vol. IV, edited by S. A. Stouffer, L. Guttman, E. A. Suchman, P. F. Lazarsfeld, S. A. Stor, and J. A. Clausen. Princeton, NJ: Princeton University Press.

———. 1959. "A Structural Theory for Intergroup Beliefs and Action." *American Sociological Review* 24:318–28.

Hall, P. M. 1987. "Interactionism and the Study of Organization." *Sociological Quarterly* 28:1–22.

———. 1991. "In Search of Meso Domain: Commentary on the Contributions of Pestello and Voydanoff." *Symbolic Interaction* 14:39–47.

Hamblin, R. L. 1966. *Ratio Measurement and Sociological Theory: A Critical Analysis.* St. Louis, MO: Washington University.

———. 1971a. "Ratio Measurement for the Social Sciences." *Social Forces* 50:191–214.

————. 1971b. "Mathematical Experimentation and Sociological Theory: A Critical Analysis." *Sociometry* 34:423–52.

Hammersley, M. 1989. *The Dilemma of Qualitative Method: Herbert Blumer and the Chicago Tradition.* London: Routledge.

Haney, C. 1976. "The Play Is the Thing: Notes on Social Simulation." Pp. 177–90 in *The Research Experience,* edited by P. Golden. Itasca, IL: F. E. Peacock.

Hanson, B. G. 1990. "Human Rulers: A Meta-Theoretical Analysis of Reliability Based on Inter Rater Agreement." Paper presented at the annual meeting of the American Sociological Association, Washington, DC.

Hanson, D. J. 1965. "Notes on a Bibliography on Attitudes and Behavior." Unpublished paper.

————. 1969. "Letters: Ideological Orientations and Sociological Facts." *American Sociologist* 4:160.

Hatt, P. K. 1952. *Backgrounds of Human Fertility in Puerto Rico.* Princeton, NJ: Princeton University Press.

Helson, H. 1947. "Adaptation-Level as a Frame of Reference for Prediction of Psychological Data." *American Journal of Psychology* 30:1–29.

Hemingway, E. 1963. "Interview with Ernest Hemingway." Pp. 215–41 in *Writers at Work: The Paris Review Interview,* 2nd series, vol. 2, George Plimpton, interviewer. New York: Viking Press.

Heritage, J. 1984. *Garfinkel and Ethnomethodology.* Cambridge: Polity Press.

Hewitt, J. P. and R. Stokes. 1975. "Disclaimers." *American Sociological Review* 40:1–11.

Hilbert, R. A. 1990. "Ethnomethodology and the Micro-Macro Order." *American Sociological Review* 55:794–809.

Hill, D., G. Gardner, and J. Rassaby. 1985. "Factors Predisposing Women to Take Precautions Against Breast and Cervix Cancer." *Journal of Applied Social Psychology* 15:59–79.

Hill, R. J. 1981. "Attitudes and Behavior." Pp. 347–77 in *Social Psychology: Sociological Perspectives,* edited by M. Rosenberg and R. H. Turner. New York: Basic Books.

Hill, R. J. and K. S. Crittenden (eds.). 1968. *Proceedings of the Purdue Symposium on Ethnomethodology.* West Lafayette, IN: Institute for the Study of Social Change, Department of Sociology, Purdue University.

Himmelstein, P. and J. C. Moore. 1963. "Racial Attitudes and the Action of Negro- and White-Background Figures as Factors in Petition-Signing." *Journal of English Psychology* 61:267–72.

Hochschild, A. R. 1983. *The Managed Heart: Commercialization of Human Feeling.* Berkeley: University of California Press.

————. 1989. *The Second Shift: Working Parents and the Revolution at Home.* New York: Viking-Penguin.

————. 1990. "Ideology and Emotion Management: A Perspective and Path for Future Research." Pp. 117–42 in *Research Agendas in the Sociology of Emotions,* edited by T. D. Kemper. Albany: State University of New York Press.

Hoffling, C. K., E. Brotzman, S. Dalrymple, N. Graves, and C. M. Pierce. 1966. "An Experimental Study in Nurse-Physician Relationships." *Journal of Nervous and Mental Disease* 143:171–80.

Holland, C.H. 1967. "Sources of Variance in the Experimental Investigation of Behavioral Obedience." Unpublished doctoral dissertation. University of Connecticut, Storrs.

Hovland, C. J. 1959. "Reconciling Conflicting Results Derived from Experimental and Survey Studies of Attitude Change." *American Psychologist* 14:8–17.

Hughes, E. C. and H. M. Hughes. 1952. *Where Peoples Meet: Racial and Ethnic Frontiers*. Glencoe, IL: Free Press.

Humphreys, L. 1975. *Tearoom Trade: Impersonal Sex in Public Places*, enlarged edition. Chicago: Aldine.

Hunt, W. H., W. W. Crane, and J. C. Wahlke. 1964. "Interviewing Political Elites in Cross-Cultural Comparative Research." *American Journal of Sociology* 70:59–68.

Hunter, C. H. 1984. "Aligning Actions: Types and Social Distribution." *Symbolic Interaction* 7:155–74.

Hyman, H. 1949. "Inconsistencies as a Problem in Attitude Measurement." *Journal of Social Issues* 5:38–42.

_____. 1954. *Interviewing in Social Research*. Chicago: University of Chicago Press.

Insko, C. A. and J. Schopler. 1967. "Triadic Consistency: A Statement of Affective-Cognitive Consistency." *Psychological Review* 74:361–76.

Irwin, J. 1987. "Reflections on Ethnography." *Journal of Contemporary Ethnography* 16:41–49.

Jaccard, J. and M. A. Becker. 1985. "Attitudes and Behavior: An Information Integration Perspective." *Journal of Experimental Social Psychology* 21:440–65.

Jaccard, J. and D. Sheng. 1984. "A Comparison of Six Methods for Assessing the Importance of Perceived Consequences in Behavioral Decisions: Applications from Attitude Research." *Journal of Experimental Social Psychology* 20:1–28.

Jacobs, J. 1967. "A Phenomenological Study of Suicide Notes." *Social Problems* 15:60–72.

Jaschik, S. 1992. "Campus 'Hate Speech' Codes in Doubt after High Court Rejects a City Ordinance." *Chronicle of Higher Education* (July 1):A19, A22.

Jones, E. L. 1963. "Courtesy Bias in South-East Asian Surveys." *International Social Science Journal* 15:70–76.

Jones, J. H. 1981. *Bad Blood: The Tuskegee Syphilis Experiment*. Glencoe, IL: Free Press.

Jordan, N. 1963. "Some Critical Thoughts Concerning Public Opinion Polls." Discussion Paper HI-188-DP:4. Hudson Institute, Indianapolis, IN.

_____. 1965. "The 'Asymmetry' of 'Liking' and 'Disliking': A Phenomenon Meriting Further Reflection and Research." *Public Opinion Quarterly* 29:315–22.

_____. 1968. *Themes in Speculative Psychology*. London: Tavistock.

Kantola, S. J., G. J. Syme, and N. A. Campbell. 1982. "The Role of Individual Differences and External Variables in a Test of the Sufficiency of Fishbein's Model to Explain Behavioral Intentions to Conserve Water." *Journal of Applied Social Psychology* 12:70–83.

Kantola, S. J., G. J. Syme, and A. R. Nesdale. 1983. "The Effects of Appraised Severity and Efficacy in Promoting Water Conservation: An Informational Analysis." *Journal of Applied Social Psychology* 13:164–82.

Kantrowitz, B. 1992. "Sociology's Lonely Crowd." *Newsweek* (February 3):55.

Katz, J. 1982. "The Impact of Time Proximity and Level of Generality on Attitude-Behavior Consistency." *Journal of Applied Social Psychology* 12: 151–68.

———. 1985. "The Role of Behavioral Intentions in the Prediction of Behavior." *Journal of Social Psychology* 125:149–55.

———. 1988. *Seductions of Crime.* New York: Basic Books.

Katzev, R. D. and A. K. Averill. 1984. "Knowledge of the Bystander Problem and Its Impact on Subsequent Behavior." *Journal of Social Psychology* 123:223–30.

Keesing, F. M. and M. M. Keesing. 1956. *Elite Communications in Samoa: A Study of Leadership.* Stanford: Stanford University Press.

Kegeles, S. M., N. E. Adler, and C. C. Irwin. 1988. "Sexually Active Adolescents and Condoms: Changes over One Year in Knowledge, Attitudes and Use." *American Journal of Public Health* 78:460–61.

Kelman, H. C. 1958. "Compliance, Identification, and Internalization: Three Processes of Attitude Change." *Journal of Conflict Resolution* 2:51–60.

Kendler, H. H. and T. S. Kendler. 1949. "A Methodological Analysis of the Research Area of Inconsistent Behavior." *Journal of Social Issues* 5:27–31.

Kirk, J. and M. L. Miller. 1986. *Reliability and Validity in Qualitative Research.* Beverly Hills, CA: Sage.

Klandermans, B. 1985. "Individuals and Collective Action: Rejoinder to Schrager." *American Sociological Review* 50:860–61.

Kohn, M. and R. Williams. 1956. "Situational Patterning in Intergroup Relations." *American Sociological Review* 21:164–74.

Kreiger, S. 1979. *Hip Capitalism.* Beverly Hills, CA: Sage.

Kriesberg, L. 1956. "National Security and Conduct in the Steel Gray Market." *Social Forces* 34:268–77.

Kurtz, L. R. 1984. *Evaluating Chicago Sociology.* Chicago: University of Chicago Press.

Labov, W. 1966. "The Effect of Social Mobility on Linguistic Behavior." *Sociological Inquiry* 36:186–203.

Lacey, R. 1986. *Ford: The Men and the Machine.* New York: Ballantine.

Lalljee, M., L. B. Brown, and G. P. Ginsberg. 1984. "Attitudes, Dispositions, Behavior, or Evaluation?" *British Journal of Social Psychology* 23:233–44.

LaPiere, R. T. 1928. "Race Prejudice: France and England." *Social Forces* 7:102–11.

———. 1934. "Attitudes vs. Actions." *Social Forces* 13:230–37.

———. 1936. "Type-Rationalizations of Group Antipathy." *Social Forces* 15:232–37.

———. 1969. "Comment on Irwin Deutscher's 'Looking Backward.'" *American Sociologist* 4:41–42.

LaRossa, R. 1988. "Renewing Our Faith in Qualitative Family Research." *Journal of Contemporary Ethnography* 17:243–62.

Lastrucci, C. L. 1970. "Looking Forward: The Case for Hard-Nosed Methodology." *American Sociologist* 5:273–75.

Lauer, R. H. 1971. "The Problems and Values of Attitude Research." *Sociological Quarterly* 12:247–52.

Lawton, M. P. and A. E. Goldman. 1958. "Cigarette Smoking and Attitude Toward the Etiology of Lung Cancer." *American Psychologist* 13:342.

Lee, A. M. 1978. *Sociology for Whom?* New York: Oxford University Press.

Lengermann, D. M. 1988. "Robert E. Park and the Theoretical Content of Chicago Sociology: 1920–1940." *Sociological Inquiry* 58:361–78.

Lerner, D. 1956. "Interviewing Frenchmen." *American Journal of Sociology* 62: 187–94.

Lewis, J. D. and R. L. Smith. 1980. *American Pragmatism: Mead, Chicago Sociology, and Symbolic Interaction.* Chicago: University of Chicago Press.

Lewis, O. 1951. *Life in a Mexican Village: Tepoztlan Restudied.* Urbana: University of Illinois Press.

Lieberson, S. 1985. *Making It Count: The Improvement of Sociological Theory and Research.* Berkeley: University of California Press.

Liebow, E. 1967. *Tally's Corner: A Study of Negro Streetcorner Men.* Boston: Little, Brown.

Likert, R. 1932. "The Method of Constructing an Attitude Scale." *Archives of Psychology* 140:44–53.

Linn, L. S. 1965. "Verbal Attitudes and Overt Behavior: A Study of Racial Discrimination." *Social Forces* 43:353–64.

Lipset, S. M. 1990. "A Unique People in an Exceptional Country." Pp. 3–29 in *American Pluralism and the Jewish Community,* edited by S. M. Lipset. New Brunswick, NJ: Transaction.

Liska, A. E. 1984. "A Critical Examination of the Causal Structure of the Fishbein/Ajzen Attitude-Behavior Model." *Social Psychology Quarterly* 47:61–74.

Liska, A. E., R. B. Felson, M. Chamlin, and W. Baccaglini. 1984. "Estimating Attitude-Behavior Reciprocal Effects Within a Theoretical Specification." *Social Psychology Quarterly* 47:15–23.

Lobel, T. E. 1982. "The Prediction of Behavior from Different Types of Beliefs." *Journal of Social Psychology* 118:213–23.

Lohman, J. D. and D. R. Reitzes. 1954. "Deliberately Organized Groups and Racial Behavior." *American Sociological Review* 19:342–48.

Lord, C. G., M. R. Lepper, and D. Mackie. 1984. "Attitude Prototypes as Determinants of Attitude-Behavior Consistency." *Journal of Personality and Social Psychology* 46:1254–66.

Luchins, A. S. and E. H. Luchins. 1955. "On Conformity with True and False Communications." *Journal of Social Psychology* 42:283–303.

———. 1961. "On Conformity with Judgments of a Majority or an Authority." *Journal of Social Psychology* 53:303–16.

Lynd, R. S. 1948. *Knowledge for What: The Place of Social Science in American Culture.* Princeton, NJ: Princeton University Press.

Maines, D. R. 1977. "Social Organization and Social Structure in Symbolic Interactionist Thought." *Annual Review of Sociology* 3:235–60.

———. 1981. "Recent Developments in Symbolic Interaction." Pp. 461–86 in *Social Psychology through Symbolic Interaction,* 2nd ed., edited by G. P. Stone and H. A. Farberman. New York: Wiley.

———. 1982. "In Search of Mesostructure: Studies in the Negotiated Order." *Urban Life* 11:267–80.

———. 1987. "The Significance of Temporality for the Development of Sociological Theory." *Sociological Quarterly* 28:303–12.

Manstead, A. S. R., C. E. Plevin, and J. L. Smart. 1984. "Predicting Mother's Choice of Infant Feeding Method." *British Journal of Social Psychology* 23: 223–31.

Manstead, A. S. R., C. Profitt, and J. L. Smart. 1983. "Predicting and Understanding Mothers' Infant-Feeding Intentions and Behavior: Testing the Theory of Reasoned Action." *Journal of Personality and Social Psychology* 44: 657–71.

Marquis, K. H. 1970. "Effects of Social Reinforcement on Health Reporting in the Household Interview." *Sociometry* 33:203–15.

Martin, H. H. 1963. "Why She Really Goes to Market." *Saturday Evening Post* (September 28):40–43.

Martin, J. D. 1970. "Suspicion and the Experimental Confederate: A Study of Role and Credibility." *Sociometry* 33:178–92.

Marwell, G. 1991. "On Bias in *American Sociological Review:* A Reply to Scheff." *Footnotes* 19:7, 13.

Masserman, J. 1968. "Debatable Conclusions." *International Journal of Psychiatry* 6:281–82.

Mayhew, B. 1968. "Behavioral Observability and Compliance with Religious Proscriptions on Birth Control." *Social Forces* 47:60–70.

McCall, M. M. and J. Wittner. 1990. "The Good News about Life History." Pp. 46–89 in *Symbolic Interaction and Cultural Studies*, edited by H. S. Becker and M. M. McCall. Chicago: University of Chicago Press.

McDonald, M. S. and E. Monroe. 1981. *A Follow-Up Study of the 1966 Head Start Program.* Rome, GA: Rome City Schools.

McPhail, C. and C. Rexroat. 1979. "Mead vs. Blumer: The Divergent Methodological Perspectives of Social Behaviorism and Symbolic Interactionism." *American Sociological Review* 44:449–67.

Mead, G. H. 1934. *Mind, Self and Society.* Chicago: University of Chicago Press.

———. 1936. *Movements of Thought in the Nineteenth Century*, edited, with an introduction, by M. H. Moore. Chicago: University of Chicago Press.

Mead, M. 1928. *Coming of Age in Samoa: A Psychological Study of Primitive Youth for Western Civilization.* New York: W. Morrow.

Melton, A. W. 1962. "Editorial." *Journal of Experimental Psychology* 64:553–54.

Meltzer, B. N. and J. W. Petras. 1970. "The Chicago and Iowa Schools of Symbolic Interactionism." Pp. 3–18 in *Human Nature and Collective Behavior: Papers in Honor of Herbert Blumer*, edited by T. Shibutani. Englewood Cliffs, NJ: Prentice-Hall.

Merton, R. K. 1940. "Fact and Factitiousness in Ethnic Opinionnaires." *American Sociological Review* 5:13–27.

———. 1949. "Discrimination and the American Creed." Pp. 49–126 in *Discrimination and National Welfare*, edited by R. M. McIver. New York: Harper.

———. 1957. *Social Theory and Social Structure.* Glencoe, IL: Free Press.

Milgram, S. 1961. "Nationality and Conformity." *Scientific American* 215:45–51.

———. 1964. "Group Pressure and Action Against a Person." *Journal of Abnormal and Social Psychology* 69:137–43.

———. 1965. "Some Conditions of Obedience and Disobedience to Authority." *Human Relations* 18:57–75.

_____. 1968a. "Some Conditions of Obedience and Disobedience to Authority." *International Journal of Psychiatry* 6:259–76.

_____. 1968b. "A Reply to Critics." *International Journal of Psychiatry* 6:294–96.

Miller, D. 1986. "Milgram Redux: Obedience and Disobedience in Authority Relations." Pp. 77–105 in *Studies in Symbolic Interaction*, Vol. 7, Part A, edited by N. K. Denzin. Greenwich, CT: JAI Press.

Miller, N., D. C. Butler, and J. A. McMartin. 1960. "The Ineffectiveness of Punishment Power in Group Interaction." *Sociometry* 32:24–41.

Mills, C. W. 1939. "Language, Logic, and Culture." *American Sociological Review* 4:670–80.

_____. 1940a. "Methodological Consequences of the Sociology of Knowledge." *American Journal of Sociology* 46:316–30.

_____. 1940b. "Situated Actions and Vocabularies of Motive." *American Sociological Review* 5:904–13.

_____. 1954. "IBM Plus Reality Plus Humanism = Sociology." *Saturday Review* (May 1):22–23, 54–56.

_____. 1959. *The Sociological Imagination*. New York: Oxford University Press.

_____. 1963. "The Language and Ideas of Ancient China." Pp. 469–520 in *Power, Politics, and People: The Collected Essays of C. Wright Mills*, edited by I. L. Horowitz. New York: Oxford University Press.

Mills, T. and S. Kleinman. 1988. "Emotions, Reflexivity and Action: An Interactionist Analysis." *Social Forces* 66:1009–27.

Minard, R. D. 1952. "Race Relationships in the Pocahontas Coal Field." *Journal of Social Issues* 8:29–44.

Mishler, E. G. 1990. "Validation in Inquiry-Guided Research: The Role of Exemplars in Narrative Studies." *Harvard Educational Review* 60:415–41.

Mitchell, R. E. 1965. "Survey Materials Collected in the Developing Countries: Sampling, Measurement and Interviewing Obstacles to Intra- and International Comparisons." *International Social Science Journal* 17:665–85.

Mullen, B. 1989. *Advanced Basic Meta-Analysis*. Hillsdale, NJ: Lawrence Erlbaum Associates.

Myrdal, G. 1944. *An American Dilemma*. New York: Harper.

Newcomb, T. 1948. "Discussion." *American Sociological Review* 13:550.

Nickerson, C. A. E. 1990. "The Attitude/Behavior Discrepancy as a Methodological Artifact: Comment on Sexually Active Adolescents and Condoms." *American Journal of Public Health* 80:1174–78.

Ogburn, W. F. 1957. "Cultural Lag as Theory." *Sociology and Social Research* 41:167–74.

Oliner, S. and P. Oliner. 1988. *The Altruistic Personality: Rescuers of Jews in Nazi Europe*. New York: Free Press.

Orne, M. T. 1962. "On the Social Psychology of the Psychological Experiment: With Particular Reference to Demand Characteristics and Their Implications." *American Psychologist* 17:776–83.

_____. 1969. "Demand Characteristics and the Concept of Quasi-Controls." Pp. 143–79 in *Artifact in Behavioral Research*, edited by R. Rosenthal and R. Rosnow. New York: Academic Press.

———. 1970. "Hypnosis, Motivation, and the Ecological Validity of the Psychological Experiment." Pp. 187–265 in *Nebraska Symposium on Motivation,* edited by W. J. Arnold and M. M. Page. Lincoln: University of Nebraska Press.

Orne, M. T. and C. H. Holland. 1968. "On the Ecological Validity of Laboratory Deceptions." *International Journal of Psychiatry* 6:282–93.

Osgood, C. E. 1952. "The Nature and Measurement of Meaning." Pp. 1–3 in *Semantic Differential Technique: A Sourcebook,* edited by J. G. Snyder and C. E. Osgood. Chicago: Aldine.

Osgood, C. E., G. Suci, and P. Tannenbaum. 1957. *The Measurement of Meaning.* Urbana: University of Illinois Press.

Pagel, M. D. and A. R. Davidson. 1984. "A Comparison of Three Social- Psychological Models of Attitude and Behavioral Plan: Prediction of Contraceptive Behavior." *Journal of Personality and Social Psychology* 47:517–33.

Park, R. E. and E. W. Burgess. 1921. *Introduction to the Science of Sociology.* Chicago: University of Chicago Press.

Pavlov, I. P. 1927. *Conditional Reflexes: An Investigation of the Psychological Activity of the Cerebral Cortex.* London: Oxford University Press.

Peneff, J. 1988. "The Observers Observed: French Survey Researchers at Work." *Social Problems* 35:520–35.

Perinbanayagam, R. S. 1991. *Discursive Acts.* Hawthorne, NY: Aldine de Gruyter.

Pestello, F. G. and F. P. Pestello. 1991. "Ignored, Neglected, and Abused: The Behavior Variable in Attitude-Behavior Research." *Symbolic Interaction* 14:341–51.

Pestello, F. G., F. P. Pestello, and I. Deutscher. 1992. "The Four Flaws in Attitude-Behavior Research." Paper presented at the Annual Meetings of the Midwest Sociological Society, Kansas City, MO.

Pestello, F. G. and P. Voydanoff. 1991a. "In Search of Mesostructure in the Family: An Interactionist Approach to Division of Labor." *Symbolic Interaction* 14:105–28.

———. 1991b. "Continuing the Quest for Meso Domain: Response to Peter M. Hall." *Symbolic Interaction* 14:135–37.

Pestello, F. P. 1985. "Principles and Practices in a Food Cooperative." Unpublished doctoral dissertation, University of Akron, Ohio.

———. 1987. "The Social Construction of Grades." *Teaching Sociology* 15:410–14.

———. 1991. "Discounting." *Journal of Contemporary Ethnography* 20:26–46.

Pestello, F. P. and F. G. Pestello. 1991 . "Precision and Elusion: The Saga of the Attitude Variable in Attitude-Behavior Research." *Studies in Symbolic Interaction* 12:255–80.

Phillips, D. L. 1971. *Knowledge from What: Theories and Methods in Social Research.* Chicago: Rand McNally.

Polanyi, M. 1958. *Personal Knowledge.* Chicago: University of Chicago Press.

Pollner, M. 1991. "Left of Ethnomethodology: The Rise and Decline of Radical Reflexivity." *American Sociological Review* 56:370–81.

Potter, J. and M. Wetherell. 1987. *Discourse and Social Psychology: Beyond Attitudes and Behavior.* London: Sage.

Prothero, J. and L. R. Beach. 1984. "Retirement Decisions: Expectations, Intention, and Action." *Journal of Applied Social Psychology* 14:162–74.

Punch, M. 1986. *The Politics and Ethics of Fieldwork*. Beverly Hills, CA: Sage.

Raden, D. 1977. "Situational Thresholds and Attitude-Behavior Consistency." *Sociometry* 40:123–29.

———. 1985. "Strength-Related Attitude Dimensions." *Social Psychology Quarterly* 48:312–30.

Ransford, H. E. 1968. "Isolation, Powerlessness and Violence: A Study of Attitudes and Participation in the Watts Riot." *American Journal of Sociology* 73:581–91.

Raven, B. H. 1959. "Social Influence on Opinions and the Communication of Related Content." *Journal of Abnormal and Social Psychology* 58:119–28.

Raymond, C. 1991. "Overuse of College Students in Psychology Studies Said to Result in Flawed View of Human Nature." *Chronicle of Higher Education* (June 26):A5.

Razran, G. H. S. 1939. "A Quantitative Study of Meaning by a Conditioned Salivary Technique (Semantic Conditioning)." *Science* 90:89–90.

Redfield, R. 1930. *Tepoztlan, a Mexican Village*. Chicago: University of Chicago Press.

Rhoades, L. J. 1981. *A History of the American Sociological Association 1905–1980*. Washington, DC: American Sociological Association.

Richardson, L. 1988. "The Collective Story: Postmodernism and the Writing of Sociology." *Sociological Focus* 21:199–209.

Riesman, D. 1958. "Some Observations on the Interviewing in the Teacher Apprehension Study." Pp. 277n in *The Academic Mind*, edited by P. F. Lazarsfeld and W. Thielens, Jr. Glencoe, IL: Free Press.

Riesman, D. and R. Denny. 1950. *The Lonely Crowd: A Study of Changing American Character*. New Haven, CT: Yale University Press.

Riess, B. F. 1946. "Genetic Changes in Semantic Conditioning." *Journal of Experimental Psychology* 36:143–52.

Rochberg–Halton, E. 1982. "The Real Relation Between Pragmatism and Chicago Sociology." *Contemporary Sociology* 11:140–42.

Rodman, H. 1963. "The Lower-Class Value Stretch." *Social Forces* 42:205–15.

———. 1966. "Illegitimacy in the Caribbean Social Structure: A Reconsideration." *American Sociological Review* 31:673–83.

Roebuck, J. and S. L. Spray. 1967. "The Cocktail Lounge." *American Journal of Sociology* 72:388–95.

Rokeach, M. 1970. *Beliefs, Attitudes and Values: A Theory of Organization and Change*. San Francisco: Jossey-Bass.

Rose, A. M. 1956. "Intergroup Relations vs. Prejudice: Pertinent Theory for the Study of Social Change." *Social Problems* 4:173–76.

———. 1961. "Inconsistencies in Attitudes Toward Negro Housing." *Social Problems* 8:286–92.

Rosensweig, S. 1933. "The Experimental Situation as a Psychological Problem." *Psychological Review* 40:337–54.

Rosenthal, R. 1966. *Experimenter Effects in Behavioral Research*. New York: Appleton-Century-Crofts.

Rosenthal, R. and R. L. Rosnow. 1975. *The Volunteer Subject*. New York: Wiley.

Roth, J. A. 1965. "Hired Hand Research." *American Sociologist* 1:190–96.

Roy, D. 1952. "Quota Restrictions and Goldbricking in a Machine Shop." *American Journal of Sociology* 57:427–42.

Sacks, J. J., W. M. Krushat, and J. Newman. 1980. "Reliability of the Health Hazard Appraisal." *American Journal of Public Health* 70:730–32.

Salancik, G. R. 1982. "Attitude-Behavior Consistencies as Social Logics." Pp. 51–73 in *Consistency in Social Behavior: The Ontario Symposium*, Vol. 2, edited by M. P. Zanna, E. T. Higgins, and C. P. Herman. Hillsdale, NJ: Lawrence Erlbaum Associates.

Salomon, A. 1945. "German Sociology." Pp. 586–614 in *Twentieth Century Sociology*, edited by G. Gurvitch and W. E. Moore. New York: Philosophical Library.

Schatzman, L. and A. Strauss. 1955. "Social Class and Modes of Communication." *American Journal of Sociology* 60:336–37.

Scheff, T. J. 1968. "Negotiating Reality: Notes on Power in the Assessment of Responsibility." *Social Problems* 16:3–17.

———. 1983. "Toward Integration in the Social Psychology of Emotions." *Annual Review of Sociology* 9:333–54.

———. 1990. *Microsociology: Discourse, Emotion, and Social Structure*. Chicago: University of Chicago Press.

———. 1991. "Is There Bias in *American Sociological Review* Article Selection?" *Footnotes* 19:5.

Schlenker, B. R. 1982. "Translating Actions into Attitudes: An Identity-Analytic Approach to the Explanation of Social Conduct." Pp. 193–247 in *Advances in Experimental Social Psychology*, Vol. 15, edited by L. Berkowitz. New York: Academic Press.

Schlenker, B. R. and H. J. Goldman. 1982. "Attitude Change as a Self-Presentation Tactic Following Attitude-Consistent Behavior: Effects of Choice and Role." *Social Psychology Quarterly* 45:92–99.

Schuman, H. and M. P. Johnson. 1976. "Attitudes and Behavior." Pp. 161–207 in *Annual Review of Sociology*, edited by A. Inkles, J. Coleman, and N. Smelser. Palo Alto, CA: Annual Reviews.

Scott, M. B. and S. M. Lyman. 1968. "Accounts." *American Sociological Review* 33:46–62.

Scott, R. A. and A. R. Shore. 1979. *Why Sociology Does Not Apply: A Study of the Use of Sociology in Public Policy*. New York: Elsevier.

Scully, D. and J. Marolla. 1985. "Riding the Bull at Gilley's: Convicted Rapists Describe the Rewards of Rape." *Social Problems* 32:251–63.

Shanab, M. and K. A. Yahya. 1977. "A Behavioral Study of Obedience in Children." *Journal of Personality and Social Psychology* 35:530–36.

Shepherd, G. J. and D. J. O'Keefe. 1984. "Separability of Attitudinal and Normative Influences on Behavioral Intentions in the Fishbein-Ajzen Model." *Journal of Social Psychology* 122:287–88.

Sherif, M. 1958. "Group Influences on the Formation of Norms and Attitudes." Pp. 219–32 in *Readings in Social Psychology*, edited by E. Maccoby, T. Newcomb, and E. Hartley. New York: Henry Holt.

Sherman, S. J. and R. P. Fazio. 1983. "Parallels between Attitudes and Traits as Predictors of Behavior." *Journal of Personality* 51:308–45.

Shilts, R. 1987. *And the Band Played On: Politics, People and the AIDS Epidemic.* New York: St. Martin's Press.

Sieber, S. D. 1981. *Fatal Remedies: The Ironies of Social Intervention.* New York: Plenum.

Silverman, I. and A. D. Shulman. 1970. "A Conceptual Model of Artifact in Attitude Change Studies." *Sociometry* 33:97–107.

Simey, T. S. 1946. *Welfare Planning in the West Indies.* Oxford: Clarendon Press.

Sivacek, J. and W. D. Crano. 1982. "Vested Interest as a Moderator of Attitude-Behavior Consistency." *Journal of Personality and Social Psychology* 43:210–21.

Sjoberg, L. 1982. "Attitude-Behavior Correlation, Social Desirability and Perceived Diagnostic Value." *British Journal of Social Psychology* 21:283–92.

Skinner, B. F. 1957. *Verbal Behavior.* New York: Appleton-Century-Crofts.

Smith, A. C. and S. Kleinman. 1989. "Managing Emotions in Medical School: Students' Contacts with the Living and the Dead." *Social Psychology Quarterly* 52:56–69.

Smith, T. W. and W. Carter. 1989. "Observing 'The Observers Observed': A Comment." *Social Problems* 36:310–12.

Snyder, M. and D. Kendzierski. 1982a. "Acting on One's Attitudes: Procedures for Linking Attitudes and Behavior." *Journal of Experimental Social Psychology* 18:165–83.

————. 1982b. "Choosing Social Situations: Investigating the Origins of Correspondence between Attitudes and Behavior." *Journal of Personality* 50:280–95.

Social Science Research Council. 1954. "Narrowing the Gap between Field Studies and Laboratory Experiments in Social Psychology." *Social Science Research Council Items* 8:38–39.

Sorokin, P. 1956. *Fads and Foibles in Modern Sociology and Related Sciences.* Chicago: Henry Regnery.

Spencer, H. 1862. *First Principles.* New York: Burt.

————. 1874. *The Study of Sociology.* New York: D. Appleton.

Steffensmeier, D. J. and R. M. Terry. 1975. *Examining Deviance Experimentally.* Port Washington, NY: Alfred.

Stokes, R. and J. P. Hewitt. 1976. "Aligning Actions." *American Sociological Review* 41:838–49.

Strauss, A. 1978. *Negotiations: Varieties, Contexts, Processes, and Social Order.* San Francisco: Jossey-Bass.

Strauss, G. 1952. "Direct Observation as a Source of Quasi-Sociometric Observation." *Sociometry* (February/May):141–45.

Stricker, L. J., S. Messick, and D. N. Jackson. 1969. "Evaluating Deception in Psychological Research." *Psychological Bulletin* 71:343–51.

Stryker, S. 1980. *Symbolic Interactionism: A Social Structural Version.* Menlo Park, CA: Benjamin/Cummings.

————. 1982. "Editor's Comment." *American Sociological Review* 47:iii.

Stults, D. M. and L. A. Messé. 1985. "Behavioral Consistency: The Impact of Public Versus Private Statements of Intentions." *Journal of Social Psychology* 125:277–78.

Stults, D. M., L. A. Messé, and N. L. Kerr. 1984. "Belief Discrepant Behavior and the Bogus Pipeline: Impression Management or Arousal Attribution." *Journal of Experimental Social Psychology* 20:47–54.

Stutzman, T. M. and S. B. Green. 1982. "Factors Affecting Energy Consumption: Two Field Tests of the Fishbein-Ajzen Model." *Journal of Social Psychology* 117:183–201.

Suchman, L. and B. Jordan. 1990. "Interactional Troubles in Face-to-Face Survey Interviews." *Journal of American Statistical Association* 85:232–41.

Sutherland, E. H. and D. Cressey. 1978. *Criminology.* Philadelphia: J. B. Lippincott.

Sykes, G. M. and D. Matza. 1957. "Techniques of Neutralization: A Theory of Delinquency." *American Sociological Review* 22:664–70.

Tarter, D. E. 1970. "Attitude: The Mental Myth." *American Sociologist* 5:276–78.

Tausky, C. and E. B. Piedmont. 1968. "The Sampling of Behavior." *American Sociologist* 3:49–51.

Taylor, S. J. and R. Bogdan. 1984. *Introduction to Qualitative Research Methods: The Search for Meaning, 2nd ed.* New York: Wiley.

Thomas, J. 1984. "Some Aspects of Negotiated Order, Loose Coupling and Mesostructure in Maximum Security Prisons." *Symbolic Interaction* 7:213–31.

Thomas, W. I. and F. Znaniecki. 1918. *The Polish Peasant in Europe and America.* Boston: Badger.

Thornton, A., D. Alwin, and D. Camburn. 1983. "Causes and Consequences of Sex-Role Attitudes and Attitude Change." *American Sociological Review* 48:211–27.

Thurstone, L. L. 1928. "Attitudes Can Be Measured." *American Journal of Sociology* 33:529–44.

Tittle, C. R. and R. J. Hill. 1967. "Attitude Measurement and Prediction of Behavior: An Evaluation of Conditions and Measurement Techniques." *Sociometry* 30:199–213.

Trow, M. 1958. "Comment on 'Participant Observation and Interviewing: A Comparison.'" *Human Organization* 16:33–35.

Van Maanen, J. (ed.). 1990. *The Presentation of Ethnographic Research.* Special Issue, *Journal of Contemporary Ethnography* 19.

Vaughn, S. M. 1983. "The Normative Structure of College Students and Patterns of Drinking Behavior." *Sociological Focus* 16:181–93.

Vissing, Y. M. and M. A. Straus. 1989. "Verbal Aggression by Parents and Psycho-Social Problems of Children." Paper presented at the annual meeting of the Society for the Study of Social Problems, Berkeley, California.

Wachter, K. W. and M. L. Straf (eds.). 1990. *The Future of Meta-Analysis.* New York: Russell Sage Foundation.

Warner, L. G. and M. L. DeFleur. 1969. "Attitude as an Interactional Concept: Social Constraint and Social Distance as Intervening Variables between Attitudes and Action." *American Sociological Review* 34:153–69.

Warriner, C. K. 1958. "The Nature and Functions of Official Morality." *American Journal of Sociology* 64:165–68.

Warshaw, R. R. and F. D. Davis. 1985. "Disentangling Behavioral Intention and Behavioral Expectation. *Journal of Experimental Social Psychology* 21:213–28.

Watts, W. A. and W. J. McGuire. 1964. "Persistence of Induced Opinion Change and Retention of the Inducing Message Contents." *Journal of Abnormal and Social Psychology* 68:233–41.

Webb, E. J., D. T. Campbell, R. D. Schwartz, and L. Sechrest. 1966. *Unobtrusive Measures: Nonreactive Research in the Social Sciences.* Chicago: Rand McNally.

Webb, E. J., D. T. Campbell, R. D. Schwartz, L. Sechrest, and J. B. Grove. 1981. *Nonreactive Measures in the Social Sciences,* 2nd ed. Boston, MA: Houghton Mifflin.

Weber, M. 1949. *Max Weber on the Methodology of the Social Sciences,* translated and edited by E. Shils and H. Finch. Glencoe, IL: Free Press.

Weigert, A. J. 1970. "The Immoral Rhetoric of Scientific Sociology." *American Sociologist* 43:422–25.

Wells, R. and J. S. Picou. 1981. *American Sociology: Theoretical and Methodological Structure.* Washington, DC: University Press of America.

Westie, F. R. 1965. "The American Dilemma: An Empirical Test." *American Sociological Review* 30:527–38.

Wheeler, S. 1961. "Role Conflict in Correctional Institutions." Pp. 229–59 in *The Prison,* edited by D. R. Cressey. New York: Holt, Rinehart and Winston.

Whyte, W. F. 1984. *Learning from the Field: A Guide from Experience.* Beverly Hills, CA: Sage.

Wicker, A. W. 1969. "Attitudes Versus Actions: The Relationship of Verbal and Overt Behavior Responses to Attitude Objects." *Journal of Social Issues* 25: 41–78.

———. 1971. "An Examination of the 'Other Variables' Explanation of Attitude-Behavior Inconsistency." *Journal of Personality and Social Psychology* 19:18–30.

Williams, F. and H. Cantril. 1945. "The Use of Interviewer Rapport as a Method of Detecting Differences between 'Public' and 'Private' Opinion." *Journal of Social Psychology* 22:171–75.

Wilson, T. D., D. S. Dunn, J. A. Bybee, D. B. Hyman, and J. A. Rotondo. 1984. "Effects of Analyzing Reasons on Attitude-Behavior Consistency." *Journal of Personality and Social Psychology* 47:5–16.

Wittenbraker, J., B. L. Gibbs, and L. R. Kahle. 1983. "Seat Belt Attitudes, Habits, and Behaviors: An Adaptive Amendment to the Fishbein Model." *Journal of Applied Social Psychology* 13:406–21.

Woodward, J. 1948. "Discussion." *American Sociological Review* 13:552–54.

Wrong, D. H. 1961. "The Oversocialized Conception of Man in Modern Society." *American Sociological Review* 26:183–93.

Wuebben, P. L., B. C. Straits, and G. L. Schulman. 1974. *The Experiment as a Social Occasion.* Berkeley: Glendessary Press.

Wuelker, G. 1963. "Questionnaires in Asia." *International Social Science Journal* 15:35–47.

Wurtele, S. K., M. C. Roberts, and J. D. Leeper. 1982. "Health Beliefs and Intentions: Predictors of Return Compliance in Tuberculosis Detection Drive." *Journal of Applied Social Psychology* 12:128–36.

Zajonc, R. B. and N. K. Waki. 1961. "Conformity and Need Achievement Under Cross-Cultural Norm Conflict." *Human Relations* 14:241–50.

Zetterberg, H. 1965. *On Theory and Verification in Sociology,* 3rd ed. Totowa, NJ: Bedminster Press.

Zimbardo, P. G. 1972. "Pathology of Imprisonment." *Transaction/Society* 9 (April):4–8.

Zuckier, H. 1982. "Situational Determinants of Behavior." *Social Research* 49:1973–97.

Zunich, M. 1962. "Relationship Between Maternal Behavior and Attitudes Toward Children." *Journal of Genetic Psychology* 100:155–65.

Zurcher, L. A. 1984. "The War Game: Organizational Scripting and the Expression of Emotion." *Symbolic Interaction* 8:191–206.

Index

Abramson, P. R. 95
Acock, A. 33, 38, 154, 167, 173, 184, 200, 201, 205, 216, 217
Adler, N. E. 230
Adler, P. 113
Ageton, S. S. 34
AIDS 45
Ajzen, I. 44, 52, 57, 78–85, 110, 134, 181, 182, 193, 194, 198, 200, 205
Albrecht, S. L. 4, 167, 177
Alexander, C. N. 122
Aligning actions 217
Alker, H. 205
Allen, H. E. 180
Allen, V. L. 178
Allport, G. W. 194–196
Almond, G. 103
Alwin, D. 184, 205
Anderson, B. 95
Anderson, R. B. 100
Anomie 36, 144
Asch, S. E. 115, 121, 125, 178
Ataöv, T. 34, 73–75
Atkinson, P. 37, 38, 215, 216, 222
Attitudes and behavior
  alcohol 143
  central problem 32–37
  cigarette smoking 82, 205
  compartmentalization 144–147, 205
  conceptual clarity 3, 14, 203
  conceptual confusion 185, 187, 201–205
  consistency 58

  inconsistency of 56, 58
  racial 6, 53, 82, 95, 126, 132–134, 174, 176, 177, 192, 231, 232
  relationship between 44, 47, 50, 53, 54, 58–61, 65, 78, 109, 129, 131–137, 170, 174, 177, 181, 184
Autokinetic effect 122, 150
Averill, A. K. 10, 45, 47, 52–54, 56, 82, 83, 97, 124, 129, 136, 137, 174, 187, 201, 205, 230

Baccaglini, W. 184
Bad company 141
Baer, D. J. 179
Bagozzi, R. P. 183, 194, 205
Bakan, D. 123, 124
Bannister, R. C. 20, 29
Barber, B. 227
Barkan, S. E. 134
Barnes, H. E. 207
Bass, B. 228
Bastide, R. 133, 192
Baumann, K. E. 33, 184, 205
Beach, C. R. 205
Beck, B. 77
Becker, H. S. 26, 28, 75, 87, 100, 109–111, 184, 205, 207
Begley, T. M. 205
Behavior
  changes in 95
  conditioning of 163, 164
  courtesy 102

definition of 188, 189, 193, 198, 199, 224
direct measure of 201, 224
direct observation of 73–75
emotional aspects of
influence of others on 141–145
in experiments 51, 116–124, 148–150, 169
intentions 34, 58, 60, 63, 64, 70, 74, 175, 180–182, 187, 198– 200, 205, 213, 219, 224, 225, 229, 230
interracial 133
intersubjective 38
measurement of 15–19, 23, 27, 40, 48, 50, 230
military 180
overt behavior 29, 51, 54, 93, 141, 173, 187
prediction of 45–46, 54, 161
scaling 47, 52, 131–137
self-reports 34, 198, 200, 224, 145, 187, 192
smoking 179
and surveillance 175
theory of 152–155, 181–183
verbal 50
volitional 199, 222
voting 92, 97
Behaviorism 210
Behaviorists 131, 132, 146, 147, 204
Benney, M. 37, 88, 101, 104
Berelson, B. 13
Berger, P. L. 212
Berghe, P. van den 133, 192
Bergman, G. 78, 81
Bernstein, B. 107, 108
Bindman, A. M. 95
Blacks 17, 18, 44, 50, 94, 95, 132, 134, 145, 146, 152, 169, 177, 178, 191–192
Blake, J. 190

Blalock, H. M. 48, 201
Blum, A. F. 212, 217
Blumer, H. 5, 18, 20, 22–24, 29, 32, 36, 45–47, 96, 97, 105, 107, 152, 156, 164–168, 170, 171, 174, 175, 177, 183, 193, 197, 203, 204, 207, 209–214, 220, 222, 226, 231
Boden, D. 37, 38, 222
Bogdan, R. 113
Bonacich, E. 26
Borgida, E. 182, 205
Bortner, M. A. 77
Bossard, J. H. S. 37
Boudon, R. 13
Bourricaud, F. 13
Boyer, R. 205
Braithwaite, L. 190
Brayfield, A. 33–35
Breckler, S. J. 194, 199, 205
Bridgman, P. W. 188–191
Brinberg, D. 205
Brinkerhoff, R. O. 229
Broad, W. 56, 124, 160, 170, 203, 217, 218
Brody, J. 77
Brody, C. L. 122
Brotzman, E. 229
Brown, L. B. 183, 196, 197
Brown, R. W. 109
Brown, S. 231
Budd, R. 182, 183, 205
Bulmer, M. 209, 210
Burgess, E. W. 212
Burke, K. 109
Butler, D. C. 143
Bybee, J. A. 182, 205

Cagle, L. T. 34, 192
Camburn, D. 184, 205
Campbell, A. 23, 96
Campbell, B. 182, 205

Campbell, D. T. 10, 17, 47, 69,
    72, 73, 78, 119, 129, 130, 131–
    134, 136, 138
Campbell, N. A. 33
Cantril, H. 94, 95
Carter, W. 97
Chamlin, M. 184
Chassin, L. 199, 205
Cheating 34, 73, 75, 89, 90, 92,
    153
Chein, I. 136
Chen, J. M. 205
Chenowith, R. L. 33, 184, 205
Chicago 20, 21, 132, 175, 209,
    210, 212, 221, 232
Chinese 16, 17, 32, 53, 56–58, 79,
    103, 129, 130
Cicourel, A. V. 38, 99, 100, 106–
    108, 166
Cloward, R. A. 179
Cohen, A. K. 107
Cohn, S. F. 134
Coleman, J. W. 179, 222
Coles, R. 144, 145
Collective behavior 152
Collins, R. 37, 38
Competence 4, 167, 215
Conditioned stimuli 163
Conformity 126, 127, 148, 152,
    157, 178
Congressional Record 92
Consistency
    assumption of 40
    attitude-behavior 58, 60, 182,
        191
    and compartmentalization 152
    conceptual 11, 202
    discounting of 137
    and interaction 217, 218
    intraindividual 63
    and prediction 60
    psychological need for 4, 35,
        223, 224, 225

and science 146, 147, 176, 191,
    224, 225
and social constraint 177
and survey methodology 92,
    94, 199
Conversation 37, 38, 99, 108, 144,
    215, 222
Conversation analysis 38, 215
Converse, P. E. 105
Correlation analysis 52, 82
Corty, E. 205
Coser, L. A. 207, 211, 212, 222
Couch, C. J. 118
Crane, W. W. 39, 102
Crano, W. D. 182, 205
Crawford, T. J. 205
Credibility
    and convergence 174
    and demand characteristics
        115
    and discounting 7, 10, 11, 13,
        14, 65, 70, 83, 111
    methodological 27, 55, 56, 59,
        60, 82, 87, 98, 119–122, 127,
        138, 150, 203, 223
    and theory 153
Cressey, D. 142
Crew, K. 38
Criminal statistics 76
Crittenden, K. S. 40
Crockett, D. M. 33–35
Cultural lag 36, 204
Cultures
    Arabic 39
    as background characteristics
        156, 160
    and interviewing 101, 104
    monolithic 149
    and obedience 152
    and phenomenology 204
    subcultures 174
    and theory 122, 142, 154–156,
        214

Dalrymple, S. 229
Dalton, M. 6
Dalton, D. R. 205
Dannick, L. 33, 151
Darley, J. M. 169
Darroch, R. K. 52
Davidson, A. R. 33, 182, 184, 205
Davis, R. A. 184
Davis, F. D. 205
Dawes, R. M. 83, 181, 194–196
Daytin Daily News 100
DeFleur, M. L. 43, 49–58, 60, 61,
    74, 79, 80, 82–84, 137, 154,
    167, 174–177, 188
DeFriese, G. H. 167, 174
Delaney, H. R. 209
DeLuca, D. R. 205
Demand characteristics 51, 115–
    117
Denny, R. 122
Denzin, N. K. 8, 27
Desroches, F. J. 113
Determinism 149, 156
Deutscher, I. 3, 11, 16, 21, 22, 26,
    29, 34, 39, 45, 58, 65, 78, 95,
    97, 107, 145, 168, 184, 187,
    192, 197, 228, 232
Dillon, W. R. 194
Discounting
  aligning action 217
  methodological 3, 9–11, 49, 65,
    121, 127
Discrimination 6, 32, 129, 133,
    230, 231
Doob, L. W. 205
Dossett, D. L. 33, 184, 201, 205
Doubt, K. 208
Douglas, J. D. 77, 78, 112, 146
Drabek, T. E. 118
Duke, L. 231
Dunn, T. S. 182, 205
Durand, J. 205
Durkheim, E. 36, 76–78, 174

Education 12, 22
Ehrlich, H. J. 10, 74, 137, 167–
    170, 175, 178, 179
Elliot, D. S. 154
Emerson, J. P. 216
Emerson, R. M. 101, 112
Emotions, 156–160
Employee 33, 34
Epistemology 19, 23, 208, 226
Erickson, M. 120
Ethnomethodology 38, 40, 41,
    109, 207–209, 211, 212, 215,
    221, 222
Etzioni, A. 84, 120
Everyday life 28, 40, 41, 83, 120,
    154, 157, 159, 176, 189, 199,
    214, 220, 230
Ewans, W. L. 44

Fazio, R. H. 24, 182, 205
Felson, R. B. 184
Fendrich, J. M. 167, 173, 174
Filstead, W. J. 112
Fishbein, M. 15, 23, 52, 181, 182,
    193, 194, 198–200
Fisher, W. A. 205
Fiske, D. W. 69
Ford, W. S. 167, 174
Frank, A. W. 43, 191, 215, 221
Fredericks, A. J. 33, 184, 201, 205
Freeman, D. 25, 85
Freeman, L. C. 31, 34, 73–75, 168
Frideres, J. S. 167
Friedman, N. 89, 118
Frost, R. T. 34
Fuller, T. 33, 184, 201, 205
Functionalism 208

Gallant, M. J. 215
Galliher, J. F. 29
Gardner, G. T. 33, 205
Garfinkel, H. 38, 40, 77, 146, 149,
    207–209, 212–214, 216, 222

Geer, B. 26, 28, 75, 87, 109–111, 205
German idealism 207, 211
Gibbons, F. X. 182, 205
Gibbs, B. L. 184, 205
Ginsberg, G. P. 183, 196, 197
Glaser, B. 7, 26, 28, 84, 111
Glass, G. R. 7
Glazer, M. P. & P. M. 157
Glenn, E. S. 39
Goffman, E. 27, 36, 37, 113, 122
Gold, D. 123
Goldman, A. E. 179, 205
Goldstein, I. 148
Goode, W. J. 190
Gorden, R. L. 126, 127, 147, 153
Gordon, L. 44
Gordon, R. A. 119, 227
Gordon, S. L. 158
Gorsuch, R. L. 182, 199, 205
Gould, L. C. 205
Gould, S. J. 99
Gouldner, A. W. 11
Graves, N. 229
Green, S. B. 199, 205
Gregory, S. W. 215
Grimshaw, A. D. 37, 108
Group pressure 115, 116, 124, 126, 148
Grove, J. B. 72
Gusfield, J. 32
Guttman, L. 20, 47, 130, 132–134, 136, 195, 196

Haas, J. E. 118
Hagan, R. A. 29
Hall, P. M. 155, 216
Halteman, W. A. 134
Hamblin, R. L. 107
Hammersley, M. 107
Haney, C. 28, 118
Hanson, B. G. 111
Hanson, D. J. 29, 119

Hatt, P. K. 190
Helson, H. 119, 120, 150
Hemingway, E. 9
Heritage, J. 208, 215
Herr, P. M. 205
Hewitt, J. P. 217
Hilbert, R. A. 215, 221
Hill, D. 33, 205
Hill, R. J. 5, 40, 136, 179–181, 193, 200
Himmelstein, P. 28, 120, 150
Hired help 89
Hochschild, A. R. 112, 158, 159
Hodges, H. M. 107
Hoffling, C. K. 229
Holland, C. H. 120, 121
Hornick, J. A. 52
Hovland, C. J. 127
Huang, G. 215
Hughes, E. C. 37, 88, 101, 104, 111, 156, 161, 188, 212, 233
Hughes, H. M. 37, 111, 161, 188, 233
Humphreys, L. 112, 113
Hunt, W. H. 39, 102, 103
Hunter, C. H. 217
Husserl, E. 207, 208, 211
Hyman, D. B. 182, 205
Hyman, H. 15, 25, 94

Inconsistency
    between knowledge and action 179
    and compartmentalization 145
    and methodology 35, 47, 52, 55, 56, 62, 91, 142, 168, 177, 199, 200
    nonproblematic 4
    pseudoinconsistency 10, 17, 37, 129–137, 169, 203
    and sociology 204
    in assumptions 220
Insko, C. A. 124

Irwin, C. E. 230
Irwin, J. 111

Jaccard, J. 184, 205
Jackson, D. N. 121
Jacobs, J. 38
Jaschik, S. 231
Johnson, M. P. 5, 181, 195, 229
Jones, E. L. 101, 102
Jones, J. H. 227
Jordan, N. 48, 97, 104, 107, 203
Jordan, B. 90, 91

Kahle, L. R. 184, 205
Kant, I. 207–209, 211, 212
Kantola, S. J. 33, 182, 184, 205
Kantrowitz, B. 222
Katovich, M. A. 118
Katz, J. 156, 179, 205
Katzev, R. D. 201, 205
Keesing, F. M. & M. M. 102
Kegeles, S. M. 230
Kelman, H. C. 148
Kendler, H. H. & T. S. 132, 146
Kendzierski, D. 182, 205
Kerr, N. L. 184, 205
Kirk, J. 70
Klandermans, B. 205
Kleinman, S. 158, 215
Kohn, M. 28, 149
Kreiger, S. 153
Kriesberg, L. 33, 145, 146
Krushat, W. M. 96, 200
Kumar, A. 194
Kurtz, L. R. 209, 210

Labov, W. 108
Lacey, R. 33
Lalljee, M. 183, 196–198
Language
  and emotions 158–161
  and meaning 163, 171, 217
  public 32
  and social research 37–39, 222, 226
  and surveys 98–101, 106–110, 113
LaPiere, R. T. 6, 8, 16–20, 22, 27, 29, 31, 32, 36, 40, 43, 53–60, 65, 74, 79, 80, 82, 129–131, 167, 230
LaRossa, R. 112
Lastrucci, C. L. 44
Latané, B. 169
Lauer, R. H. 203
Lawton, M. P. 179
Lee, A. M. 227
Leeper, J. D. 201, 205
Lengerman, D. M. 212
Lepper, M. R. 16, 43, 58–65, 74, 79, 80, 205
Lerner, D. 102, 103
Lewis, J. D. 210
Lewis, O. 25, 85
Lieberson, S. 48, 119
Liebow, E. 154
Likert, R. 38, 91, 136, 195, 196
Linguistics 37, 39
Linn, L. S. 43, 44, 46–58, 60–62, 64, 65, 74, 79, 80, 82, 84, 132, 173
Lipset, S. M. 192
Liska, A. E. 24, 182–184, 194
Lobel, T. E. 205
Lohman, J. D. 8, 132, 146, 148
Lord, C. G. 16, 43, 58–65, 74, 79, 80, 205
Luchins, A. S. & E. H. 178
Luckmann, T. 212
Lyman, S. M. 38, 217
Lynd, R. S. 227

Mackie, D. 16, 43, 58–65, 74, 79, 80, 205
Maines, D. R. 27, 37, 38, 155, 216, 221

Manstead, A. S. R. 34, 184, 205
Marijuana 177
Marolla, J. 39
Marquis, K. H. 95, 96
Martin, H. H. 34
Martin, J. D. 117, 121
Marwell, G. 26
Marx, K. 155, 208, 232
Masserman, J. 120
Matza, D. 217
Mayhew, B. 175, 176
McCall, M. M. 38
McDonald, M. S. 228
McDonel, E. C. 205
McGaw, B. 7
McGinnies, E. 148
McGuire, W. J. 148
McHugh, P. 212, 217
McMartin, J. A. 143
McPhail, C. 210
Mead, G. H. 36, 37, 99, 109, 156, 157, 164, 175, 204, 209, 210, 211–213
Mead, M. 25, 85
Melton, A. W. 123
Meltzer, B. N. 212
Merton, R. K. 11, 17–20, 24, 29, 32, 56, 70, 133, 134, 147
Mesostructure 155, 216
Messé, L. A. 184, 205
Messick, S. 121
Methodology
   confederates 53, 99, 115, 121, 126, 152, 178
   and cumulative knowledge 57–65, 78–85, 180, 196, 202
   double screen 3, 7–14, 83, 137, 203
   and ethnomethodology 41, 72
   experimenter effect 57, 88
   experiments 95, 100
   conditioning 163

and demand characteristics 51, 112, 115, 123, 229
and field studies
and Head Start 228
laboratory 10, 28, 58, 61, 73, 74, 83, 127, 201
and phenomenology 177, 178, 219
and publication policies 148–153
and sampling
and scaling 48
as a social situation 89
field studies (see participant observation)
interviewer effect 88, 94, 95
interviews 10, 90–92, 95, 98, 99, 100, 102, 104, 107–109, 113
meta-analysis 7, 8
observer effect 88
operational definitions 28, 78, 165, 202, 223
participant observation 77, 87, 98, 99, 109–113, 210
qualitative 19, 26, 69, 90, 112, 163, 170
quantitative 7, 8, 19–22, 26, 45, 69, 163, 170, 195, 210
surveys 10, 23, 37, 84, 88, 91, 94, 95, 98, 103, 104, 108, 119, 128, 226
and theory 136, 142
Milgram, S. 28, 115, 116, 118, 120, 121, 144, 147, 150–152, 157, 169, 229
Miller, D. E. 118
Miller, M. 9, 70
Miller, N. 143
Mills, C. W. 7–9, 12, 14, 18–20, 25, 37, 87, 90, 165, 217, 226
Mills, T. 158
Minard, R. D. 132

Mishler, E. G. 69
Mitchell, R. E. 102, 104, 108
Monroe, E. 228
Montague, A. 145
Montano, D. E. 33, 205
Moore, J. C. 28, 120, 150
Morality 32–34, 143, 227
Morrison, D. M. 205
Mullen, B. 7
Myrdal, G. 191

Needs 18, 48, 101, 121, 131, 137,
    169, 225, 225, 226, 231
Negroes (see Blacks)
Nesdale, A. R. 182–205
Newcomb, T. 22, 23, 97
Newman, J. 96, 200
Nickerson, C. A. E. 230
Nonreactive indicators 88
Norwood, M. 33, 205
Null hypthesis 63, 84, 123, 124

O'Keefe, D. J. 205
Obedience 115, 120, 144, 151, 152
Ogburn, W. F. 204
Ohlin, L. E. 179
Oliner, S. & P. 157
Olney, T. J. 205
Olshavsky, R. W. 205
Opinion
    measurement of 17, 18, 20, 27,
        39, 97, 119, 195
    public 22, 23, 32, 46, 91, 95,
        104, 105
    private 92, 97, 118, 126, 127,
        141, 148
    change 150
    mental orientations 189
Orne, M. T. 51, 115–118, 120,
    121, 150
Ortberg, J. 182, 199, 205
Osgood, C. E. 195, 196

Pagel, M. D. 182, 184, 205
Park, R. E. 21, 212, 232
Pavlov, I. P. 163, 171
Peneff, J. 90, 91, 97
Perinbanayagam, R. S. 158, 159
Personality 59, 62, 103, 119, 122,
    142, 150, 154–156, 160, 161
Pestello, F. G. 3, 124, 155, 168,
    180, 193, 197, 198, 216
Pestello, F. P. 3, 33, 77, 124, 135,
    153, 168, 180, 193, 197, 198,
    217
Petras, J. W. 212
Phenomenology 106, 109, 146,
    207–209, 211, 212, 221, 226
Phillips, D. L. 11, 13, 24, 91, 200,
    227
Picou, J. S. 15
Piedmont, E. B. 27
Pierce, C. M. 229
Plevin, C. E. 34, 184, 205
Polanyi, M. 6
Pollner, M. 221
Positivistic 6, 20, 100, 211–213,
    218–221, 225
Postmodernism 221
Postmodernist 8
Potter, J. 101
Powell, M. C. 205
Pragmatism 210
Prediction 44–46, 51, 53, 54, 60,
    75, 78, 81, 156, 166, 173,
    188
Prejudice 230
Presson, C. C. 205
Process
    intervening 4, 5, 50, 165, 167,
        168, 170, 173, 174, 176–180,
        198, 216, 225, 226
    social 24, 40, 41, 75, 77, 154,
        169, 212, 219, 220
    action as 37, 45, 201, 223
    socialization 158

Process (*cont.*)
  interpretive 166, 167, 171, 204
  negotiation 216
Profitt, C. 34, 184, 205
Prothero, J. 205
Punch, M. 112

Questionnaires 17, 37, 44, 98, 99,
    108, 113, 182, 196, 228
  Thurstone 20, 136, 195, 196

Raden, D. 182
Ransford, H. E. 33, 169
Rassaby, J. 33, 205
Raven, B. H. 125–127, 153
Raymond, C. 83, 123
Razran, G. H. 164
Reactivity 46, 47, 87, 88, 99, 101,
    107, 112, 119, 122, 126, 207,
    211, 226
Reasoned action 181
Redfield, R. 25, 85
Reference groups 4, 36, 167, 174
Reitzes, D. R. 8, 132, 146, 148
Reliability 19, 24–26, 65, 69–72, 74,
    76, 81, 85, 90, 94, 95, 111, 223
Research finance 19
Research methods 19, 135
Responsibility 123, 232
Rexroat, C. 210
Rhoades, L. J. 22
Richardson, L. 8
Riesman, D. 39, 104, 105, 122,
    151, 152, 161
Riess, B. F. 164
Rinehart, J. W. 74
Roberts, M. C. 201, 205
Rochberg-Halton, E. 210
Rodman, H. 11, 190–192
Roebuck, J. 27
Rokeach, M. 37, 177, 203
Role theory 36

Rose, A. M. 36, 144, 145, 221
Rosensweig, S. 118
Rosenthal, R. 51, 118
Rosnow, R. L. 51
Roth, J. A. 89–91, 94, 134
Rotondo, J. A. 182, 205
Roy, D. 134, 135

Sacks, J. J. 96, 200
Salancik, G. R. 143
Salomon, A. 208, 211
Sampling procedure 55, 96
Scale analysis 20, 52, 130, 131,
    133
Scaling 20, 47, 52, 55, 61, 133,
    138, 189, 195, 198
Schatzman, L. 37, 106, 107
Scheff, T. J. 6, 26, 109, 158, 216
Schlenker, B. R. 196, 205
Schnedlitz, P. 205
Schopler, J. 124
Schulman, G. L. 89
Schuman, H. 5, 181, 195
Schwartz, R. D. 72, 189
Scott, M. B. 38, 217
Scott, R. A. 227
Scully, D. 39
Sechrest, L. 72
Sentiments and Acts (*See*
    Attitudes and behavior)
Sex talk 103
Shanab, M. 152
Sheng, D. 205
Shepherd, G. J. 205
Sherif, M. 122, 150, 178
Sherman, S. J. 24, 182, 205
Shilts, R. 45
Shore, A. R. 22
Shulman, A. D. 118, 143
Sieber, S. D. 227
Significant others 141, 167, 174
Silver, B. D. 95

Silverman, I. 118, 143
Simey, T. S. 190
Simmel, G. 211, 212
Simonsen, C. E. 180
Situational sociology 146, 156, 160, 164, 207, 218, 225
Sivacek, J. 182, 205
Sjoberg, L. 16, 205
Skinner, B. F. 188
Smart, J. L. 34, 184, 205
Smith, A. C. 158
Smith, M. L. 7
Smith, R. L. 210
Smith, T. L. 181, 194–196
Smith, T. W. 97
Snyder, M. 182, 205
Social change 157, 160, 165, 227, 232
Social disorganization 36
Social Science Research Council 73, 128
Social structure 19, 38, 122, 142, 154–156, 160, 161, 222
Social world 12, 38, 165, 210, 213, 218
Sociological Research Association 21, 29
Sociologists 9, 12, 13, 15, 20–23, 26, 28, 31, 37, 38, 40, 41, 45, 71, 76, 98, 109, 142, 146, 152, 154, 159, 165, 175, 208, 210–212, 216, 219, 227, 232
Sorokin, P. 227
Steffensmeier, D. J. 28
Spencer, H. 87, 182, 183, 193, 205
Spray, S. L. 27
Stanley, J. C. 28, 78, 115
Steiner, G. 13
Stokes, R. 217
Stolwijk, J. A. J. 205
Straf, M. L. 7
Straits, B. C. 89

Strauss, A. 7, 26, 28, 37, 84, 106, 107, 111, 112, 216
Strauss, G. 16
Stricker, L. J. 121
Structure 13, 19, 37, 38, 122, 142, 154–156, 160, 161, 196, 208, 219, 221, 222
Stryker, S. 26, 212, 221
Stults, D. M. 184, 205
Stutzman, T. M. 199, 205
Suchman, L. 90, 91
Suci, G. E. 195
Suicide 76, 77, 155, 213
Suicide statistics 76
Sutherland, E. H. 142
Sykes, G. M. 217
Symbolic interactionism 38, 207, 209, 210, 222
Syme, G. J. 33, 182, 205

Talk 18, 25, 27, 31, 37, 38, 40, 81, 103, 105–108, 127, 142, 158, 159, 169, 204, 214–217, 222, 224, 226, 229, 230
Tannenbaum, P. 195
Tarter, D. E. 188, 203
Tausky, C. 27
Taylor, S. J. 113
Temporality 38
Terry, R. M. 28
Thomas, J. 156, 160, 161, 175, 177, 193, 210
Thornton, A. 184, 201, 205
Thurstone, L. L. 20, 136, 195, 196
Tiemann, A. P. 205
Time and motion studies 27
Timko, C. 44, 205
Tittle, C. R. 136
Todor, W. D. 205
Training 12, 13, 160
Trow, M. 87, 113

Validity 4, 8, 25–28, 50, 52, 56,
  61, 64, 69–79, 81–83, 85, 88–
  90, 94, 95, 102, 111, 125, 196,
  200, 223, 224, 227–229
  construct 24, 59, 71, 78, 149,
    175, 232
  convergent 65, 72, 73, 78, 83,
    85, 95, 125, 151, 223
  face 6, 36, 50, 71, 77, 129–131,
    144, 158, 217, 224
Van Maanen, J. 109
Variable(s)
  analysis 4, 24, 165–168, 170,
    171, 183, 218, 220
  intervening 4, 5, 10, 45, 50,
    166, 167, 169–171, 173, 174,
    176–180, 204, 213, 220, 225,
    226
  moderating 24, 183
Vaughn, S. M. 205
Verba, S. 103
Verbalization 37, 97
Vetter, H. J. 180
Vissing, Y. M. 231
Voydanoff, P. 155, 216

Wachter, K. W. 7
Wade, N. 124
Wahlke, J. C. 39, 102
Waki, N. K. 152
Warner, L. G. 167, 174–177
Warriner, C. K. 8, 32, 35, 142
Warshaw, R. R. 205
Watts, W. A. 148, 169
Webb, E. J. 72, 75, 88, 125
Weber, M. 155, 208, 211
Webster, S. 215
Weigert, A. J. 24, 45, 70, 71

Wells, R. 15
Westie, F. R. 11, 43, 49–58, 60,
  61, 74, 79, 80, 82–84, 137,
  145, 146, 188, 190–192
Wetherell, M. 101
Wheeler, S. 143, 148
White, J. B. 8, 18, 33, 44, 47, 50,
  52, 94, 101, 132, 133, 146,
  179, 192, 205, 228, 231
Whyte, W. F. 16, 112
Wicker, A. W. 4, 166, 168, 192,
  203
Wicklund, R. A. 182, 205
Widdison, H. A. 209
Williams, F. 94, 95
Williams, R. 28, 149
Wilson, T. D. 182, 205
Wittenbraker, J. 184, 205
Wittner, J. 38
Woodward, J. 22, 23, 97
Wrong, D. H. 24, 25, 46, 73, 74,
  83, 121, 131, 134, 142, 149,
  156, 165, 178, 232
Wuebben, P. L. 89, 119
Wuelker, G. 104
Wurtele, S. K. 201, 205

Yahya, K. A. 152
Yantis, S. 33, 205

Zajonc, R. B. 152
Zetterberg, H. 84
Zimbardo, P. G. 28
Znaniecki, F. 193
Zucker, L. G. 122
Zuckier, H. 183
Zunich, M. 33
Zurcher, L. A. 160